STARDOM IN POSTWAR FRANCE

Polygons: Cultural Diversities and Intersections
General Editor: **Lieve Spaas**, *Professor of French Cultural Studies, Kingston University, UK*

STARDOM IN POSTWAR FRANCE

Edited by
John Gaffney and Diana Holmes

Berghahn Books
New York • Oxford

First published in 2007 by
Berghahn Books
www.BerghahnBooks.com

© 2007, 2011 John Gaffney and Diana Holmes
First paperback edition published in 2011

Library of Congress Cataloging-in-Publication Data

Stardom in postwar France / edited by John Gaffney and Diana
Holmes.
    p. cm. -- (Polygons: cultural diversities and intersections ; v. 12)
Includes bibliographical references and index.
  ISBN 978-1-84545-020-5 (hbk) -- ISBN 978-0-85745-160-6 (pbk)
  1. France--Social life and customs--20th century. 2. Celebrities--
France--History--20th century. 3. France--Intellectual life--20th
century. 4. France--Civilization--1945- 5. Fame. I. Gaffney, John.
II. Holmes, Diana.

  DC402.S73 2007
  305.5'2--dc22

                                                            2007040252

British Library Cataloguing in Publication Data

A catalogue record for this book is available
from the British Library.

Printed in the United States on acid-free paper.

ISBN 978-1-84545-020-5 (hardback)
ISBN 978-0-85745-160-6 (paperback)

The editors would like to express their gratitude to Peter Kramer and Chris Warne, without whose contributions to the discussion of stardom and French cultural history in the early stages of the project, the book would never have been written.

They would also like to thank Lieve Spaas for her help and advice as Series Editor.

CONTENTS

Introduction

John Gaffney and Diana Holmes

The aim of this book is to examine the concept and the practice of stardom in the France of the 1950s and 1960s,[1] a period of French history that saw dramatic economic, social and cultural change. Our premise is that the 'stars' of a given historical period or moment capture their era for us in a range of ways: that the preoccupations, values, conflicts and contradictions of a particular culture, its 'climate of feeling', are vividly expressed through its celebrities. Stardom may be read as a symbolic portal into the nature of a culture, stars as that culture's ultimate expression. At the same time, stars, by their very nature, are what most people are not, are symbolic *negations* of a given culture: they offer the new in place of the old; excitement where it has been lacking; the urbane to the provincial; glamour where there is none; and dreams to those whose dreams are unrealised. In our relationship to stars, there is often an element of idealised self-recognition, but there is also aspiration, desire and sometimes nostalgia. A study of stardom in a period of particular social change can reveal what is becoming and what is being left behind; what is being aspired to and what is being forgotten or denied. Stars can restate, often in new and modern forms, old identities and values, as well as calling a society towards newer, and perhaps confused, emergent values and value systems. The combination of the old and new was encapsulated in the phenomenon of French post-World War II stardom.

Stardom has been theorised mainly in relation to the cinema, and it is film stars who first come to mind when the word 'star' is used. Yet it is unmistakeably the case that stardom goes well beyond the movies. Film theory has defined the star as 'a performer in a particular medium whose figure enters into subsidiary forms of circulation and then feeds back into future performances' (Ellis 1982: 1). The mass appeal of film stars is argued as guaranteeing their capacity to reflect and express a given culture: '[s]tars matter because they act out aspects of life that matter to us; and performers get to be stars when what they act out matters to enough people' (Dyer 1987: 19). Each of these statements can be applied not just to stars of the big screen, but also to that select number of musicians, sportsmen and -women, politicians, writers and intellectuals who seize the public imagination not just as exceptional achievers in a particular sphere, but also as part-mythified characters, at once compellingly different and reassuringly recognisable. Françoise Sagan, for example, represented a new kind of tough but vulnerable femininity for a vast national audience, not just for her readers, just as Poulidor meant strength, talent and the capacity to fail nobly for a public that far exceeded cycling fans.

Writers and intellectuals are rarely thought of as stars, but they are an essential element of our study. Particularly in this period, the intellectual dimension of stardom distinguished France from most other countries in character, and all others in scale. We find in the 1950s and 1960s a range of intellectuals who were household names, including Barthes and Lévi-Strauss. With Jean-Paul Sartre and Simone de Beauvoir, indeed, the intellectual and the popular cross paths, for they were themselves part of trendy Paris café society, along with celebrities such as the singer Juliette Greco. Even political stars such as de Gaulle were major intellectual figures, and the treatment, as we shall see, of a Poulidor race as a highly elaborate analogy of Manon Lescaut by a sports journalist borders on the surreal when one imagines Anglo-Saxon equivalents. The intellectual life as a hallmark of Frenchness, in fact, was one of the cohesive elements of this period of postwar stardom, from intellectuals as stars to politicians as intellectuals, from the intellectualism of cycling – originally France's truly working class sport – to the intellectual aspirations of singers such as Greco, or singer-songwriters like Brassens and Brel and even, to a minor extent, yé-yé singers such as Françoise Hardy. If this particularity provided France with a sense of superiority over its giant, Anglo-Saxon cultural rivals, this needs to be seen in the context of a deep and growing opposite complex, namely, the anxiety of a cultural empire that was besieged from without and mined from within by repressed self-doubt, and fuelled by the literal end of empire.

The array of very different celebrities discussed in this book all functioned as stars in 1950s and 1960s France, and attracted the passionate interest of a large public, not just because of their beauty, talent or power, but because they combined performance in their field with the capacity to embody issues or emotions that felt relevant to people's lives. Although there is, of course, a world of difference between the ordinary citizen's relationship with a film star, a famous writer or a politician, in each case the public was fascinated not just by what they did, but by what they were, or what they seemed to be.

The study of what determines a star's appeal – the conditions of production, the qualities of performance – together with the analysis of the star-making process, should therefore provide an illuminating perspective on an era, as well as on the phenomenon of each individual star. The two decades that followed France's defeat and humiliating occupation were a period of intensive reconstruction, at both a material and a cultural level. Supported by US investment (Marshall Aid), France plunged forward into the consumer age, rapidly modernising industrial production and working practices, developing an ever-growing market in everything from domestic appliances to cars to beauty and leisure goods, rehousing the increasing population of the baby-boom years in great new suburban estates, and informing and entertaining most of the nation through the developing media of glossy magazines, French and Hollywood cinema, radio, and later television. Perhaps because of the dizzying speed of social change, the 1950s and 1960s also constituted a moment in French history when stars of cinema, sport, literature, popular music, intellectual life and politics all appear to have fulfilled vital symbolic functions for mass audiences, and to have formed a major part of the fabric of everyday culture. A comprehensive study of the important stars of the period would have demanded a book of encyclopaedic proportions. We have aimed, rather, to provide a set of case studies that 'capture' the period, framed by a theoretical and historical overview of stardom and of the era, that includes (in Chapter 2) a discussion of how stardom first came to be theorised in France in the 1950s by intellectuals, one of whom (Barthes) was himself to become an iconic figure. The sheer number of major celebrities in those decades made choices difficult. Though there were many other contenders from the cinema (Jeanne Moreau for example), Brigitte Bardot was the French female star whose face and style most marked her era, internationally as well as nationally. Johnny Hallyday was the face and voice of French rock and roll, and Françoise Sagan the author whose fame went way beyond literary circles to make her a household name, as the best-known literary representative of 1950s youth culture. Raymond Poulidor was not the only iconic sportsman of his era, but he was particularly representative of some of the contradictions and tensions played out in the period's sport; nor was Jean-Luc Godard the only French director whose fame extended well beyond the public who appreciated his films, though he was more dramatically iconised than that other celebrity-director, Truffaut. Claude Lévi-Strauss is only one of the internationally celebrated French intellectuals whose impact on their era transcended, by far, their readership. Jean-Paul Sartre, Albert Camus and Simone de Beauvoir shone still more brightly in that intellectual firmament of 1950s France; here we have chosen a less obvious case of the intellectual as national celebrity, in order to demonstrate how deeply stardom penetrated French intellectual life beyond its three most famous exponents. A more exhaustive study would also extend to stars from other fields and media: French *chanson*, for example, produced its own stars in Georges Brassens, Juliette Greco, Jacques Brel and many others, and from the early 1960s, Guy Lux attained star status on the increasingly ubiquitous TV screen. Our case studies, then, are precisely that, and make no claim to cover the whole field.

Our first chapter explores the nature and function of stardom, seen not as a phenomenon limited to cinema or even the entertainment industries, but rather as a form of extreme, iconic celebrity that can be achieved by or ascribed to individuals from many spheres of public life, including politics and – particularly in France – intellectual production. Stardom in the postwar decades is set in the context of the period's dizzying economic growth and intensive modernisation, with all the social tensions and contradictions that this entailed. Susan Weiner's chapter shows how mass culture and its creation of new mythologies became a key object of inquiry for the new social sciences, most famously through the work of Barthes and Morin. Her analysis contrasts Barthes's critical focus on the alienating, mystifying function of mass culture, with Morin's insistence on the active participation of the consumer, and willingness to position himself, as theorist, with, rather than above, the fans who make the stars. Morin identified teenagers and women as the main consumers of star culture; Diana Holmes asks what pleasures (and displeasures) could be found by women spectators – especially young ones – in watching and reading about 'BB', a star who was the iconic object of male desire, yet appeared to claim 'masculine' freedoms unavailable to her female fans. In the years preceding the renaissance of French feminism, did Bardot (as Beauvoir suggested) look forward to the post-1968 movement for sexual liberation, or merely add a new gloss to a traditionally objectified female sexuality? The popularity and success of Johnny Hallyday, the French Elvis, is seen by Chris Tinker in terms of the development of a technological, consumer and leisure-oriented society. Rock and roll music provided a focus around which young people began to forge collective identities, with terms such as *fan* and *copain* entering popular usage. Exploring how Hallyday reworks the tradition of the 'rebel star', Tinker's chapter questions the extent to which he promotes youthful aspirations to autonomy and subverts traditional notions of gender and national identity.

If film and pop music were the most obvious sites of stardom, sport played a more vital role in the imagination of a large, predominantly male, and cross-class public. Philip Dine's chapter explores the representation of France's pre-eminent sports star of the 1960s, the cycle road-racer Raymond Poulidor. At the core of the sporting persona of 'Poupou' was the publicly enacted transition from authentic rural poverty to media-friendly superstardom, which effectively mirrored the general social mobility and growing affluence of the postwar decades. The late 1950s and early 1960s also saw the rise of 'auteurism', or the glorification of the film director as a recognised way of approaching cinema. Alison Smith focuses on the most iconic figure of the New Wave group, Jean-Luc Godard, whose significance in French culture is disproportionate to his film production (and audiences). She examines how a director comes to project a specific persona that is so clear and compelling as to have something like star quality, how this persona functions in both popular and academic culture, and what particular features of the period led to the emergence of a film director as a seminal figure.

As we have argued, in France the intellectual can be elevated to a 'star' status that would be unthinkable in many other countries. Christopher Johnson shows how the anthropologist

Lévi-Strauss is a prime example of this phenomenon, and examines how his celebrity status rested on concentric circles of legitimation: first an acclaim limited to his own discipline of anthropology, then, with structuralism, a much wider intellectual recognition, and finally, through his bestselling autobiography and the tailoring of his profile to the times, a level of mediatised fame that went well beyond the academic and intellectual spheres. French national culture already had a long tradition of literary celebrity, but Françoise Sagan, who burst onto the national (later international) scene in 1954, was never just a famous writer but, in the phrase that she coined to describe herself, a 'starlette de la littérature'. Heather Lloyd examines how a complex variety of factors – from Sagan's own literary merit and exploits, to modernising trends in the book trade, to the role of the media and the emergence of a mass culture that was youth and leisure-oriented – meshed in the creation and commodification of Sagan as star.

In the postwar period one political leader stands out as central to both the political destiny of France and the national imagination. John Gaffney charts the way in which Charles de Gaulle, through his discourse and through symbolism, deployed a mythology of leadership and of national identity that would reshape French political culture. As the political star of the era, de Gaulle embodied in particular that fusion of old and new, national tradition and radical modernity, that marks the years between World War II and 1968. The exceptional political personality may function as a star when his role in the popular imagination extends beyond any practical political function.

The decades between the Liberation and May 1968 were, among so many other things, an age of stars, and in bringing together some of the diverse figures from that remarkable constellation, we can throw new light on a vital period of the cultural history of modern France, on the stars themselves, and on the nature of stardom.

Note

1. Our main emphasis is on the period of intense economic growth and development between the early 1950s and the cultural watershed of 1968. However, where a star's story demands a slightly wider timeframe (e.g. Hallyday, Godard, Poulidor), we have not imposed a strict definition of the period.

CHAPTER 1

STARDOM IN THEORY AND CONTEXT

John Gaffney and Diana Holmes

Stardom

A star is a performer on a public stage whose image, produced through the available media, appeals to and fascinates a mass audience. To qualify as a star, the scale of celebrity must be such that the performer's name and image are familiar not just to those within their specialised field (for example, film enthusiasts, sports fans, intellectuals), but to the general public. For a society to produce stars, and for stars to play an important role in the definition of values and identities, certain conditions are required. Not all human cultures have privileged individualised personality over social function in a way that fosters a culture of celebrity, but as Richard Sennett argues, from the mid-nineteenth century on, the industrialised Western world developed a strong tendency to envisage public, collective issues in terms of the personal. In response to a public world of uncontrolled capitalism, rapid urbanisation and growing secularity, Sennett argues, the public sphere became devalued, the private space of the home and personal life correspondingly idealised. Politicians and other public figures came to be judged less in terms of their effectiveness, than in terms of perceived personal qualities. This personalisation of public life, and the 'transmut(ation of) political categories into psychological categories' (Sennett 2002: 259) is certainly one of the social trends that feeds into the modern phenomenon of stardom. But for individuals from a range of fields to occupy that central place in the public imagination defined as stardom, there must also be a mass media to transmit their image and stories about their lives, and a political and economic system that can make ideological use of the extreme celebrity of selected personalities. 'The star system', Edgar Morin wrote in 1957, 'is an institution specific to advanced capitalism'.[1]

Morin was writing as France underwent an extraordinarily rapid transformation from a predominantly rural, economically conservative, Catholic, colonial nation into an urban, largely secular, decolonised and highly industrialised one: the star system was one element in that process. The swiftly developing, mass consumer culture provided both the means to disseminate star images, news and gossip, through a range of media, and a complex but coherent set of motivations for doing so. At the simplest commercial level, star figures functioned to sell newspapers, magazines (such as the new postwar *Paris Match* and *Elle*), books, films and all kinds of other products that could play on the consumer's desire to acquire something of the star's aura. At a broader ideological level, a culture of stardom works to promote belief in the supreme importance of individual qualities and choices, rather than the determining power of class or income, and in the free, perfectible individual ('you too can be like the star') who is the ideal consumer. Or, in the case of star politicians or intellectuals, the individual's compelling aura may work to legitimate political choices, or to popularise (and sell the books associated with) intellectual movements. Consumer capitalism and the liberal democratic regimes that, at least in the West, have accompanied it, have had a clear stake in the promotion of a star system; stars became a central element of the collective imagination during the mid-years of the twentieth century, at a time of rapid economic growth, urbanisation and the development of a consumer economy.

However, star theory within film studies has been at pains to avoid a simple 'top-down', exploitation model of the relationship between a capitalist film industry and the public who consume the star image. In this, the conceptualisation of celebrity has followed Morin rather than Barthes for, as Susan Weiner demonstrates below (Chapter 2), Morin's work on stars develops the model of an active and individualised encounter between spectator/fan and star. Morin's approach captures the complexity of relations between stars and audiences more adequately than does a view of the public as merely passive and mystified. Stars do not simply function to maximise consumption and support the political and economic status quo. In order to achieve stardom, celebrities have to appeal to a range of different audiences, and it can be precisely their representation of opposition and contestation that gains the allegiance of dispossessed, marginalised or simply rebellious social groups. Despite the recuperative power of advanced capitalism, and its capacity to harness subversive forces to its own ends, the relationship between the star's image and the public that consumes it remains a complex, interactive one. What a star signifies for her or his public is not simply predetermined. Like the film spectator, the consumer of the star image brings his or her own hopes, desires and dreams to the encounter, and plays an active role in selecting which aspects of the star matter. At a period of intense and conflictual social change, the capacity of a star to give expression to different, and often contradictory, fears and aspirations may be what determines their success.

As we shall see, all of the conditions for stardom outlined above pertain strongly to 1950s and 1960s France. France was part of a capitalist, industrialised Western world that had long fostered a culture of celebrity: Paris, in particular, had produced stars in theatre, sport, music hall and the 'higher' arts for a century and a half before the 1950s. These were, by and large, stars with a restricted audience of Parisian elites,[2] but nonetheless, they existed, were particularly marked in French society and, in the twentieth century, became more universal with the emergence of media celebrities such as sports heroes (in boxing, for example), cinema idols (of specifically *French* cinema), nationally known music-hall and radio and recording artists, such as Charles Trenet and Edith Piaf, and writers such as Colette. Moreover, France, perhaps more than other comparable countries, has a very strong tradition of *personalisation* in all aspects of social and political life, from the absolute monarchy, through revolutionary adventurers, to imperial and war heroes. Even throughout its many republics, individuals often encapsulated the impersonal *res publica* itself; in politics as in art, France teems with the lives of its heroes (and occasionally heroines) and villains. The dramatic expression of many social, political or cultural moments in the form of a person is a quintessentially French characteristic.

The development of a consumer culture and the growth and diversification of the mass media now provided the conditions that would foster the emergence of star figures in a range of different cultural fields. If initial qualities or talents are the starting point for stardom – physical beauty or skill, intellectual or artistic originality, political acumen – they are not, of themselves, sufficient. The star persona must be constructed by a process that interweaves the performer's achievements in their specific fields with the dramatisation of their own lives and persons. Publishers, publicists and agents, together with an expanded and diverse new media, were very much part of the new France, and it is through their interventions that localised renown in a specific field spread through what we might term 'concentric circles', to reach a national, and often international, public.

The secularisation of society may also help to explain the vital symbolic role played by stars in conceptualising and coming to terms with new forms of modernity. France had long been profoundly Catholic, and had personalised religion through Madonna and saint worship: the postwar decades saw a vertiginous drop in church attendance (only 25 percent of the population attended Church regularly in 1955, 15 percent by 1970). Religious disenchantment coincided with the elevation of secular figures to the position of national icons. Like the saints, star figures could embody ideals, providing a form for dimly perceived aspirations to better forms of selfhood; but as flesh-and-blood individuals with continuing life stories, they could also act out the risks and conflicts of an age of sudden change.

France from the Liberation to May 1968: reconstruction of a nation

The two decades that followed the end of World War II were a period of unprecedented change in France. During the war, France had lost 600,000 lives in battle, and an estimated further 500,000 from unhealthy living conditions and poor medical care. By 1945, the country had seen the destruction of fifty thousand factories and 300,000 buildings, all of its ports, one quarter of its trains, most of its ships, over one hundred railway stations, nearly ten thousand bridges, and half of its motorised vehicles (Berstein and Milza 1991: 90). In the aftermath of war, a divided and weakened nation was totally dependent on US and UK support (ironically, the two countries largely responsible for the destruction as they freed France from German control). But reconstruction was rapid: by 1950, France had already reached the same levels of economic activity as in 1938. At the beginning of the 1950s, an economic boom began which only slowed down some twenty-five years later. In the period 1959–1970, France had a higher average national growth rate (5.8 percent) than any country in the world, apart from Japan. This economic boom was accompanied by social and cultural changes of great magnitude. In 1945, France's population of forty million was virtually the same as it had been in 1900, but over the next decade it was to grow to forty-five million, and then to fifty million by the end of the 1960s. Demographic expansion supported the development of an economics of consumption, which in turn contributed to an accelerated move to the towns and cities with their opportunities for employment and new forms of leisure. Statistics tell the story clearly. In 1946, with a ruined economy, there were 700,000 private cars in France, many of them old and in disrepair. In 1957, there were four million. In 1945, nearly half of the population still lived on the land rather than in a town – and the definition of 'town' included communities as small as two thousand inhabitants. In most rural households, three generations or more had lived together in one household, or in very close proximity, the situation unchanging down the centuries. Over the next thirty years, the rural population would halve, with the urban population now also living in much larger towns (Paris went from one tenth of the national population to one fifth), and on the whole in nuclear family units. The psychological significance of this will be discussed below, for it was not simply that rural France disappeared, but rather that the 'rural imagination' was itself carried suddenly forward into the 'new France'.

Change was dramatic, sudden, deep: France seemed to be transforming before its population's very eyes. Cities not only grew, but were also redesigned, with older districts being demolished in the name of progress and their populations frequently being moved out (as in Paris) to new, more salubrious if soulless suburbs. In terms of the acquisition of consumer goods, and the changing lifestyles they engendered, the gradually accumulating changes of the 1950s turned into an avalanche in the 1960s. Already between 1950 and 1960 the consumption of personal hygiene products (soaps, shampoos, deodorants) had risen by 86 percent (Ross 1995: 86). Between 1954 and 1957, household ownership of refrigerators went from 7 percent to percent, washing machines from 7 percent to 18 percent and vacuum cleaners from 14 percent to 22 percent. Ten years later, by the end of the 1960s, all of these were close to universal.

The essential socio-economic and psychocultural background to the 1950s and 1960s, therefore, is one of fast-paced change, with an underlying sense of vulnerability inherited from both dislocating social change and France's still vivid collective memory of the disasters of the two world wars. Moreover, the nation's developing and sustained economic prosperity and growth were accompanied by political uncertainty and instability. The year 1944 saw a raft of historic social reforms, a national economic plan, family policies, the nationalisation and the modernisation of banks, gas, electricity, car manufacturing, coal and steel, and the creation of Air France (the world-renowned *Caravelle* aeroplane came into production in 1955). These were followed by a huge, new nuclear programme, both civil and military. All these changes, however, were accompanied by inflation and a weak currency, and dependence on massive US aid. This was a very unusual phenomenon in any country: two processes, one restoring and one undermining the healthy self-confidence France needed so badly. In 1946 (and this after the dramatic resignation of de Gaulle in January, as if he were abandoning the country[3]), the new Fourth Republic constitution was voted in by referendum by only nine million people. Eight million voted against the constitution and another eight million did not bother to vote at all, so unloved was the new republic only one year on from the heady days of national liberation. Between 1946 and 1958, no government lasted for any length of time; there were sometimes two, even three in one year, and chronic political instability stumbled on until the regime broke upon the catastrophe in Algeria, when de Gaulle was called back again to power, in May 1958. De Gaulle's immense appeal to the national imagination owed much to his capacity to incarnate a positive, unified sense of Frenchness, however much division and conflict this in fact concealed.

French identity was threatened not just by political instability and economic dependence on the USA, but also by the massive influx of American films, goods, music and fashions, with all of the new and foreign values that these implied. Postwar Europe as a whole experienced the onslaught of US culture – pervasive, optimistic, glittering – as also a deep and difficult experience of the new entering the old. And France, with its anti-Americanism, its rural, small-town identity and sense of wounded pride (France would accept huge Marshall Aid like all western European countries, but with a sullenness unseen elsewhere), would experience US culture in a particular way. In one sense, France was as enthusiastic as any European country, as the short-lived but ecstatic welcoming of GIs into liberated Paris showed. Pop singers like Johnny Hallyday and Eddy Mitchell would become devoted ambassadors for US culture in the 1950s and 1960s.[4] Nonetheless, the US was experienced as a far more alien (and also utopian) culture in France than it was elsewhere. For the whole of western Europe, the US represented everything that was both glamorous and missing from a world of postwar gloom, from nylons to fridges, brightly coloured cars and neon signs.[5] In postwar (western) Europe generally, including the UK, the US became a truly mythical, other place. But in France – the French being among the least travelled Europeans, particularly to the United States – this mythologisation was doubly the case (as was the diabolisation of the US by the highly influential Communist Party). In the arena of the everyday, the relationship between established French cultural traditions and the mingled threat and promise of the American Other remained uneasy, and the capacity to signify a distinctly *French* identity whilst embodying the energy, style and openness to modernity associated with the USA was one determining feature of stardom. Bardot's style of beauty connoted a guilt-free eroticism that drew on a very French vision of *l'amour* whilst capturing a sense of as yet scarcely articulated sexual emancipation. Bardot both shocked and delighted US audiences, to the extent that her iconic status could rival that of Marilyn Monroe.[6] Her refusal to go to Hollywood confirmed her capacity and will to embody a distinctly French version of the modern. The New Wave – and notably Godard – fused the conventions of Hollywood genre films with their own innovative and stylish cinematography, effectively reconciling the thrill and energy of the new world with the poetic and experimental tradition of French film culture. In another significant cultural domain of the period, car design succeeded, at its best, in bringing together space-age modernity and French *haute couture* elegance: the star car of the 1950s was undoubtedly the out-of-reach-for-most Citroen DS (1956; *Déesse* = goddess), with its imaginative aesthetic boldness, and its almost futuristic air of modernity that made even American cars look ordinary.

Unity and difference: the old and the new

In certain respects, therefore, France telescoped into one generation what other countries had taken several generations to complete. One of the reasons why France was able to do this was its longstanding political and administrative centralisation. In many ways, and despite the instability of the Fourth Republic, it was the state that led France into modernity through government initiatives, the national plan, nationalisations and a powerful, centralised bureaucracy. Political structures embedded a sense of shared national identity and cultural developments in the postwar decades developed and intensified this. Radio, television and new, glossy magazines distributed nation-wide all contributed to the development of a collective sense of a specifically French modernity, and it was through these media that stars could enter the domestic intimacy of people's lives and become, to adapt the words of Edgar Morin, mediators between the 'heaven' of a glamorous public world and the 'earth' of quotidian reality.[7]

Until this time, radio had been the most significant mass medium, and had played an important social role in the twentieth century. Along with the education system (and conscription), the radio had acted in many ways as a unifier, a 'nationaliser' of France and its citizens. For Marshal Pétain, the radio had been a major propaganda tool during the Vichy period, and de Gaulle was also to use the radio, well into the 1960s. Widespread recognition of Lévi-Strauss as an intellectual authority outside the narrow realm of the university came, in part, from his 1959 radio interviews. Radio would play a vital role, too, in the construction of a teenage audience with its own music and its own sense of values and style – embodied, notably, in Johnny Hallyday – particularly from 1959 with the influential pop programme *Salut les copains!* But radio ownership was now developing slowly, from 72 percent in 1954 to 78 percent in 1958. By contrast, the growth in TV ownership was sudden and dramatic. In 1958, only 6 percent of the population had a TV set (one million sets). Within the next decade, this increased to 70 percent. In the 1960s, television brought both star performances and news and gossip about star lives, into the home.

But from the immediate postwar period on, a new style of glossy magazine was perhaps the most important vehicle of both a national sense of specifically French modernity, and of star culture.[8] From 1949, the weekly *Paris Match* chronicled national life, from changes of government and colonial wars to the *Salon de l'auto* (Motor Show) and the marriages of famous actors, in large, visually appealing photo spreads and up-beat, reader-friendly articles. *L'Express*, cofounded in 1953 by Françoise Giroud and the dashingly handsome americanophile Jean-Jacques Servan-Schreiber, presented political, business and cultural news in a stylish format with the emphasis on youth, progress and prosperity. The new and oh-so-modern women's magazine *Elle*, founded in 1945 and edited from 1946 to 1953 by Françoise Giroud, invited its readers to see themselves as a new generation of emancipated women, now (at last) full citizens of their country with the right to vote finally won in 1944, but also as specifically *French* women, elegant, domestically competent, culturally aware and willingly responsible for the quality of their (heterosexual) relationships. The reader evoked and addressed by *Elle* was either single and working, or young married and part of a 'modern' couple; in either case her aspirations were towards stylish and well equipped domestic efficiency (including culinary expertise), elegance and good grooming, and a feminine identity that combined social equality with the maintenance of a very traditional role as (sooner or later) wife and mother. At one time or another, *Elle* evoked, quoted or reviewed all of the stars discussed here, but Bardot and Sagan, constructed as ideal cases of the *femme moderne*, appeared regularly in the magazine's colourful pages.[9] The *vous* collectively addressed by *Elle* assumed a common sense of identity and set of priorities that connected a (broadly middle-class) generation of French women across the nation.

In a real sense, then, popular culture built on the infrastructure of a politically centralised country to bring together in an 'imagined community' (Anderson 1991), a population whose life experience nonetheless continued to vary widely, depending on a number of different factors including place of residence, class, generation and gender. 'National' French culture also remained localised, and life was undoubtedly very different depending on whether one lived in Paris, the provinces, the new suburbs of developing cities or small rural communities. Though the majority saw the world, at least in part, through the new mass media, they also saw it through the prism of their locality (inherited from the Revolution, there remain 36,000 administrative communes in France), and one of the factors that determined where one lived was class. Kristin Ross argues for the dynamic role played by social class in this period, but also identifies a generalised will to deny its importance (Ross 1996: 13), for the myth of modernity was one of seamless, conflict-free access to the material advantages of an efficiently technocratic society. Class difference undoubtedly was very evident, however, for example in the vast disparity between the rural poor and the urban bourgeoisie, or in the fact that France remained a country of huge income difference. By 1963, most workers enjoyed four weeks' paid holiday, but only 30percent of the French could afford to take a holiday away from home. Twenty years later this had risen to 60percent, a still relatively low figure, we should note, in a land of such prosperity. The homes that people left – or did not leave – to take holidays also varied widely. The government-sponsored housing/apartment-building programme began in earnest in the mid-1950s. By 1958, however, 37 percent of the population still lived in severely overcrowded conditions; one-third of families of four in only one or two rooms. There were vast slum areas. Around most large cities there were shantytowns of tarpaulin and corrugated iron. Ninety percent of dwellings in Paris had no bath or shower; 70 percent had no lavatory. In France as a whole, the figures were all around 50 percent (Gildea 1996: 81). In the 1940s and 1950s, there had been some haphazard, often private, building initiatives, but these often led to estates with no facilities, roads or public transport. By the 1960s, huge municipal apartment blocks on a Soviet scale were being thrown up. The vast, concrete Parisian suburb of Sarcelles was the prototype. In 1959, 300,000 homes were built, and by 1962 and until 1969, the figure was at half a million homes per year. It is arguable, however, which of these situations – the inadequate housing or the concrete jungle – was ultimately the more depressing. The new estates represented modernity in its more brutal form.

The overall result of social surveys between 1959 and 1969 (Berstein 1989: 213) was not one of great happiness and satisfaction, as one might imagine given the statistics of greater wealth, leisure, education and so on, but of unease and upheaval. For many, the stars in chic Paris and trendy St Tropez were indeed light years away. And we should bear in mind that although stars such as Raymond Poulidor and Johnny Hallyday came from very modest backgrounds, they were exceptions to the social status quo rather than indications of tectonic shifts within it as regards movements between social classes. Before this period and well after it, France remained a country where upward social mobility was rare and restricted to movement from the peasantry and proletariat into the lower middle class, where income differences were pronounced and where class differences, in spite of all the country's social revolutions, characterised social relations.

Generational difference attained a new importance too in the 1950s. Most periods after a war create dramatic rifts between generations. The post-World War II 'generation gap' was huge, partly because the demographic stagnation of the interwar years was quite suddenly replaced by a high birth rate and hence a large 'baby-boom' generation. For a century, the French had seen themselves as being in danger of dying out as a nation. After the war, the state, the Catholic Church and not least de Gaulle himself called repeatedly for a good, healthy, family-oriented baby boom. Family legislation became a hallmark of the Fourth (and later Fifth) Republic and, as we have seen, the French responded with an unprecedented rise in the birth rate. By 1958, eleven million of the French population were aged under fifteen, and their immediate elders whose teenage or young adult years coincided with the birth of the new, modern France also felt themselves to be significantly *different* from their parents and grandparents. Retail and cultural industries targeted this new market and defined *les jeunes* as a special generation needing their own products, music, films and stars: the enterprising publisher René Julliard was already making stars of his young female authors in the early 1950s by using their youth (and gender) as a marketing strategy, and the appeal of both Bardot and Hallyday rested in large part on their capacity to incarnate a mood of vaguely defined but passionate youthfulness. In 1957, Françoise Giroud organised a large-scale national survey for *L'Express* on a youth generation she called 'the New Wave' (*la Nouvelle Vague*): though responses revealed a decided absence of political engagement or social radicalism among the young, it confirmed that their sense of identity emphasised the generational rather than, for example, class affiliation.[10]

The effects of class and locality on the lived experience of being French in the postwar decades apply, of course, equally to the young, and although for the majority of French youth the decades after World War II meant more leisure, education, consumer goods and travel, this was by no means a universal trend. Christiane Rochefort's 1961 novel *Les Petits Enfants du siècle* (Children of the Century), a story of urban greyness and a teenage girl's (doomed) efforts to transcend it, captures an essential quality of life in this period. Many of this generation found themselves yearning for a range of ill-understood liberations, but trapped in the mundane, the urban and the dull. Stars represented the pleasures of 'otherness' and fantasy; they seemed to live in a world a million miles from the lived experience of many of the new generation. But elements of fantasy could also be brought into the everyday: reading Sagan's slim, desultory tales of Parisian love, listening to Johnny's music, following Poulidor's epic feats, for the most educated reading Sartre, Beauvoir, Camus and Lévi-Strauss, provided models of sophistication, stylish rebellion, courage against the odds and intellectual adventure that shaped young people's own self-image and sense of how to love, or dress, or move, or think.

For all generations and not only the young, in a society that was still firmly patriarchal, responses to the stars – like the whole sense of what it meant to be French in the postwar era – were inevitably shaped by gender. For women, this was a period of profound contradictions. On the one hand, a new equality was enshrined in the constitution, encouraged by the economy-driven expansion of educational and employment opportunities. On the other, pro-natalist policies, combined with the new imperative to sell consumer goods, laid the emphasis overwhelmingly on women as mothers, domestic consumers and objects of desire. The female stars studied here – Bardot and Sagan – both offered some degree of challenge to the prescribed, normative model of femininity, appropriating certain 'masculine' elements of style and behaviour into their portrayal of the feminine. At the same time, their stories (novels, films – and mediatised personal lives) maintained a focus on love and relationships with men that was in keeping with a traditional sense of feminine priorities. Their appeal for a female audience rested in part on this capacity to express a sense of contradiction. Their relevance for their female contemporaries extended too to the specific domain of sexual behaviour. There was also a darker side to the policies that produced France's demographic revival. The persuasive strategies of family allowances and benefits were only half the story: women were also dissuaded from making choices about maternity by the continuing illegality of abortion, and by the prohibition (until 1967) of information about or provision of contraception. In this period, one third of pregnancies were 'unwanted', and there were an estimated half a million back-street abortions per year. In fact, thousands of these did not even qualify as 'back street', a great many abortions and attempted abortions in the period being self-administered at home. It is estimated that such practices resulted in the deaths of twenty thousand women per year (Larkin 1997: 179–80). Both Sagan and Bardot represented an aspiration to a greater sexual freedom – already famously and notoriously articulated by Beauvoir in her 1949 book *The Second Sex* (Beauvoir 1972 [1953]) – that was, in practical terms, unavailable to most women. The shock value of their stories derived in part from this disparity between imagined freedoms and real constraints, and contributed to their celebrity. Bardot herself lived out the gap between fiction and fact, by undergoing – in 'real' life – illegal abortions followed by an unwanted pregnancy and birth, the latter acclaimed by the media as BB's final discovery of true feminine fulfilment.[11] Sagan publicly claimed to have undergone an illegal abortion when she signed the 1971 *manifeste des 343*, the manifesto of female celebrities in support of legalised abortion.[12]

Ideologies of masculinity were scarcely contested in this period: politics, industry, culture, sport – the public realm – remained a largely male sphere, and male roles were correspondingly defined. Nonetheless, the seeds of a post 1968 questioning of male identity, and of compulsory heterosexuality, may perhaps be glimpsed in such phenomena as the opposition to conscription and to militarism generally that arose from the Algerian war, or in the spectacular, semifetishised representations of Hallyday as sexy, sultry rock star. On the whole, though, male stars – including even Godard, with his interest in the politics of sex – offered variations on traditional constructions of masculinity, rather than their *mise en question*. De Gaulle, the political architect of the new France, managed to incorporate in his persona several of the most potent and durable male archetypes: soldier, knight errant, consort, patriarch.

The period is characterised, then, by a mixture of strongly shared national identity and division along the lines of class, age and gender, and by the ubiquitous juxtaposition of the old and the new. To take one concluding and summarising example, as a generation of young women embraced the *Elle* world of co-education, the right to vote, off-the-peg fashion and relaxed social mores, there remained literally millions of World War I widows and spinsters,[13] many of whom were now only in their early sixties (in 1958, there were five million people over sixty in France). Dressed head to toe in black, with no hint of make-up, sweeping their doorsteps, sitting in the shade in their doorways, in every small town and village in France they bore witness to the continuing existence of one age while witnessing the coming of another, perhaps in the form of the tanker trundling through the main street on its way through France, or the arrival of the roadies and electricians setting up the local hall for a concert by the young Johnny Hallyday.

Algeria

In her analysis of this period, Kristin Ross argues that the iconic glamour of cars – like, perhaps, that of stars – functioned in part to mask a deeper unarticulated knowledge, almost like a psychically repressed nightmare: the horrors of France's decolonisation process. Throughout the period 1954–1962, many young men (as conscripts) experienced the underside of France's modernisation, in the frightening experience for all concerned of Algeria and the brutal decolonisation process.[14] And we can say, moreover, that much of this process, and particularly its mediatisation – for example, media coverage of the horrific bombings of cafés, bus queues and other, everyday, civilian spaces that were taking place mainly in Algiers, but also in Paris – were both awful and *new*.

Analysis of the Algerian conflict lies outside our project here, but it is essential to note that the war was central to the French experience of the 1950s and 1960s.[15] This was a bitter armed struggle that provoked intense controversy and called the political regime itself into question. The conflict (or, more precisely perhaps, the crisis of authority that it provoked within the French state) brought the Fourth Republic regime down in 1958, and the country to the brink of a military coup and arguably civil war. Not only did the increasingly ubiquitous media make events in Algeria a part of daily French experience, but military conscription meant that all French families were potentially involved in a more direct way, if their sons were sent to North Africa. The revelations about the use of torture by some elements of the French army led to an uncomfortable questioning of national morality, at a time when memories of the Nazi occupation were still close. The war came closer still when, in the late 1950s and early 1960s, demonstrations in France pitted Algerian workers and French civilians against the police in confrontations that were often violent and sometimes murderous; once it became clear that de

Gaulle was going to grant independence, in 1962, fear of the Algerian National Liberation Front (FLN) was replaced by fear of the French settlers' OAS (*Organisation de l'Armée Secrète*), with its use of terror tactics both in Algeria and on the mainland.

It goes without saying that the French intellectual community was particularly involved in the passionate debate over the rights and wrongs of colonialism, and of the conduct of the war itself. From the Dreyfus Affair[16] through to the 1950s, French intellectuals had played a vital and very public role in political life. Not all intellectuals were pro-Algerian independence, but the most prominent of them were. Sartre and Beauvoir led intellectual opposition to French policy and then backed vigorously the decision to withdraw, once it came. In September 1960, many intellectuals and artists signed the *Manifeste des 121* in favour of military insubordination, given the use of torture and mistreatment by the French army.[17] Signatories included Françoise Sagan, who went on to support the cause of Algerian women fighters ill-treated by their French captors, and thus became a target for the OAS. Godard's gradual politicisation as a film-maker both mirrored and contributed to a developing mood of left-wing *engagement* in sections of the younger generation: his second feature film, *Le Petit Soldat,* ambivalent as its politics were, was kept off the screen from 1960 to 1963 because it dealt with the Algerian situation, and *Pierrot le fou* (1965) aligned the Algerian war with that other bloody drama of decolonisation, the war in Vietnam. Lévi-Strauss chose the path of detachment from immediate political events, but his engagement with the issues of Eurocentrism and racial inequality was central to his work and to his impact on a nation and a world dealing with the painful changes of a postcolonial age.

It was by no means only the 'intellectual' stars whose fame was interwoven with the conflict in Algeria. De Gaulle's career from the mid-1950s to 1962 was defined by Algeria. At the other end of the scale, as it were, Raymond Poulidor was known to have been severely affected emotionally by his period of conscript service in Algeria: his sense of alienation on his return echoed that of a generation, and in part motivated his self-investment in cycling as a form of 'redemption'. The significance of stars like Bardot and – slightly later – Hallyday owed something to their capacity to represent that sense of generational alienation shaped, in part, by the war, and particularly by the experience of conscription. With characteristic ambivalence, playing on

both the new and the old, Bardot also benefited from a wave
of patriotic approval in 1961 when she stood up to the OAS,
who tried to extort money from her by threatening both her
and her baby son. Instead of paying up, Bardot published
their threatening letter in *L'Express*, using her celebrity to
encourage opposition to their terror campaign. Thus the stars
of the period did not only function to distract national
attention from the traumas of a violent decolonisation, but
were also seen to be touched by or involved with the war, and
provided public representations of the conflicting emotions it
provoked.

Conclusion

We have noted the *scale* of change that France went through
in the decades after World War II, from ruin and deprivation
to prosperity and modernity. We have also stressed the *speed* of
the scale of change at all levels of society and the economy,
and that such speed was dramatic, while not being universal.
It did not carry all before it, though it may have appeared to
do so. In many ways, and this has been our third point,
although the 'new' was brought in on a massive scale – from
the state, by the state, by the Americans and the culture that
flooded in behind them, from Europe, from and by Paris to
and upon the provinces – it was indelibly affected by the 'old'.
The speed of change, in fact, assured the *survival of the old*, or
more precisely, the entry of the old into the new, of 'deep
France' into the 'new France'. Old and new France; France and
Europe; France and the US; democratic France and its very
recent authoritarian, near-fascist Vichy experience; the bright
France of exciting, fashionable Paris and the darker side of
the Algerian (and other decolonisation) nightmares: all co-
existed. If the period is characterised by tension between the
old and the new, it is also charged with the contradictions
between difficult and opposing kinds of newness.

The old France, 'deep France', survived in the midst of
change, so that for many the 'new France' was lived mainly at
a symbolic level; a new way of life, glamorous, modern, chic
and colourful, lived vicariously alongside the old, through
magazines and radio shows. For most people, though in
varying proportions, the new nation was in part lived
experience, in part a spectacle viewed from the outside. The
capacity to appeal at once to the yearning for a new, rootless

modernity, and to a nostalgic respect for tradition, home and region played its part in the success of many stars of the 1950s, as some of the chapters below will argue. Brigitte Bardot embodied a new sexual freedom, but both on and off screen her assertion of female desire was firmly recuperated for a more traditional politics of gender. Johnny Hallyday was at once rebellious teen hero and sober, patriotic conscript; Raymond Poulidor's national celebrity rested on his combination of a very modern talent as sporting entrepreneur with the traditional values of the French peasant. De Gaulle himself also incarnated this juxtaposing of old and new. In 1958, when he came back to power, he was sixty-seven years old, had fought in World War I, was in many respects an almost nineteenth century figure, and yet was the instrument of France's dramatically fast political and economic modernisation, and – although in part to his own incomprehension – its social and cultural modernisation too. It was in the year that preceded his return to power in 1958, that Françoise Giroud coined the term 'New Wave' to describe the emerging culture. We can see, therefore, that the old and the new were not just interwoven, but in some respects were expressed simultaneously in the same person or same moment.

Stars condense fantasies, star image reflects notions of identity within society, and a star system helps a society reconcile or appear to reconcile contradictions. Clearly the cross-class appeal of the stars of entertainment (here Bardot, Hallyday and Poulidor) or of a national political leader (de Gaulle) was very different from the address to an elite audience made by a Lévi-Strauss, a Godard or even a Sagan. But given the popular celebrity of intellectuals and artists peculiar to French culture, in each of these three cases critical or academic acclaim was able to develop – albeit to differing degrees – into mass recognition, and a star status that crossed class boundaries. At one level, stardom reflected the optimism of what was perceived as a major step away from the misery and deprivation of the 1930s and the war: new homes, colourful consumer goods, more income and leisure, better health care, employment, better food. But stardom also betrayed signs of the loss of a former world and the disappointments of the new, of displacements to grey council estates and the frustrations (and anxieties) of a new and booming generation of teenagers, arguably both emotionally and morally at sea, and prey to a strong sense of the mundane and the dull at best, the horrific (Indochina, Algeria) at worst; all hidden, denied and repressed as well as revealed, celebrated and expressed by the star system, itself bathing the land in glorious Technicolor as the monochrome France of the Fourth Republic moved into the bright and swinging sixties.

Notes

1. 'La star-system est une institution spécifique au grand capitalisme' (Morin 1972 [1957]: 99).
2. There were, arguably, some exceptions to this in the nineteenth century, for example Napoleon's nation-wide – and distinctly glamorous – celebrity, or that of Victor Hugo.
3. In January 1946, De Gaulle – so recently the leader of French resistance to the German Occupation, hence seen as the saviour of national honour – resigned his presidency of the provisional government. De Gaulle disagreed profoundly with plans for the new Constitution, which would return power to parliament, rather than (as De Gaulle recommended) establish a strong executive.
4. Hallyday and Mitchell, in their choice of songs as well as costume – blue jeans, check shirts, sometimes cowboy hats – invoked the glamorised myth of the rural USA, whereas singers in the French *chansonnier* tradition, like Charles Aznavour and Yves Montand, brought back to France images of Manhattan. From the late 1950s, the New Wave directors also promoted – in a spirit of what François Truffaut termed 'respectful pastiche' (Houston 1961: 64) – the urban mythologies of the American B-movie.
5. One is reminded that for intellectuals like Simone de Beauvoir, the UK barely existed, but the US was a fascinating place even if in political terms it was the enemy (see for example Beauvoir's Goncourt prize-winning *Les Mandarins*, 1954); and that for journalists such as Jean-Jacques Servan-Schreiber and Françoise Giroud, the US represented a bright, optimistic future.
6. *L'Express* of 19 December 1957 proudly proclaims that 'Bardolatry' is sweeping the United States, with *And God Created Woman* (*Et Dieu créa la femme*) showing at twenty New York cinemas.
7. Morin, writing in 1957, refers only to film stars, though his comment is more widely applicable. His actual words are 'Stars now participate in the everyday life of mere mortals. They are no longer inaccessible but mediators between the heaven of the screen and the earth below' ('Les stars participent dès lors à la vie quotidienne des mortels. Ce ne sont plus des étoiles inaccessibles mais des médiatrices entre le ciel de l'écran et la terre') (Morin 1957: 33).
8. Kristin Ross sees the widespread reading of these self-consciously modern, visually appealing magazines as a central element in the creation of a new sense of national identity, or what Benedict Anderson has termed a 'nationally imagined community' (Ross 1995: 144).
9. See below, chapters 3 and 8.
10. Questions on political issues attract a lot of 'don't know' answers. For example to 'Would you like to see a socialist society in France?' 47 percent answered 'Don't know' (*L'Express* 5.12.57).
11. See below, Chapter 3.

12. The manifesto, published in the magazine *Le Nouvel Observateur* on 5 April 1971, stated that a million women each year underwent illegal and often dangerous abortions in France, and declared support for free access to contraception and the legalisation of abortion. The 343 well-known women who put their names to the manifesto all declared that they themselves had undergone illegal abortions, and thus implicitly dared the state to prosecute them. Simone de Beauvoir and Christiane Rochefort were among the signatories, as were actresses Jeanne Moreau and Delphine Seyrig. Abortion was finally legalised in France in 1975.

13. Well over 1.25 million young Frenchmen had been killed between 1914 and 1918, and a further four million wounded, one million of these permanently maimed.

14. See Philip Dine's chapter in this volume for Poulidor's reaction to the experience.

15. A useful point of comparison would be the conflict in Northern Ireland (1969–): for all its dramatic and harrowing nature, that conflict has never called the UK regime into question, nor triggered so bitter a controversy outside Ulster itself. The USA's experience of the war in Vietnam would be a more appropriate analogy.

16. The Dreyfus Affair was a political scandal that divided France at the end of the nineteenth century. It began with the prosecution for treason of a French Jewish Army officer, Alfred Dreyfus, in 1894: after a passionate and deeply divisive national debate, his innocence was proved and antisemitism proved to be the real cause of his conviction. Intellectuals, and in particular the writer Emile Zola, played a major role in the whole affair.

17. A countermanifesto from intellectuals supporting France's continuing presence in Algeria followed.

CHAPTER 2

1950s POPULAR CULTURE: STAR-GAZING AND MYTH-MAKING WITH ROLAND BARTHES AND EDGAR MORIN

Susan Weiner

'Barthes is back', announced the 4 December 2002 cover story of *Les Inrockuptibles*, a weekly dedicated to international high and popular culture trends for the would-be plugged-in reader. The occasion was multiple: an exhibition dedicated to this major intellectual at Beaubourg, the revised edition of the complete works, as well as the first-time publication of his Collège de France seminars, also available on CD-ROM (fourteen and twenty-one hours of listening time).[1] Barthes may have been back in France, but for Anglo-Americans, he had never gone away. In academe, Barthes was among the first emissaries of 'Theory,' via the English translations in the 1960s and 1970s of *Sur Racine* (Barthes 1960a; *On Racine,* 1964), *Le Degré zéro de l'écriture* (Barthes 1953a; *Writing Degree Zero,* 1967), *Eléments de la sémiologie* (Barthes 1960b; *Elements of semiology,* 1967), and *Mythologies* (Barthes 1957; *Mythologies,* 1972). Unlike Derrida, Foucault and Lacan, Barthes does not go in and out of style, but remains a consistent reference in literary and cultural studies, as well as film theory. Outside the ivory tower, his writings have made a significant impact in marketing and advertising – ironically so, since Barthes sought to dissect and not encourage the dissemination of the consumer mentality and the world of images.

With Barthes under the influence of Ferdinand de Saussure, intellectuals on both sides of the Atlantic began to take what Richard Rorty in 1967 dubbed 'the linguistic turn' (Rorty 1967), the tendency to see and read everything as a system of signs, as a language unto itself. The aforementioned *Mythologies* applies Saussurian linguistics to the novelties and familiarities of everyday life in post-war France. The combination of subject and method make it simultaneously accessible and subtly difficult in its humour and style. *Les Inrocks* calls it 'dated and extremely topical' ('daté et terriblement actuel') (Gabriel 2002: 40). Roland Barthes has shaped several generations of critics, inside and outside academia.

But for cultural studies, at least in its sense as the study of everyday life through popular cultural forms and practices, the Barthesian critical stance in its 'everything is text' ('tout est textuel') mode has proven itself insufficient. The elitism of its 'us/them' mentality leaves little room for 'them', the participants or consumers of popular culture. Today Barthes' semiotic aloofness in *Mythologies* is synonymous with the beginnings of theoretical reflection on mass culture in postwar France. Its 1957 publication, however, coincided with that of an essay taking a different approach to the subject: Edgar Morin's *Les Stars* (Morin 1957).[2] *Les Stars* represents the early stages of a body of work Morin would later call his 'sociology of the present' (Morin 1984: 199). In contrast to Barthes, Morin sought to examine both the outer world and the inner experience of mass culture, and to account for a pleasure in which the researcher, too, might very well take part. Over the decades in an Anglo-American context long enthralled with Marxist theory, Morin's approach has generated little interest. Only four of his books are available in translation: not the mass-culture essays, but two field studies and a volume on the philosophical and scientific paradigm of self-organisation, the latter representing the interdisciplinary direction his work took from the 1970s on.[3] Yet intellectual history has recently turned its attention to this long-neglected thinker, with the publication of Myron Kofman's *Edgar Morin: From Big Brother to Fraternity* (Kofman 1996: 102)[4] and a 1997 issue of the British journal *French Cultural Studies* devoted to Morin's life and work. Kofman's title carries with it the reason for our new interest. Rather than the critical stance, Morin speaks from a place of sympathy, consistently eradicating the distance between the phenomena he studies, from mass culture to the self-organisation of the physical world, and himself. Nor does

Morin indulge in Hoggart-style populism in his approach to
mass culture. A Sephardic Jew, son of a Sentier shopkeeper, he
turned to intellectual life and activism; Morin was the name
he took in the Resistance.[5] Morin joined the French
Communist Party in 1942, and left in 1951 following reactions
to an article he wrote for *L'Observateur* (Morin 1992a[1959]:
178). In the mass culture essays of the 1950s and 1960s, his
sympathy is not an expression of class identity, but a
methodological choice to understand the 'bio-social origin
and character' (Kofman 1996: 104) of groups constituted by
gender and generation rather than social class.[6] Morin called
his approach 'anthropo-socio-historical' (Kofman 1996: 159);
later critics have termed Morin an anthropological humanist
(Rigby 1997: 333–340). In the current climate of cultural
studies, motivated by the desire to understand individual
experience and response rather than begin and end with the
text, Morin has found his appeal at long last alongside,
though not in placement of, Barthes.

The movie-star culture that is Morin's single subject is one of
many for Barthes, but *Les Stars* and *Mythologies* come to a more
complex point of convergence. Both observed the same odd
principle at work in mass culture, odd in light of the apparent
thrall of technology in the postwar period. That principle was
myth: technology, paradoxically, had the power to renew
the ancient imaginative function of mythic thinking in
contemporary industrial society. Through the mass media, the
mythic was rendered visible, palpable, legible and ubiquitous.
For Morin, movie stars were contemporary society's gods, their
personae and movements on and off screen rendered mythic by
worshipful fans; for Barthes, media reports on the marriage of
stars to mortals created new myths and reinvented familiar
ones, just as did the plastic industry touting the alchemical
properties of the material, or a general's call for steak and fries
upon return to his native land. Reclaiming myth from the
exoticising ahistoricism of Lévi-Strauss's structuralist analysis,
Morin and Barthes instead examined myth's cultural work,
conscious and unconscious, in the formations of contemporary
industrial society. Their agreement on myth as the generative
principle of mass culture stands as a determinative moment in
intellectual history: the site of the linguistic turn and the
anthropological humanist alternative (the latter long-ignored),
two approaches cultural studies brings together today.

Barthes and Morin: culture as text and the sociohistoric determinants of culture

Barthes and Morin came to their views of mass culture within a shared New Left trajectory.[7] Friends and collaborators, the two men initially made contact through Morin's responses to a 1952 survey Barthes had devised with Maurice Nadeau for *France-Observateur*. By 1952, Morin had become increasingly disenchanted with the hard line of the French Communist Party. His approach to the Sartrian 'what is literature?' question (he saw the importance of Proust's *Recherche* as fundamentally sociological, for example) had a significant impact on Barthes's analysis of the survey's results, and, one can imagine, on Barthes's own response to *littérature engagée* in the 1953 *Degré zéro de l'écriture*. Both men wrote for Nadeau's dissident Left *Lettres nouvelles*, with Morin contributing for the most part articles on cinema. And both were affiliated with the *Centre National de la Recherche Scientifique* (CNRS) research council. In the mid-1950s, Barthes was appointed to its sociology section to research fashion. Morin abandoned the area of his initial research from the beginning of the decade, the 'aesthetics of labour', in order to study cinema, using social science methods. Fashion and cinema: equally unorthodox areas of sociological research at the time. In 1956, when Morin launched the research bulletin *Arguments*, a voice for the nonCommunist Left, he chose Barthes as associate editor. Barthes would again participate in a sociological endeavour of Morin's with the 1960 creation of the *Centre d'études de communications de masse* (CECMAS) and its journal *Communications*, intended to study the phenomenon of the media event.

Barthes and Morin were on the same page intellectually and politically: anti-Stalinist and antistructuralist – while conceding their debt to both '-isms' (Stafford 1997: 293). They differed profoundly, however, in their commitment to industrial mass culture as an object of study. After *Les Stars* and the preceding 1956 essay, *Le Cinéma ou l'homme imaginaire*, Morin went on to analyze in the two-volume *Esprit du temps* (Morin 1976) the more general postwar phenomenon of the transformation of leisure into what he called a *Tierce Culture* ('Third Culture'). He was, as he himself laid claim, the first French sociologist to treat popular culture seriously, its forms as well as its audiences. In a two-part article on the first page of *Le Monde* in July 1963, he prophetically hailed the concert of Johnny Hallyday and his *yé-yé* peers at the Place de la Nation as a 'collective phenomenon,' the sign of the emergence of a new social type, the teenager, poised between consumerism and revolt (Morin 1963).

No youngster himself, Morin nevertheless took a pleasure best described as vicarious in the music made by young Americanophiles who retained a certain something French, and the fans who resembled them. Morin believed he held the key to understanding the mass culture that French intellectuals, pedagogues, and moralists typically despised. The only way to render descriptive justice to the object was to take pleasure in it oneself.[8] In a parenthetical aside in *Les Stars* following a reference to Marilyn Monroe by first name only, he asks for the reader's tolerance: 'the reader is asked to forgive this familiarity coming from an author who lives the myths he analyses'[9] (Morin 1957: 32). Morin was part of the crowd – or at least he wanted to be.

Outside of collaborative work with CECMAS, Barthes would not return to the study of cultural life after *Mythologies* until the 1967 *Système de la mode*, a semiotic analysis of the language of fashion where the garments themselves practically disappeared. In the interim, he turned his attention to literary theory.[10] For Barthes, the mode of analysis was always more meaningful than the object itself. This first period of his work in the 1950s and 1960s was marked by a dual attention to language and ideology – the work of language being always more interesting than the ideological content transmitted. Barthes would only begin to address the question of the reader's, and writer's, pleasure in the 1973 *Le Plaisir du texte*. Barthes' approach in *Le Plaisir du texte*, though not a sociology of reading, does bring to mind Morin's insistence on pleasure rather than aloofness in the intellectual's analysis of mass culture, a filiation that has gone unremarked in intellectual history. In their 1957 essays, the agreement on myth as the generative principle of postwar mass culture was complemented by the shared methodological choice to appropriate key concepts of Marxist thought for its analysis. *Mythologies* saw Barthes working with the Marxist theory of demystification.

Classic Marxist thought defines demystification as a means to transcendence or social change. Barthes appropriated the term to show how contemporary French culture was a network of messages, some familiar, some not, which he called myths: 'myth is a language' (Barthes 1957a: 9) generated by the Right – for the Left does not make myths, according to Barthes, in what Michael Kelly terms one of his more 'embarrassing' statements (Kelly 2000: 89). Myth is an incessant but always subtle promotion of 'Nature', 'la Norme [two capital Ns] bourgeoise', in the form of messages received uncritically, thus lived, by the reader-consumer: 'the reader lives myth as a story both true and imaginary'[11] (Barthes 1957: 202). It is the task of the mythologist (*mythologue*) to demystify myth on the level of its language. The mythologist is none other than the semiotician, the intellectual offspring of Saussurian linguistics; *Mythologies* is effectively Barthes's call to semiological arms for a cultural moment poised between the old and the new: 'the development of advertising, of major newspapers, the radio, glossy magazines, not to mention the survival of an endless number of communication-related rites (rites of social appearance) make more urgent than ever the constitution of a semiological science'[12] (Barthes 1957: 185). True to his tendency to place the mode of analysis before the social or literary text, Barthes relegated the rise of the mass media and the accompanying sociopolitical *immobilisme* in postwar France to a footnote.

Only semiotics can expose the relaying of bourgeois ideology by mass culture and the public's ritualistic participation in the mythic form it takes. Ordinary language is the vehicle for mythic messages. To take an example Barthes himself did not use, we have only to think of the 1950s advertisement for Moulinex: 'Moulinex liberates woman' ('Moulinex libère la femme'). Nothing to 'interpret' here; the words are all ordinary. Barthes insisted upon the fact that the demystification of cultural myths is not interpretation. Interpretation would imply a latent presence, and as he wrote, 'nothing hides behind myth' ('le mythe ne cache rien') (Barthes 1957: 194). Rather, demystification involves the work of decoding the arbitrary – yet motivated – relationship between signifier and signified to identify ideological messages, which have been on the surface all along. Moulinex frees woman: from what? What kind of 'saviour' does such an advertisement posit Moulinex to be? How are women, plural rather than singular, paradoxically re-enslaved by the glamorisation of Woman and her accessory appliances? Barthes wrote, for example, of advertising's opposition between powdered and liquid detergent and the true abrasive qualities of both formats, of recipes in *Elle* as fantasies for the magazine's modest readership, and of the new Citroën as the contemporary Gothic cathedral. Omo, Moulinex, Citroën, cherry-studded roast partridge, Marlon Brando (via his humble French fiancée): these were the stars of 1950s France.

Yet the public did not realise that such a continuum of adoration had become the stuff of everyday life – and vice versa. The artifice of a belief system composed of media messages was not apparent to those who lived their myths as an inductive rather than semiological system (Barthes 1957: 204). Obliviousness to domination is the definitive condition of the consumer public Barthes described, whose only distinguishing mark was their relationship to the bourgeois norm.[13]

Demystification led Barthes right back to alienation, not of labour, but first of language, then necessarily of everyday life. It was not *his* alienation, however. 'What I have looked for in all this material is signification' ('Ce que j'ai cherché en tout ceci, ce sont des significations'[Barthes 1957: 10]), he explained. The search for the signifier positioned Barthes the mythologist as one who stood outside of alienated language, who 'excludes himself from all of the consumers of myth' (Barthes 1957: 209) – a far cry from Morin's enthusiasm for 'Marilyn.' Such a person can only relate to the world through what he admits to be a kind of soulless cleverness: 'his connection to the world is a sarcastic one' ('sa liaison au monde est d'ordre sarcastique') (Barthes 1957: 231). Lest he get too comfortable in his prophet's shoes, the mythologist, Barthes warned, is not in a 'Mosesian situation' and does not get the chance to lay eyes on the Promised Land: 'he is forbidden to imagine what appreciably the world will be like, when the immediate object of his critique will have disappeared'[14] (Barthes 1957: 231). Ultimately, the situation of the mythologist is even more distressing than that of the oblivious public living their myths: no longer believing in the revolution, the mythologist is condemned to forever read – perhaps just another form of alienation.

Morin: Myth and Anthropology

For Morin, myth was a category of human experience whose mystery was meant to be left intact. In the 1972 preface to the third edition of *Les Stars*, he placed his essay in opposition to what he called the 'official' sociological mode of analysis of movie fan culture. 'In this book,' he wrote, 'we have taken the phenomenon seriously'.[15] As Morin went on to define it, the 'serious' approach did not dismiss the masses as naïve or deceived, but considered them with respect. Respect meant the treatment of the relationships between the film-going public and the actors they adored as a culture unto itself, structured by mythic thinking and practices. Morin borrowed freely from the discourse of anthropology, analysing the minutiae of fan behaviour much as if they were the rites of a remote tribal culture. Borrowing freely does not mean borrowing naïvely: Morin ultimately put anthropological discourse on display, effacing the distance between so-called primitive and civilised people, both of whom, as he showed, held to their own myths. Underlying Morin's anthropological humanism is the appropriation of the Marxist dialectic – remarked on, moreover, by Barthes, who saw in Morin's mode of analysis the workings of a 'dialectical imagination' (Barthes 1993: 1534–5).[16] Its origin and reference were Hegel and Marx, but a different vision motivates Morin's 'actively imagining work' ('oeuvre imaginante'): the synthesis of social realities alongside what should and should not exist: 'what is, what should not be, and what should'[17] (Barthes 1993: 1535). The Barthes who appreciated Morin's synthesis of intellect and imagination could not similarly assess the French public, whose consumption of media messages as 'true and imaginary stories', as we have seen, was rather a sign of their passivity.

'True and imaginary' are the terms of Morin's general definition of myth as well, but seen in dynamic relation to each other. Myth was the effect of the human imagination as it was lived in the world, and the star system was its ideal contemporary illustration. Film stars, like their counterparts in ancient Greece and Rome, were an amalgam of traits both human and divine; the identities of cult actor and fictional character were in constant synthesis between real life and the screen, from one film to the next. Morin illustrated this phenomenon through a neologism inspired by Gary Cooper, who '*garycooperise*'-es his roles. Fans engaged with the various manifestations of actors and characters in a mode that combined entertainment, quasireligious devotion, and psychological identification (Morin1972 [1957]: 8). Among the 'ensemble of imaginary practices and situations' (Morin 1972 [1957]: 38) of fan culture were magazines, clubs and obsessive letter-writing, and multiple viewings of favourite films. The Cannes film festival was holy ground, the 'mystical site of identification of the imaginary and the real' (Morin 1972 [1957]: 57), a terrestrial Olympus where fans had the real chance to see their gods. Such fervour was unequalled among devotees of theatre, dance or music – though this would not long be the case for the latter. For the star system was the culture of the 'impossible dream': the imagined encounter with the star or the dream of becoming a star oneself, the *why not me?'* (*'pourquoi pas moi?'*). Any fairly attractive, ordinary person might be 'discovered' on the street – but at the same time stardom was a closed system: 'myth begins here … at the very heart of reality'[18] (Morin 1972 [1957]: 49). Whereas Barthes diagnosed 'the French' in terms of the bourgeois norm, Morin incorporated verbatim British, US, and French samples of fan mail and stars' responses, letting real people speak for themselves. Letters between Luis Mariano and his fans published weekly in *Cinémonde* are the basis for observations about the nature of gifts to latter-day gods – symbolic, religious, secular, fetishistic – and the types of communication fans initiate with them: requests for work, money, or clothing the star has worn; sentimental, familial, and professional confessions, to which the star replies with advice or consolation. Gifts and letters are the most intimate means of approaching the star, a union both imaginary and real which Morin compares to cannibalism and communion:

> Moreover, the faithful always want to consume their god. From the time cannibals ingested their ancestors, ever since totemic meals where believers would eat the holy animal, up to our own communions and eucharists, every god is made in order to be eaten, that is to say incorporated, assimilated. The first assimilation is through knowledge. The fan wants to know everything, wants to mentally possess, manipulate, digest the total image of the idol. In this instance, knowledge is a means of magical appropriation[19] (Morin 1972 [1957]: 82).

Little difference, then, between the devout Christian, the tribal initiate, and the fan. Adoration of the screen's immortals was simply the newest manifestation of the magic of religion.

Yet the fan was a specific sociohistorical phenomenon as well. Morin cited UK and US researchers who found that 75–90 percent of movie fans were under the age of 21, and that 80 percent were female. The significance of the statistics lay in Morin's conclusions. Who else but women and teenagers, he queried, were most inclined to feel and express the uncensored fervour characteristic of the fan? The man who imitates his favourite actor rarely turns imitation into devotion: 'he has a preference for the star, but without adoring them' ('il la préfère [la star] mais sans la révérer') (Morin 1972 [1957]: 94). Teenagers, on the other hand, look to stars in the self-conscious process of identity formation. Nowhere was this more apparent than in the apprenticeship of gender roles and sexuality:

> They are the ones who model themselves on film heroes, in order to better affirm their identity. They are the ones who assimilate the imaginary star into their real romantic life. The star is not only informative, but formative, not only instigative, but initiatory[20] (Morin 1972 [1957]: 130).

The interplay between the imaginary and the real acquires all the more urgency for teenagers watching love scenes in a darkened theatre. Morin was the first sociologist to identify adolescence in the France of the 1950s and 1960s as both a category of psychosocial identity and a consumer group in its own right, forged in no small part by the mass media. *Les Stars* was just the beginning of his reflection on the subject. Morin's explanation as to why women would continue to worship stars well after the initiations and incitations of adolescence was nowhere near as celebratory. Adult female fans, he suggested, were necessarily unhappy in their lives. Across the spectrum of the middle classes, in the country and the city, they suffered and delighted masochistically, in the throes of a latter-day Bovaryism:

> However, the star's influence can persist, after adolescence, where personality has weakly established its internal boundaries between dream and reality, that is to say in adult women more than men, and more often in the middle social sectors. That is to say, ultimately, especially in women of those sectors: low-paid shopgirls, lower-middle class women, dreamy, unsatisfied provincial types, their faces all made-up[21] (Morin 1972 [1957]: 132).

Morin's fascination for the rituals of the film fan gives way here to a kind of fastidiousness in the face of female fantasy. At her worst, the woman who fantasises about film stars exhibits signs of a personality disorder; at best she inspires pity. Notable in their absence from Morin's formula are working-class and white-collar professional women, whose minds, he implies, were necessarily more sensibly occupied.

Film studies has since given a much more nuanced view of gender, class, and spectatorship. Lest we dismiss Morin's point of view too quickly, however, the fact that he even considered the female fan worthy of sociological attention is itself significant. The concept of 'projection-identification' introduced in *Le Cinéma ou l'homme imaginaire* in 1956 has become one of the cornerstones of theories of spectatorship and cultural studies in general. Theorists today assume there exists an individual experience of the products of mass culture determined by a variety of factors, among them gender. Morin was the first to introduce this idea.

Popular culture and the new generation

In the late 1950s, Morin held the view that fantasy was age-appropriate: acceptable and even natural in the formation of adolescent identity; but a sad sign of the middle-class woman's tenuous grip on reality. When Barthes turned to the question of gender and generation in the context of cinema, the result was a good deal more subtle. Unlike Morin, Barthes was no film fan; movement on screen interested him less than the film still. In 'Visages et figures' ('Faces and Figures'), excerpted in *Mythologies* and published in full in *Esprit* in July 1953, he traces the development of cinematic icons in France in terms of a 'sociology of the human face' ('sociologie du visage humain' [Barthes 1993: 224]). Valentino was the 'first historical face' of cinema, miraculous, inimitable and divine (Barthes 1953b). With the advent of sound, cinemas proliferated and with them the new genre of the fan magazine. An entire gallery of faces came to be displayed in Paris and the provinces, 'broadcast', wrote Barthes, 'with a level of insistence and amplitude never before possible'[22] (Barthes 1993: 225). Though the cinephilia of the 1930s spread geographically and found new forms of expression in print media, it remained a world unto itself. This separate status would change after World War II. Changes in the industry engendered physiognomical changes on screen. With the nationalisation of French cinema, faces on the screen and faces on the street came to resemble each other. Once divine and singular, the cinematographic face underwent what Barthes called its 'vulgarisation'. Actors now signified archetypical Frenchness: 'a euphoric anthropology of salespeople, shopboys, loveable spendthrift boys from good families ... In one fell swoop, the human face is secularised, and at the lowest level'[23] (Barthes 1993: 229). Everyone looked like a star; stars looked like everyone. Barthes's observations are more dramatic than Morin's theory of projection-identification; he saw social life and cinema changing in tandem, on the very level of a shared morphology.

Of prime value in the new iconographic type of the postwar face was the capacity to signify interiority, 'a less distressed and more youthful intellectuality' ('une intellectualité moins souffrante et plus juvénile'). For the 'birth of the intellectual face' ('naissance du visage intellectuel' [Barthes 1993: 230]) coincided with the new visibility – and new exemplarity – of adolescence in late 1940s France. From 1946 on, the streets and screens of France had undergone a simultaneous adolescent invasion. 'What is new', wrote Barthes, 'is the recognition of adolescence as an age unto itself, complete with a human dimension that can even be exemplary'[24] (Barthes 1993: 230). There is no causality to be established between adolescence real and represented, but rather the workings of culture's own dialectical imagination. Thus the rise of Gérard Philippe, Brigitte Bardot (eventually) and their myriad lookalikes.

The newest version of the sensitive young man, cinematic and no longer literary, made new roles possible for young women as well. Long suspended in the timeless status of pure concept, pure myth, femininity became generation-specific on screen. Screenwriters realised that the vulnerability and interiority specific to youth could be the feminine province as well: 'a completely new symmetry' ('symétrie toute nouvelle') (Barthes 1993: 231), whose implications passed back and forth from the domain of representation to the world of lived experience. This was not, Barthes hastened to add, a new reign of androgyny, but a recognition of a shared identity across the boundaries of gender: 'the sense of a fragility particular to the age, as a matter of fact given to both sexes, an identical sociology for male and female students'[25] (Barthes 1993: 232). The interchangeable physiognomy of film stars and real people redefines demystification yet again, and puts the critic into the role of observer of popular culture as representation as well as practice. 'Visages et figures' ('Faces and Figures') is the mythology where the influence of Morin is most apparent, and where Barthes goes beyond *Les Stars*. For Barthes's description of the interplay of faces on- and off-screen works on the level of suggestion. Morin gives transcriptions of fan mail; Barthes's reader must instead imagine the psychic process of the exchange, and is thus drawn into the very work of description. Barthes would later call this 'the pleasure of the text' ('le plaisir du texte', see Barthes 1975), by which the text itself, through its ellipses, calls upon the reader to complete it. And so we should read Morin, with *later* Barthes, in the current cultural studies climate. For everything in the world is not textual – inner and outer human experiences have their place as well – but Barthes has also shown us the creative potential of the encounter that follows that of the intellectual and popular culture: the encounter between reader and text, and the role of psychic processes therein.

Notes

1. See Gabriel 2002: Barthes 2002a and 2002b. The CD-ROMs are available through *La Procure librairie* (www.laprocure.com).
2. For a comparative overview of Morin and Barthes, see Rigby 1991: 168–180.
3. *Les Stars* (out of print) was published in translation in 1960. See also Morin 1970; 1971; 1992b. Also see *New Trends in the Study of Mass Communication* (Birmingham, Occasional Papers, 1968). Morin's mass culture essays other than *Les Stars* include *Le Cinéma ou l'homme imaginaire: essai d'anthropologie* ('The cinema or the imaginary man: an essay in anthropology' (Morin 1956) and *L'Esprit du temps I* and *II* ('The Spirit of the Times', Morin 1976).
4. According to Kofman, 'fraternity' is the mythic name Morin gives to his ultimate values: humanity and love. He makes the astute connection between the 'golden age of Marxist theory in Anglo-American culture' in the 1970s and the accompanying lack of interest in Morin (Kofman 1996: 4).
5. Morin has written several autobiographical works. For his Sephardic roots, see *Vidal et les siens* (Morin 1989); for his journey to and from communism, see *Autocritique* (Morin 1992a).
6. From the mid-1960s on, Morin became interested in regional identity as another expression of identity not based on class. See his *La Commune en France. La Métamorphose de Plodémet* (Morin 1967), and *La Rumeur d'Orléans* (Morin 1969), written with Bernard Paillard and others. For a discussion of Morin as a populist thinker, see Rigby 1991.
7. I am indebted to Andy Stafford's article (1997) in the volume of *French Cultural Studies* dedicated to Morin for the biographical information that follows.
8. On the notion of descriptive justice, see Grignon and Passeron 1989.
9. 'que le lecteur pardonne cette familiarité à un auteur qui vit les mythes qu'il analyse'.
10. *Sur Racine, Essais critiques,* and *Critique et vérité,* 1960a, 1964 and 1966 respectively.
11. 'le lecteur vit le mythe à la façon d'une histoire à la fois vraie et irréelle'.
12. 'le développement de la publicité, de la grande presse, de la radio, de l'illustration, sans parler de la survivance d'une infinité de rites communicatifs (rites du paraître social) rend plus urgente que jamais la constitution d'une science sémiologique'.
13. 'Romans et enfants' ('Novels and children') is an exception to this rule: here Barthes recognises the myth of the woman writer as offered in *Elle* magazine, the myth that children are necessary to her identity and always come before novels.

14. 'il lui est interdit d'imaginer ce que sera sensiblement le monde, lorsque l'objet immédiat de sa critique aura disparu'.
15. 'Ici le phénomène a été pris au sérieux'.
16. Text originally published in *Combat*, 5 July 1965.
17. 'ce qui est, ce qui ne doit pas être et ce qui doit être'.
18. 'ici, le mythe commence ... au coeur même de la réalité'.
19. 'Bien plus, le fidèle veut toujours consommer son dieu. Depuis les repas cannibales où l'on mange l'ancêtre et les repas totémiques où l'on mange l'animal sacré, jusqu'aux communions, et eucharistes religieuses, tout dieu est fait pour être mangé, c'est-à-dire incorporé, assimilé. La première assimilation est de connaissance. Le *fan* veut tout savoir, c'est-à-dire posséder, manipuler et digérer mentalement l'image totale de l'idole. La connaissance est ici moyen d'appropriation magique.'
20. 'Ce sont eux qui prennent pour modèles les héros de films pour mieux s'affirmer. Ce sont eux qui assimilent la star imaginaire pour se conduire dans l'amour réel. La star est non seulement informatrice mais formatrice, non seulement incitatrice mais initiatrice.'
21. 'Toutefois l'influence de la star peut persister, après l'adolescence, là où la personnalité a mal tranché ses frontières intérieures entre le rêve et le réel, c'est-à-dire plutôt chez les femmes que chez les hommes, et plutôt dans les couches sociales intermédiaires. C'est-à-dire, en fin de compte, surtout chez les femmes de ces couches sociales intermédiaires: petites employées, petites bourgeoises, provinciales rêveuses et inassouvies, fardées ...'
22. 'diffusés avec une insistance et une ampleur jusque-là impossibles'.
23. 'une anthropologie euphorique de petits employés, de calicots, de fils de famille aimables et dépensiers ... Le visage humain est d'un seul coup sécularisé, et au plus bas'.
24. 'Ce qui est nouveau c'est que l'adolescence soit reconnue comme un âge complet, pourvu d'une dimension humaine qui peut même être exemplaire'.
25. 'le sens d'une fragilité d'âge justement impartie aux deux sexes, une sociologie identique pour l'étudiant et l'étudiante'.

CHAPTER 3

'A GIRL OF TODAY': BRIGITTE BARDOT

Diana Holmes

Brigitte Bardot – whose career as a film star ended in 1973 – has never completely ceased to command media attention. In the late 1990s, she was in a Parisian court facing a charge of 'provoking racial discrimination and hatred' for articles published in the French right-wing daily *Le Figaro*. Writing as an animal rights campaigner, she had objected to Muslim slaughter practices, but in a style that reproduced the nationalist, exclusionary rhetoric of the far-right *Front National* who supported her (Duval Smith 1996). In June 2004, she was back in court to be fined for inciting racial hatred in her best-selling book *Un cri dans le silence* (A Cry in the Silence), in which she fulminates against the 'Islamisation of France' and the mixing of 'French genes' with those of non-European immigrants. Her campaigns in support of animal welfare have merited a rather better press, but Bardot's support for animal rights often leads her into a disregard for human rights, an accusation that she counters with naïve protestations that she is 'not a politician'. At one level, this comes as no surprise, for Bardot's image was always in direct contrast to that of the articulate, committed kind of French star (such as Simone Signoret) who lent support to political causes. But at another, many of her ex-fans were saddened by the contrast between the innocently mutinous, tousle-haired Bardot of myth and memory, with her air of rebellious sensuality, and the reactionary sixty-year-old whose flouting

Brigitte Bardot in 1957 (in Une Parisienne).
Sam Lévin © ministère de la Culture – France.

of consensual standards of decency now served not the cause
of liberty, but that of prejudice.

This sense of disappointment points to some of the meanings
that Bardot's star persona held for her contemporaries. For the
purposes of this study, I distributed a questionnaire on
perceptions of Bardot to a number of French women, varied by
class and level of education but all born within a decade (either
side) of Bardot (born 1934).[1] These women mostly expressed
mild and unsurprised regret at the older Bardot's association
with the extreme-Right, just as they deplored her insensitivity to
the feelings of her son displayed in the 1996 best-selling

autobiography *Initiales B.B.* (for which she was found liable for damages for 'untrue statements and an attack on the subject's image'). Whilst most of my respondents emphasised Bardot's intellectual and moral limitations as a woman,[2] when they recalled what Bardot meant in their youth they almost all remembered her as a liberated and liberating figure with whom they strongly identified: the most frequently used words were 'liberation' and 'emancipation'. Their spontaneous memories of what Bardot meant correspond to the more theorised responses of feminist intellectuals who experienced the BB phenomenon. For the feminist film critic Françoise Audé, Bardot's contemporary, she was 'the fabulous yet authentic product of the collective imagination of the girls of her generation' (Audé 1981: 31).[3] For Simone de Beauvoir, writing at the height of Bardot's stardom, BB represented the refusal of the role of prey to man's hunter, a 'wordless affirmation of sexual equality' (Beauvoir 1972 [1959]: 22).

This chapter will examine how and why, at a particular moment in French history, Brigitte Bardot attained a degree of stardom that made her one of the international icons of the twentieth century, and how it is possible to reconcile the liberating function attributed to her by many women, with the compelling evidence that in fact her stardom worked to support a social structure that was deeply patriarchal, in the sense that it shaped women's lives primarily in terms of male needs. Bardot presented an extreme case of the glorification and fetishisation of the female body as sex object; in the late 1950s and early 1960s her fame was closely imbricated with the massive commodification of French everyday life, and with the positioning of women as consumers. The Bardot persona contributed to the dangerous confusion between women's liberation and women's (hetero)sexual availability, and the near-obsessive fascination with her body – her 'elusive, dense, corporeal' (Martin 1996: 13) presence – reinforced the myth of the 'Eternal Feminine', of woman as man's Other: as 'healing presence and sorceress; … man's prey, his downfall … everything that he is not and that he longs for, his negation and his *raison d'être*' (Beauvoir 1972 [1953]:175).[4] In these senses Bardot's star persona foreshadowed her later alliance with a political group (the *Front National*) committed to a highly conservative politics of gender. The tension between emancipation and subordination seems central to the particular phenomenon that is Bardot. Performers become stars because, as Richard Dyer puts it, they 'matter' to a very large public (Dyer 1987: 19). This study will first explore what 'mattered' to Bardot's spectators – particularly female spectators – in the 1950s and 60s, and how Bardot acted this out, both on screen and through her highly mediatised 'private' life. Secondly, it will consider the relevance to this of the central contradiction between her complicity with a culture repressive to women, and her female public's perception of her as an emancipatory figure.

The BB phenomenon – Bardot and the *zeitgeist*

Bardot is one of a very small number of internationally iconic star figures of the twentieth century, and is probably the only French woman to have achieved this status. Her celebrity conforms in every respect to Dyer's definition of the star image as 'extensive, multimedia, intertextual' (Dyer 1987: 3). It is extensive in both time and space, for though the decade between 1956 (year of *Et Dieu créa la femme*) and 1965 (*Viva Maria* with Jeanne Moreau, after which box-office returns began to drop) represents the height of her worldwide celebrity, she remains an instantly recognisable name and face and a continuing reference point for the 'look' of female sexuality, at least in the Western and Westernised countries of the world. She was a 'multimedia' figure from the early 1950s, kept in the limelight by Roger Vadim's media contacts and promotional management, and once her stardom was established through cinema she became the darling and the victim of the paparazzi, the subject in France of more press coverage than President de Gaulle,[5] a recording artist, a television performer and a semi-deity, whose adoption of St Tropez as a holiday retreat transformed the one-time fishing village into a place of pilgrimage and the glamorous site of a pre-1968 'swinging Sixties'.[6] Her stardom was intertextual in the sense that for the public there was a constant interplay between the fictional characters she played and her 'authentic' self. The stardom itself, and the mixture of complicity and antagonism in the star's relations with the media, were further mediatised through Louis Malle's film *Vie privée* (1962) in which the film-star heroine 'Jill' is a scarcely disguised version of BB.

One of the explanations provided for Bardot's fame, almost from the start, is that of her close attunement to the *zeitgeist* or spirit of the times. Such claims need to be read partially as components of a star discourse that is *performative* as well as descriptive, for to represent an artist as embodying the mood of their era is in itself a way of constructing stardom. Thus Roger Vadim, who first 'discovered' the future BB when she was a well-chaperoned fifteen-year-old, was keen to attribute his recognition of her star quality to a perception that 'she had a "now" face, she was really a girl of today'.[7] *Cahiers du Cinéma*, the film journal of the New Wave, was also eager to link Bardot into their own self-identification with a 'new, young' era: 'BB, product of our age, allows our age to invade the screen' (de Givray 1957: 43).[8] François Nourissier's 1960 essay *B.B 60* repeats the attribution of Bardot's success to her accordance with the social moment, arguing that (in 1960), 'Bardot embodies what the French like' (Nourrissier 1960: 27).[9] Retrospectively, in a book that is largely a tribute to Bardot, Yves Alion maintains the same view: 'her charm, her youth, her air of naturalness are the external signs that correspond to what a whole generation wanted. BB was the incarnation of new values ...' (Alion 1989: 11).[10] The construction of Bardot as the personification of a new, youthful modernity was highly effective and remained central to her image.

However, the *zeitgeist* argument is not only an element of promotional star discourse, it is also a significant factor in any understanding of a star's appeal for a particular audience. Bardot does seem to have 'incarnated' the 'new values' of a generation, though the definitions of both the values and the generation are more complex than Alion's formulation allows. The period of Bardot's success – mid-1950s to mid- 1960s – was, as we have seen, one of intense social change in France, as the State allied with private industry to promote rapid industrialisation and modernisation of the economy, accompanied by an accelerated growth and urbanisation of the population. At the same time France was engaged in fighting independence movements in the colonies, notably Indo-China (where the war was lost in 1954) and Algeria (1954–1962). France moved quickly 'from a rural, Empire-oriented Catholic country into a fully industrialized, decolonized and urban one' (Ross 1995: 4). Education reflected the need for an increasingly skilled workforce, and the numbers of young men and women in higher education increased steadily. The need to create and maintain new markets for consumer goods, combined with the higher levels of education of the younger generation, contributed to a redefinition of generation as a key factor in taste and culture. Fashion, music, food and beauty products gradually began to be marketed as specifically 'young'. All that was new, modern and youthful was initially viewed positively, as central to the renewal of the French economy and of French identity, tarnished by the Occupation years. With the accession to power of de Gaulle in 1958, the emphasis on a 'new, young' era (despite the venerable age of the President himself) became still more marked, and the media hailed the 'New Wave' in cinema, the 'New Novel' in literature and the 'new' baby-boom generation with its own identity and product needs.

This promotion of generational difference nonetheless carried the seeds of a more conflictual division. The conscription of young men to fight in the Algerian war led – in some social groups – to a sense of political alienation from the values and strategies of the older men who ruled the nation. The culture of the young, with its loud music (first jazz, then rock and roll), its more casual modes of address and behaviour, its borrowings from American style, provoked anxiety in the older generation, despite the widespread acknowledgment of the virtues of modernisation. Disapproval was to become more marked as the libertarian impulses implicit in the high-to-middlebrow trends of the 1950s (jazz and *chanson*, New Wave in cinema, student café culture) were more widely disseminated in the form of pop music (Johnny Hallyday), mass-market fashions and 'teen' publications such as *Salut les copains!* (1962) and, specifically for girls, *Mademoiselle* (1962). Whilst Bardot's fame belongs more to the earlier years of the period we are examining (she was twenty-eight years old by the time Johnny Hallyday's appearance at the Place de la Nation provoked mass teen hysteria),[11] the context of rapid social change and of a growing sense of generational identity is an important one. Both the effective marketing of Bardot as star, and the memory of her as enacting a daring freedom on behalf of a generation of young women, need to be seen in the context of a developing youth culture in France – a culture promoted and welcomed by commerce and government, but also containing the potential for contestation of dominant social values. Gender roles and identities were one important field of potential conflict.

Economic and social development had produced a complex mix of gains and losses for women. On the one hand, French women had finally gained the right to vote and stand for elections in 1944, and equality between the sexes had been written into the new, postwar constitution. The growth of the tertiary sector led to better educational and job opportunities, with a concomitant increase in social freedoms as young women became more mobile and integrated into 'male' environments. The new emphasis on youth culture offered girls an alternative source of identification: they might be destined to follow in the footsteps of their mothers, but they could also enjoy a provisional identification with 'youth', with all its connotations of modernity and indocility. On the other hand, the pro-natalist policies of the period firmly identified women with domesticity and motherhood and, despite the new types of job available to women in the service industries, the actual numbers of women working outside the home dropped to their lowest levels since World War I (reaching their nadir, twenty-seven percent, in 1962). The consumer culture also brought new imperatives to be constantly beautiful, well dressed and well made-up, reinforcing what Laura Mulvey has termed women's *to-be-looked-at-ness* (Mulvey 1989[1975]: 19). The imperative to be sexy co-existed awkwardly with the unobtainability of contraception and the illegality of abortion, so that sexual standards and sexual freedom remained firmly divided by gender. The legalisation of women's right to contraception and abortion, and a critique of the 'double standard', were both central themes of the French women's movement that was to take off after May 1968.

Thus for the generation of women who formed Bardot's female public, there existed a tension between, on the one hand, a prescriptive definition of modern femininity as domesticity and maternity in a more stylish guise and, on the other hand, a sense that femininity might also be compatible with citizenship, education, opportunity, mobility – and a self-defined, pleasurable sexuality. If we trace Bardot's rise from obscurity to celebrity – or how a star was made – then we can see how this contradiction found expression, and sometimes provisional resolution, both in her performance as off-screen celebrity and in the fictional roles she played on screen.

The mediation of biography

Bardot's origins were respectably, affluently middle class, her father a successful engineer, her mother a housewife with a strong interest in fashion and ballet. She attended private, single-sex schools, and (with rather more enthusiasm) ballet classes. The normal outcome of such a childhood would have been marriage to a man of the same class and a life similar to that of her mother. But the combination of her mother's interest in, and connections with, the fashion trade, and Brigitte's physical grace, developed through dancing, led to an invitation to model junior fashions in the magazine *Le Jardin des Modes*. The publication of these photos captured the attention of Hélène Lazareff, editor of the most avant-garde and influential of postwar women's magazines, *Elle*. In May 1950, aged fifteen, Bardot appeared in a 'mother and daughter' fashion spread in *Elle*, still very much the docile, parentally controlled model of a teenager; in turn these photos were seen by the film director Marc Allégret and his assistant Roger Vadim, who (at least according to Vadim's subsequent telling of the story) were seeking a new face to represent the new generation. The screen tests that Allégret managed to persuade the Bardot parents to allow were finally unsuccessful, but through them Bardot encountered a new and very different milieu: cosmopolitan, sophisticated, bohemian and tuned in to the cultural changes and commercial possibilities of the day. Through Vadim (a few years her senior, darkly handsome, well travelled and independent) the sixteen-year-old Bardot discovered sex, the pleasure of escaping parental control, and an exciting new world where lives were not predetermined by rigid familial patterns. In the extent to which this alternative world was made available to her, she was unusual. In the desire to escape into a 'modern', glamorous life that left the constraints of domesticity and decorum behind, she was perhaps more representative of her peers.

Biography is not irrelevant to the making of a star, as Thomas Harris has pointed out (Harris 1991[1957]), but it tends to be edited, inflected and reshaped in the process of star construction. From the time Bardot became engaged to Vadim (parental opposition giving way when faced with the first of her several suicide attempts) in 1951, her life and person began to be stage-managed for public consumption. Vadim almost certainly did not have any grand master-plan, but he seems to have recognised very quickly that Bardot's particular combination of extreme femininity and androgynous grace captured the ambivalence of postwar gender identities, and to have taken on the role of promoter and public-relations manager that in Hollywood would have fallen to the studio. Since his acceptance as a son-in-law depended on his being in paid employment, Vadim joined the staff of *Paris Match*, the magazine that epitomised and promoted France's new self-image as a nation proud of its traditions (though a selective view of the past excluded the recent shame of Vichy), but at ease with modernity. *Paris Match* in the early 1950s offered a carefully blended mix of features: coverage of the war in IndoChina emphasised adventure and heroism rather than politics; cars (essential symbols of the modern) figured largely with, for example, a major annual feature on the *Salon de l'Auto* (equivalent of the Motor Show); there was a good deal of national and international gossip about royals and show business celebrities, and advertising was predominantly for the 'modern' products that accompanied a hygienic, efficient and stylish lifestyle: washing machines, deodorants, beauty products and swimsuits (including bikinis) recur most frequently. At the same time as he enrolled Brigitte (briefly) in acting classes and encouraged her to accept her first film roles, Vadim ensured her introduction to a wider public by featuring their own romance in the pages of *Paris Match*.

The edition of 31 May 1952 carries a cover photo of BB, hair in a long plait, posed in a field of buttercups, of which she also carries a bouquet. She looks straight at the camera with a half-knowing smile that belies the homespun innocence proclaimed by all the other elements of the image. The same alliance of a reassuringly traditional femininity with a hint of sexual independence is evoked by the three-page feature inside. Bardot is posed in a leotard and tights, practising her ballet on the roof of the *Paris Match* building 'so as not to be disturbed', at once solitary and absorbed, and clearly displayed for the camera. The other photos show her at home in the garden with parents and grandfather, a 'symbol of adolescence' in a family 'like many French families' (as the accompanying text explains), who returns each weekend from making her first film to be reunited with her family, her bald teddy bear and her pet tortoise, but who is soon due to marry the man she loves and leave her childhood behind. The narrative is one of order, a natural progression from the father's care to that of the husband, sexuality contained by the institution of the family. The sexual provocation implied by Bardot's repeated look to camera, and the physical ease and authority of her dancer's pose, suggest alternative narratives. The tension between family order and female self-assertion is smoothed over in *Paris Match*, used merely to add a touch of eroticism to a conventional feature.

Beyond the glossy pages of the magazine, the gap between a pro-family policy that prohibited contraception and abortion, and the reality of women's sexual behaviour, produced harsher consequences. The illegality of abortion forced women into dangerous back-street operations or, if they could afford it, expensive trips to foreign clinics where the quality of care was not guaranteed. Bardot underwent her first abortion in Switzerland at the age of seventeen while her parents confidently assumed that she was still a virgin, and in her own words 'almost died for lack of medical care' (Bardot 1996: 107).[12]

The Vadim/Bardot wedding took place on 27 December 1952 and was extensively covered by *Match* under the headline 'Brigitte found her husband at *Paris Match*'.[13] The bride is described as a 'cover girl and cinema star',[14] '*la petite star*' (by now she had made two unremarkable comedies, *Le Trou normand* and *Marina la fille sans voile*), and Vadim as 'one of *Match*'s most brilliant reporters'.[15] In the presentation of the wedding as a match between the ideal feminine (the beautiful, blonde, eighteen-year-old star) and the ideal masculine (the reporter/writer, emblem of a modern, adventurous society), the coverage prefigured the wedding two years later between Marilyn Monroe and Joe di Maggio, a couple already being seen together in 1952. The sexual division of labour was the same in each case: to him activity, courage, physical (di Maggio) or intellectual (Vadim) strength; to her beauty, the power to provide the pleasure of looking.[16] At the same time, marriage and career are presented as compatible in this fairytale land of modern youth.

Vadim brought all his skills as a journalist, his insider knowledge of the cinema scene and his seductive charm to bear on the project of mediating his wife's identity and appearance for public consumption. From 1953 to 1956, his career management took Bardot through a series of minor films, most of them French and unlikely to go beyond a national market, though including the British film *Doctor at Sea* (1955) and an Italian 'peplum'.[17] The main aim – just as with the big Hollywood studios' management of promising starlets – was to keep her in the public eye, and to make her trademark style of tousled bouffant hair, big eyes and pouting mouth immediately recognisable. Her 'starlet' appearances on the beach and on the American aircraft carrier *Midway* at the 1953 Cannes film festival served the same purpose, since she received considerable media coverage, and her one theatrical venture, in Anouilh's *L'Invitation au Château* (1954), also gained attention. Bardot was clearly being marketed as an exceptionally beautiful body, an object of male desire to be consumed through cinema, photographic images and fantasy. At the same time, her unkempt *coiffure*, her preference for clothes that were revealing but also informal, and her facial expressions that frequently connoted contained resentment or frank desire, but almost never submission or anxiety to please, signified a new style of femininity that combined willing eroticism with self-assertion.

Et Dieu créa ... BB

Vadim's moment of triumph came with the film he cowrote and directed for Bardot, *Et Dieu créa la femme*. Playing a role – Juliette – written to accommodate her tendency 'not to get into the character, but to get the character into me' (Bardot 1996: 373),[18] Bardot had a whole film in which to enact the persona she had already begun to represent both on and off screen: a delectably consumable body, but also a woman uncompromising in the pursuit of her own pleasure, and who spontaneously espouses a simple ethics of authenticity (no pretence, no existentialist *mauvaise foi* [bad faith]). The opening sequence announces the film's central ambivalence of perspective: the camera follows a smart, middle-aged man (Carradine) as he enters a sunlit yard and observes a pair of naked female legs protruding from behind a sheet draped over the washing line. A reverse shot takes the viewer behind the sheet: the framing of the upper surface of Juliette's body confirms that she is lying face down and naked, basking in the sun, but also provides Juliette's perspective on Carradine, silhouetted behind the sheet. Juliette is subject as well as object. When she stands up to speak to Carradine, her relaxed engagement in a playfully provocative dialogue makes it clear that she is quite unembarassed by her nudity, as by his evident desire for her. The arrival of Juliette's outraged, furious foster mother ('showing yourself naked to men! You slut!') caricatures intradiegetically the scandalised reactions of a conservative audience to which the film implicitly opposes the young, 'modern' spectators it wishes to address. Bardot at once promises a feast for the voyeur and a scandalous representation of female sexuality as confident, desiring and free of shame. Though the film's narrative closure safely restores Juliette to the roles of wife and daughter,[19] it was her dissent from domestic and familial values that stayed with most of the spectators – that and the spectacle of her dancing body, at once repeatedly displayed to the intra- and extradiegetic (on- and off-screen) male gaze, and connoting a desperate desire to escape into the subjective pleasure of rhythmic movement, in the famous 'mambo' scene that (almost) closes the film.

Earlier French films (for example the 1950 *Caroline Chérie* starring Martine Carol, to which Bardot was to make a sequel) had played with the figure of the 'ingénue with attitude', the girl who innocently and uncompromisingly follows her heart and senses. But this was something different: actresses like Carol displayed a provocative *décolleté* but did not appear in states of casual nudity, and their hearts and senses could be counted upon to operate in harmony, so that love sanctioned desire. Juliette's sunbathing prefigures her liking for other forms of sensual pleasure, including sex, and – until her eventual punishment and return to order – the film encourages identification with her attempts to assert an equal right to sexual fulfilment and multiple partners, a right she sees as limited only by a code of mutual honesty and sympathy, rather than by the imperatives of monogamous romantic love.

Et Dieu créa was not an immediate hit in France, though it generated a good deal of interest (much of it hostile) in the press. It did, however, produce a quite unexpected *succès de scandale* in the United States where, despite the public's general dislike of subtitled foreign cinema, Bardot rapidly attained the status of major sex-symbol, exotically French, but also quintessentially 'modern' in a way that many Americans identified with their own culture. Her international success ricocheted back to France: Bardot became a major export, not only an asset to the national economy but also a representation abroad of that sexy, male-oriented femininity on which French culture has long prided itself. For the popular weekly *France Dimanche* in December 1956 Bardot was, above all, 'the French woman who is most famous abroad'.[20] Vadim was no longer her manager nor her husband, since during the shooting of *Et Dieu créa* she had begun a new relationship with her costar, Jean-Louis Trintignant, and the couple had subsequently, and fairly amicably, divorced. Bardot was now so demonstrably a marketable commodity, however, that there was no lack of film offers, nor of media attention to maintain her unmistakable (if increasingly copied by others) profile and persona in the public eye.

As argued above, the period of Bardot's stardom coincides with a period of considerable contradiction in French women's status, roles and sense of identity. Both the media discourses that constructed and maintained her as a star, and the films she made in the late 1950s and early 1960s (the years of her most intense stardom), play on these contradictions by combining a fascinated, semi-admiring representation of

Bardot as a woman in touch with modernity (mobile, acquisitive, a free agent), with a careful re-insertion of her person and behaviour into reassuringly traditional narratives. The phenomenon of film stardom demands a constant interplay between a star's on-screen performances and their off-screen, apparently 'real' personality constructed through media coverage of their private lives. Without losing sight of the interdependent nature of these different types of representation, I propose here to deal first with Bardot's star persona outside the cinema, after the success of *Et Dieu créa la femme*, and then with some of the roles she played between 1956 and 1962.

Off-screen stardom

Not surprisingly, press coverage of Bardot tended from the outset to be heavily visual, with photographs playing as important a role as text. Thus her particular style of dress – clarified and rendered more extreme in *Et Dieu créa la femme*, where Juliette's relative poverty provides a narrative justification for her simple button-through cotton dresses, jeans and tee-shirts – became well known and easily available for imitation. Physical appearance had long played a central part in the construction of femininity; the development of an increasingly consumerist culture invited women to acquire the right sort of femininity by purchasing the right products, and Bardot's style was so clearly *prêt-à-porter* rather than *haute couture* that it was possible to emulate her. In Jackie Stacey's words: 'the construction of women as cinema spectators overlaps here with their construction as consumers' (Stacey 1991: 156). Stacey's work, however, is also careful to avoid a simple positioning of women as helpless victims of capitalism; she insists upon the spectator's degree of agency and the pleasure she may find in identifying with the star through adoption of elements of her style: 'the star's identity is selectively reworked and incorporated into the spectator's new identity ... identification does not simply involve the passive reproduction of existing femininities, but rather an active engagement and production of changing identities' (Stacey 1991: 160). Bardot's gingham dresses, cotton shifts, tight jeans, bikinis and shorts all emphasised a slender but curvaceous figure that few women could fully aspire to, but also (especially when combined with the illusory but persuasive 'naturalness' of the hairstyle) implied a more radical revision of the feminine by connoting ease of movement, refusal of constraint, and identification with the rebelliously casual style of male teen idols such as James Dean and Marlon Brando.[21]

What the press was to do with her off-screen behaviour was a rather more complex matter, for in a culture that prohibited contraception and idealised fidelity and maternity in women, Bardot's rapid changes of male partner (not always straightforwardly sequential, as she continued to be seen with Vadim long after their divorce) had to be either criticised or somehow accommodated. In fact, the popular press chose a middle road, combining a fascinated and nonjudgemental chronicling of the exotic habits of BB and her companions (for example, in December 1956 when *France Dimanche* captures Vadim and BB affectionately entwined at a premiere, the text invites readers to share in a reaction that is more wondering than disapproving: 'Et pourtant si! Ils divorcent!' ['And yet it's true – the divorce is on!', *France-Dimanche* 1956] with occasional reminders that such behaviour must eventually end in tears, as in the same paper's 1960 article 'La Défaite des mauvaises femmes' ('The downfall of bad women'), which charts the abandonment of a number of female stars (Maria Callas, Brenda Lee, Eva Bartok) by the men they 'seduced': 'Sooner or later love is defeated by scandal' (*France-Dimanche*, 1960). Bardot's polygamous, pleasure-seeking behaviour is thus given a considerable amount of positive coverage, and the moralising undertones that predict her doom remain muted. As star, Bardot is to some extent licensed to live out a fantasy life of brief but authentic passions. The fantasy is both male, for the multipartnered Brigitte can be imagined as available, so that (for example) even English youths would set off for St Tropez with the hazy expectation of becoming the next lover,[22] and female, for Bardot's appropriation of 'masculine' sexual freedom, and her affairs with a series of delectable and apparently manageable men, suggested a whole new area of sexual possibility for women.

The question of the relationship between France's greatest female star and the hegemonic values of pre-1968 France nonetheless reached a crisis point with Bardot's second marriage and the birth of her son. Whatever the margin of freedom for fantasy (an essential element, after all, both of entertainment and of the consumer economy), the French state and indeed the majority of the population remained committed to the core values of marriage and family. When

Bardot married for a second time, this time to a handsome, clean-cut actor from a respectable bourgeois milieu not unlike Bardot's own, and became a mother, she appeared briefly to have resolved the contradiction between 'new' and 'old' femininities in favour of the latter. Bardot met Jacques Charrier when she starred opposite him in the comedy *Babette s'en va-t-en guerre* in 1959, and – though this was not part of the public story – soon became pregnant. Her autobiography recounts her attempts to procure a (third) abortion, and the impossibility of doing so now that she was so famous as to be instantly recognisable. Charrier persuaded her to marry him, to the delight of the media: Nicolas was born in January 1960, in a Paris flat so besieged by the media that Bardot had been imprisoned there for the preceding weeks. The marriage rapidly broke apart under the glare of press attention, and Bardot's consistent lack of enthusiasm for maternity was confirmed by her willingness to have Charrier keep the child.

Elle magazine had generally presented a positive view of Bardot, from the first cover photo in 1950, as a 'modern' young woman with style, the kind of woman to whom the magazine was addressed. What is interesting about the coverage of her maternity is the way that the magazine studiously ignores all the problematic aspects of the story and transforms it into an idealised tale of elegant young motherhood and ideal marriage, so that the star becomes part of *Elle*'s reassuring certainty that modern femininity is wholly compatible with the traditional roles of wife and mother. On 8 January 1960, BB is on the cover 'more dazzlingly beautiful than ever – BB is a modern, organised young mother and inside she shows you the nursery and all the new baby clothes that await the new arrival'.[23] The article in fact has 'Moussia-the-nanny who has helped Brigittte-the-mother-to-be to get everything ready'[24] presenting the decor and various consumables that await the Bardot baby – there is no sign of Bardot (since in fact she was in a state of angry depression as the birth approached). On 22 January 1960, the birth is announced on the cover: 'Radiant mother Brigitte introduces Nicolas to you',[25] and inside a photo spread of Bardot beautifully made-up and holding the baby is accompanied by an ecstatically pro-maternity text that could scarcely be further from the true state of affairs:

> Nicolas Charrier is nine days old and Brigitte is no longer just the BB envied, admired and criticised by all, but a mother like

any other. She can't bear to leave Nicolas. Her daily routine is organised around bottles and the regular timetable of babies the world over. With the birth of Nicolas, Brigitte has discovered something deeper and truer than the glory of stardom: maternal love.[26]

This prescriptive and wholly mendacious text uses Bardot's first name ('Brigitte') and the explicit phrasing of 'comme toutes les autres' ('a mother like any other') to enlist the star in the cause of that very maternity she had tried so hard to avoid, and was so soon to reject. She is also used to remind readers of their duty not to let maternity override the imperative to be sexually attractive: Bardot is praised for having rapidly regained her '*taille de BB*' (BB figure) by *not* 'eating for two'. In late March, when the rest of the press had already begun to devote columns to the problems in the marriage, *Elle* was still printing photos of Bardot and Charrier embracing and of Bardot with Nicolas, insisting that this remained the perfect marriage. *Elle's* agenda was not solely a conservative one: the magazine was concerned throughout these years to impress upon its (mainly middle-class) readers both the value of their domestic and maternal roles and the possibility of combining these with a degree of independence and a sense of intellectual and political engagement with the public world. Bardot's 'return to the fold', however, brings out the most conservative elements of the *Elle* ideology: the maternal instinct is universalised and idealised, all the problems (surely relevant to parts of the readership) of the conflict between freedom and motherhood, and between the female body as eroticised spectacle or reproductive machine, are simply ignored.

   Elle had recently dealt with one aspect of marital relationships that was to figure largely in popular press discourse around the marriage break-up. In 1959, the magazine carried out a major survey entitled 'La Française et l'amour' ('The Frenchwoman and love'), and one of the conclusions of this formed the subject of a lengthy article in the mid-December issue. Apparently, many women had reported that their own increased financial and emotional independence made their husbands distinctly less attractive to them: women are only sexually and emotionally attracted to men stronger than themselves, opined *Elle*; 'women have a need to admire (…) the husband must be a god'.[27] Generally well disposed to a star who provided so much valuable copy, *France Dimanche* used precisely this argument to explain the 'drama in the Bardot household' (headline of the 18–24 February 1960 edition). The 'special correspondent' sent to Chamonix where the couple were sorting out their problems 'alone' reported that Charrier wanted his wife to give up her career and devote herself to her family, but that his 'weakness' (Charrier had suffered a minor breakdown during the lead-up to the marriage) had 'meant that he lost his prestige, and a woman cannot forgive this'. Thus, whilst both the glossy women's press and the tabloid press reported Bardot's dereliction of marital and maternal duty in a fairly positive way, they each did so by reframing her story within the most conservative of narratives. Bardot is 'really' just like all women, instinctively maternal and monogamous, but has been unable to fulfil her natural role because of the shortage of appropriately strong men, for men find it hard to adjust to women's more 'modern' identity.

The media's repeated recourse to this version of events suggests not only that Bardot as star incarnated contemporary anxieties about how the modern woman could remain a wife and mother, but that her public story served to articulate a sense of crisis in masculine identity. Charrier had seemed to be the ideal mate for the nation's favourite female star: he was a handsome, yet reasonably ordinary representation of young French manhood, so that BB appeared to fall in love with the male public who adored her. The widespread perception of the divorce as a failure of Charrier's virility may be read as an expression of some collective anxiety about French masculinity itself, at a period when traditional modes of male self-assertion were under threat, with the deskilling of the workplace produced by the modernisation of industry, the intrusion of women into domains hitherto safely identified as male territory and the series of defeats suffered by the French army (World War II, IndoChina, Algeria). Interestingly, Charrier's role in the film he made with Bardot (*Babette s'en va-t-en guerre*) was that of a Free French hero, but coverage of the marriage tended to emphasise the fact that off screen, though he was the son of a military officer, he himself failed to complete his military service due to his (excessive?) anxiety about being away from the pregnant Bardot. Thus the gap between successful and failed masculinity was seen in terms of military prowess.

Press presentation of Bardot's off-screen life expressed the period's ambivalence towards the issue of female emancipation, but finally came down on the side of a safe re-insertion of BB, the sexually assertive woman, within a more traditional narrative of wifely submission and motherhood, seen as women's ideal path to self-fulfilment. Bardot's story also allowed for the expression of anxiety at the impact of changes in women's role on men and masculinity. Both the conflicted treatment of female emancipation, and the sense of anxiety around masculine identity, are equally central to Bardot's films of the same period.

Bardot on screen: the films

Bardot had made sixteen films by the time she achieved international stardom with *Et Dieu créa la femme* (referred to hereafter as simply *Et Dieu*). She went on to make over thirty more. Amongst the best and most lasting of these are two films made with major directors shortly after *Et Dieu*: *En Cas de malheur* (costarring Jean Gabin, directed by Claude Autant-Lara, 1958) and *La Vérité* (directed by Henri-Georges Clouzot, 1960). Each of these films gained a degree of cultural legitimacy from the status of its director, whilst achieving box-office success thanks to the presence on screen of (the post-*Et Dieu*) BB. The capacity to straddle the boundary between 'high' and popular cultures contributed significantly to the elaboration of Bardot's star persona. It is on these films – together with *Et Dieu* – that I will concentrate this closing analysis of Bardot as film star.

The experience of watching these films confirms the central contradiction between BB as emancipatory figure, remembered as 'liberating' and a source of positive identification, and BB as commodified fantasy, functioning to glamorise women's subordination and to address (and to some extent pacify) contemporary doubts about male authority. Bardot, like all established stars, carries into each film meanings already established by previous fictions and by her off-screen personality, with the result that despite the very different styles of the directors the films share basic structures.

There are senses in which all of the films undeniably undermine a normative model of femininity as sexual object rather than subject, as naturally maternal and as monogamous. The characters Bardot plays are all, like Juliette, the central narrative focus of the film and sympathetic to a degree that invites at least partial identification. Thus the female spectator (at least) finds herself in sympathy with characters situated outside the patriarchal family (Juliette and Yvette [*En Cas de malheur*] have no families, Dominique [*La Vérité*] leaves home early in the film) and who radically refuse the ethic of female purity and monogamy. Each of these heroines is driven primarily by a desire for sexual pleasure, for a freedom that has no aim other than '*disponibilité*' or openness to experience, and for love without the constraints of family or fidelity. In each film, these desires are connected diegetically and visually to the youth culture of the late 1950s: Juliette dances the cha-cha and the mambo; Dominique defends pop against classical music, frequents student cafes of the Left Bank, wears the jeans, duffle coats and scarves that go with the milieu and loves sports cars and motorbikes; Yvette frequents jazz musicians and bohemian cafés.

Meanwhile those characters who oppose the heroine's drive for a loosely defined freedom tend to be caricatured and ridiculed: from the foster-mother in *Et Dieu*, to the frustrated spinster secretary of *En Cas de malheur*, to the domineering father and the courtroom moralists of *La Vérité*, the defenders of a more traditional morality are represented on screen as bigoted and envious, and the spectator is invited to enjoy the heroine's irreverence and to identify to some extent with her forthright commitment to the pursuit of pleasure, including sexual pleasure. The opposition between a 'traditional' and a 'modern' sexual ethic is at its starkest in *La Vérité*, perhaps due to the fact that Christiane Rochefort, one of the 'angry young women' writers of the pre-1968 period,[28] collaborated on the script. The film centres around the trial for murder of Dominique Marceau (Bardot), and employs flashback sequences to narrate the fraught relationship between Dominique and the much more conventionally minded young musician, Gilbert Tellier, whom she eventually kills in a 'crime passionnel' motivated by his contemptuous rejection of her. Both the relationship between Dominique and Gilbert and the trial itself demonstrate the conflict between conventional and liberal, less male-centred attitudes to sex. The orthodox, normative view still construed female desire as legitimate only when expressive of love, and hence as naturally monogamous, whereas Dominique represents the view that sex is a mutually pleasurable experience involving both tenderness and camaraderie, but is not to be confused with love. Gilbert, who shares the orthodox view, is horrified by her explanation of a passing infidelity: 'We were seeing each other before,' [i.e. before they slept together] 'and still seeing each other afterwards – what difference does it make?' ('On se voyait avant, on se voyait après. Quelle est la différence?'). Gilbert's values are aligned with those of the court, itself a microcosm of orthodox society, more concerned to try Dominique for her promiscuous, amoral lifestyle than for the act of murder itself. The prurience and hypocrisy of both the lawyers and the public are contrasted to the sincerity of the accused, represented visually by Bardot's unusually sober coiffure, dress and acting style in these sequences. When Dominique cries 'I don't know what is honest about making a guy marry you', the film is undoubtedly on her side, and her comradely bed-sharing with an ex-lover (which further shocks the court) looks forward to the more relaxed sexual mores of the later 1960s with amused equanimity.

Similarly, Juliette's refusal in *Et Dieu* to play the blushing bride at her wedding breakfast and her unabashed preference for carrying the food upstairs to accompany an immediate consummation of the marriage, employs humour to engage the spectator on the side of Juliette's frank sensuality. In *En cas de malheur*, though Yvette is an inveterate liar, her puzzled declarations that she cannot see *why* she has to be faithful to either of the men in her life establish the character's underlying innocence. Though the morality of each heroine is, in any conventional terms, decidedly dubious (Juliette makes love to the brother of the husband who loves her, and repeatedly runs away from the consequences of her actions; Yvette is a prostitute, a thief, a liar and almost a murderess; Dominique wrecks her sister's life and commits murder), and though Bardot always plays women too intellectually limited to articulate a code of values, each represents an oppositional stance which the films to an extent endorse. Their unashamed pursuit of pleasure, fun and freedom is favourably compared to rigidly encoded social moralities, and to hypocrisy. Moreover, at least in terms of plot, both *Et Dieu* and *La Vérité* imagine sexual relationships in which experience and expertise are on the woman's side, and subject/object positions are equally distributed. For these reasons, the perception of one of the respondents to my questionnaire, that 'for girls, she represented the freedom to be mistress of one's own body' ('pour les jeunes filles, elle représentait la liberté d'être sa propre maîtresse dans le physique') and of another that 'she spoke on our behalf!' ('elle parlait pour nous') are supported by the films of the period.

However, these are not films with a deliberately radical agenda, but rather products of the mainstream national film industry (in the case of *En cas de malheur* of what the New Wave lambasted as *'cinéma de qualité'*),[29] and the more subversive meanings of the films are carefully counterbalanced by a re-assertion of what we might term patriarchal order. The BB character's 'liberated' sexuality frequently serves to justify the showcasing of her nude or scantily clad body, usually with an intradiegetic male gaze serving to position and determine that of the spectator. The representation of the heroine as 'subject (agent) of the narrative, initiating action and expressing her own (guiltless) desire' is offset by her representation as 'object, both of male desire *and* of the camera' (Vincendeau 1992: 86). The opening scene of *Et Dieu*, already discussed above and echoed regularly throughout the film, is a good example of how the Bardot character's 'unconventional' behaviour provides an opportunity for the camera to act as voyeur. In *La Vérité,* Dominique's refusal of order or convention is demonstrated by a sequence in which her sister's straight-laced boyfriend comes to the flat the sisters share, to find Dominique naked in bed, covered only by a sheet and listening to loud pop music. Enjoying his discomfiture, she offers him – and the camera – the spectacle of her scarcely concealed body gyrating to the music. The occasion for such display of the famous BB body is rarely lost in the films. *En Cas de malheur* contains the famous scene in which Yvette, guilty of robbery with violence, penniless but desperate to obtain the services of the eminent lawyer Maître Gobillot, played by Gabin, slowly lifts her skirt to her waist to offer him (quite literally) her sex. Filmed from behind but cross-cut to show Gobillot's controlled but (we read through the expression) profoundly shaken reaction, the scene condenses one of the film's central themes, that is the terrifying power not of a woman as individual subject (Gabin's character has only contempt for Dominique's intellect and behaviour) but of female sexuality.

Moreover, in some instances the caricaturing of conventional morality is not so much a way of seriously attacking it as a way of avoiding the debate. It is easy to laugh at the cluckings of Juliette's mean-spirited foster-mother or at the prosecutor who believes Dominique capable of murder because she frequented 'dissolute' cafés and 'ran around town with a lot of young people', but the staging of a rather facile New France / Old France opposition here has more to do with style than with substantial values, and significantly fails to address the issue of gender. Indeed, where there are any older characters who 'understand' the Bardot character, they are invariably older men: Carradine in *Et Dieu*, Maître Gobillot in *En cas de malheur*. As is traditionally the case, the static, convention-bound past tends to be represented by women (the foster-mother and the mother-in-law in *Et Dieu*; the secretary and to some extent the wife in *En cas*; the sister in *La Vérité*), suggesting that female revolt must be directed against the mother rather than the father, and that any female 'liberation' will pass through alliances with men rather than other women. Female friendship is a theme significantly missing from the Bardot films of this period, as from the extrafilmic reporting of her life which did, on the other hand, make a good deal of de Gaulle's reportedly positive views on the star ('That little girl has a nice lack of pretension' ['Elle a une simplicité de bon aloi, cette petite'], he is reported to have said [Rihoit 1986:226]).

The main feature of these films that argues against any straightforwardly 'liberating' meaning is, however, their mode of closure. In narrative terms, the rebellious BB figure always ends up being eliminated or reintegrated into the family: order is restored. *Et Dieu* concludes very clearly with the re-assertion of male authority, as Carradine (the film's father-figure) encourages Juliette's young husband to complete his rite of passage and become a man by asserting his authority as a husband: first the pointing of a (phallic) revolver, then a violent slap to the face put an end to Juliette's frenzied self-absorption in the dance, and she follows him willingly back to the marital home. *En cas de malheur*, generically a much grimmer film, has Yvette die at the hands of her young lover, at once devastating and releasing the older man (Gabin), ending her disruptive effect on his family and professional life. *La Vérité* concludes with the suicide of Dominique, on the one hand confirming her status as victim of an uncomprehending society, but on the other hand establishing her acceptance of fundamentally romantic values, since she dies out of remorse for having killed the man she loved. The elimination of the BB figure through death recurred in other films of the same period, notably in *Vie privée* (Louis Malle, 1961) and in Godard's *Le Mépris* (1963), which manages in a typically Godardian way to be at once ironically self-aware of the mechanisms of female stardom and willing to exploit them.

However, the violence with which the Bardot figure is restored to order or removed should perhaps be seen as significant in the light of the 'crisis of masculinity' that seems to appear in press coverage of BB's real-life marriage. In both

Et Dieu and *En cas de malheur*, a young man struggles against
the economic and social power of an older, wiser man to win
the woman he loves, and finally defeats his rival by an act of
violence that asserts only a fragile, imperfect authority (in the
first case re-establishing the bond with the woman, but in a
way that seems unlikely to be permanent; in the second only
by killing her). The Bardot character here serves as a pretext
for the playing out of an Oedipal narrative that expresses
anxiety about the son's capacity to accede to a viable form of
manhood – a narrative that played its part a few years later in
the confrontation between de Gaulle's government and the
(male-led) student movement of May '68. In the films, the
heroine must be defeated to produce the son's fragile victory.
In life, women found their gender-specific rights and interests
largely ignored in the battle between the old, paternalist
culture and the rebellious sons of '68: recognition of their
marginalisation would be the starting point for a new wave of
more militant French feminism.

Conclusion

If female spectators – particularly young ones – experienced the
thrill of a liberating identification with the Bardot of screen and
press, this was because her performance of femininity implicitly
claimed the right to a sexual and social independence hitherto
identified as masculine. However, neither in life (Bardot has
never displayed any interest in feminist issues) nor on screen
(the BB heroine remains materially and emotionally
dependent on men and is reclaimed or eliminated by the
films' closure) does she sustain or carry through this role.
Bardot's appeal as a star seems to have depended, at least in
part, on her capacity to hold together a tension between
contradictory discourses on sexuality and femininity: between,
on the one hand, a nascent female desire for sexual freedom
that also connoted a more generalised autonomy and that
converged in complex ways with the discourses of
consumerism, and on the other hand, a powerful ideology,
materially supported by the pro-natalist laws and by the
labour market, that defined women as by nature dependent,
monogamous and maternal. As the nature of this conflict
began to be more clearly articulated, and signs of the second-
wave feminist movement began to appear, Bardot's popularity
declined: box-office returns began to drop significantly after

Viva Maria in 1965, and Bardot retired from film-making in 1973. It was as if the need for a star who could express both the inchoate desire for 'liberation' and its impossibility faded with the more explicit definition of women's demands, and the widespread recognition that at least some of them could and should be fulfilled.

Although Bardot's films of the late 1950s and early 1960s offered considerable pleasures to female audiences, they also 'encouraged conservative views of women', the 'new values' represented by her heroines 'making few waves' because they implied in the end that 'women's liberation boiled down to (hetero)sexual promiscuity' (Vincendeau 1992: 93–4).[30] The ambivalence of both films and star persona, in terms of sexual politics, is undeniable, but my contention is that nonetheless, for her young female fans, BB's stardom had a predominantly empowering effect (as they themselves tend to perceive), encouraging a later identification with at least some of the goals of the feminist movement. Both the media discourse that shaped public perception of her life, and the film roles she played, ultimately fitted Bardot back into a traditional definition of femininity: self-assertion as a desiring subject ended either in capitulation, the acceptance of male authority (albeit an authority presented as itself in crisis) through love, or in death. Thus the real constraints on women's lives, and the resulting contradictions in their aspirations, were dramatised and acknowledged. But the pleasure of identification with a woman whose style and behaviour connoted irreverence, shame-free desire and resistance to the domestic/maternal imperative was not simply destroyed by her final recuperation. Though the BB persona was deeply unsisterly – a *femme à hommes* (a man's woman) rather than a *copine* (female friend) – the model of femininity she proposed played its part in the development of a feminist critique of the dominant culture.

Acknowledgments

Warm thanks to the following who answered my Bardot questionnaire and thus contributed to this essay: Bernadette Cristilli, Danièle Demachy-Dartin, Josette Desverchère, Janine Ferrand, Madeleine Frêne, Florette Galant, Colette Goulois, Mme. Hérault, Annie Kamina, Marie-Louise Lambillon, Elyane Lamour, Georges Maron, Mireille Millour-Dufresne,

Martine Pelloux, Bernard Pelloux, Solange Stora and Jane Tranoy, plus those respondents who preferred to remain anonymous. Special – and now, sadly, posthumous – thanks to Jacqueline Mercier for distributing her questionnaire amongst friends, and for her illuminating letter.

Notes

1. Jackie Stacey's work on Hollywood stars (Stacey 1994) highlights the way that feminist film theory has paid more attention to textual construction of the star than to audience response. Stacey herself analyses the process of identification through a study of letters from female fans, remembering the way that they felt about female stars of the 1940s and 1950s. In a similar way, though on a smaller scale, I tried to gain some sense of how women spectators remembered Bardot as star by circulating a short questionnaire to a number of French women born between 1924 and 1944 (Bardot's date of birth is 1934). I received twenty replies, some of them quite long. Whilst I would not make great claims for the scientific validity of the sample – I made use of contacts in France to distribute the questionnaire, ensuring only that it went to women from a range of backgrounds, degrees of education and regions – it did prove useful as an indicator of a certain consensus, albeit one based on memory and inevitably affected by the subsequent cultural construction of BB as an emancipatory figure.

2. One commented acerbically: 'It's a pity her cerebral hemispheres are not as developed as other parts of her body' ('Dommage que ses hémisphères cérébraux ne soient pas aussi développés que ses attributs féminins').

3. 'le produit fabuleux et néanmoins authentique de l'imaginaire collectif des jeunes femmes de sa génération'.

4. 'la guérisseuse et la sorcière … la proie de l'homme, … sa perte, … tout ce qu'il n'est pas et qu'il veut avoir, sa négation et sa raison d'être.' (Beauvoir 1976 [1949]: 242).

5. An opinion poll in 1957 concluded that BB was the subject of 47 percent of conversations in France, well ahead of politics at 41percent. (Rihoit 1986: 165).

6. St Tropez was already a popular place for holidays before BB adopted it (Colette, for example, had a house near the village and deplored the invasion of that part of Provence by tourists in *La Naissance du jour* [1928]), but it was Bardot who transformed the village into a place of pilgrimage for the 'hip' youth of the day. See for example the fourteen-page spread on 'St Trop' in *Paris Match* of 16 August 1958, which opens with a photo of Bardot.

7. 'Et puis elle avait un visage actuel, elle ressemblait vraiment à la jeune fille d'aujourd'hui' (Bernert 1991: 1086).

8. 'BB, produit de notre époque, permet à notre époque d'envahir les écrans'.

9. 'Bardot incarne ce qu'aiment les Français'.

10. 'son charme, sa jeunesse, son naturel sont sans conteste les signes extérieurs qui correspondent à l'attente de toute une génération. BB est l'incarnation de nouvelles valeurs …'.

11. See Chapter 4. The cultural differences between Bardot and the generation born some fifteen years later are strikingly apparent in a photo printed in the girls' teen-magazine *Mademoiselle Age Tendre* (slogan 'Pour les filles dans le vent' ['for girls in the groove']) in February 1968. BB (then aged thirty-four) and Sylvie Vartan (teenage pop idol and wife of Johnny Hallyday) pose together, dressed identically in hipster denim jeans and white T-shirts, both slim and leggy, blonde hair to their shoulders, BB's arm around Sylvie's shoulders. The magazine is thus reclaiming Bardot as a 'big sister' to current teenagers, but BB's more pronounced bust and hips, and her overtly sensual mouth and eyes accentuated by make-up, signify an explicit sexuality quite at odds with the androgynous, *copine* (girl-next-door) look of Sylvie.

12. 'J'avais pourtant manqué mourir, par manque de soins'.

13. 'Brigitte a trouvé son mari à *Paris Match*'.

14. 'cover-girl et vedette du cinéma'.

15. 'l'un des plus brillants reporters de *Match*'.

16. The same argument could be made about the John F. Kennedy/Jackie Lee Bouvier couple. They married in September 1953.

17. The 'peplum' is a 'sword and sandal' film, usually a tale of love and adventure set in ancient Greece or Rome, and named after the diminutive skirt worn by the male characters. The genre was popular in the 1950s: Bardot appeared in *Helen of Troy* (Robert Wise, 1954), shot in Italy.

18. 'Je ne me suis jamais mise dans la peau d'un personnage, mais ai toujours mis les personnages dans ma peau'.

19. See below. The film ends with an assertion of authority by Juliette's hitherto gentle husband and her obedient return to the marital home, with the implied blessing of the father-figure, Carradine.

20. 'la Française la plus célèbre à l'étranger'. *France Dimanche*, 21–27 December 1956.

21. Many of the women who responded to my questionnaire recalled, with pleasure, their own adoption of elements of the Bardot style, and the sense of thereby taking on a degree of 'Bardotness'. For example: 'I am just a little younger than Bardot, so for me she seemed very desirable, with a natural style that we weren't used to at the time. Girls of our age all started to try and look like her (clothes, hairstyle etc.)'. ('Je suis juste un peu plus jeune qu'elle, elle me paraissait donc très désirable, d'un naturel dont on n'avait pas l'habitude à l'époque. Les filles de nos âges se sont mises à lui ressembler [vêtements, coiffure etc.]').

22. See Andy Martin's (1996) *Waiting for Bardot*, where the author's teenage self and his friend do exactly this. On a more anecdotal level, while writing this essay I was told by two other men that as teenagers, around 1960, they had set off from England for St Tropez with the same vague aspiration to meet her.

23. 'plus éblouissante que jamais – elle est cette jeune maman moderne et organisée, et elle vous présente le nursery et la layette de son bébé'.

24. 'Moussia-la-nurse qui a aidé Brigitte-future-maman à tout préparer'.

25. 'Brigitte maman radieuse vous présente Nicolas'.

26. 'Nicolas Charrier a neuf jours et Brigitte n'est plus seulement la B.B. enviée, admirée, critiquée, mais aussi une maman comme toutes les autres. Elle ne veut pas quitter Nicolas. Sa vie de tous les jours est maintenant réglée sur les biberons, rythmée sur un horaire précis, celui de tous les bébés du monde. Avec Nicolas est né chez Brigitte quelquechose

de plus profond et de plus vrai que la gloire d'une vedette: la tendresse maternelle' (p.28).

27. 'les femmes, en effet, ont besoin d'admirer ... le mari doit être un dieu'.

28. In my essay 'Angry Young Women: Sex and Conflict in Best-selling First Novels of the 1950s' (1994) I identify the tension between the theoretical new freedoms offered to women in the 1950s and the strong ideological emphasis on the family, as a determining factor in the work of three popular young women writers of the period: Françoise Sagan, Françoise Mallet-Joris and Christiane Rochefort.

29. Claude Autant-Lara is one of the directors specifically attacked in François Truffaut's polemical article 'Une certaine tendance du cinéma' (1954). The script was also written by the most successful screenwriting partnership of the day, Aurenche and Bost, also the object of Truffaut's critical wrath. Though *Et Dieu*'s low budget and deliberate appeal to a youth audience gives it some resemblance to the New Wave films that followed, Vadim's later career confirms that he was anything but radical in his sexual politics, and *En cas de malheur*, though made by an interesting director, also serves as a vehicle for Jean Gabin's very conventionally masculine star persona.

30. See also Vincendeau 2000, where the conclusion on Bardot's overall impact on sexual politics is more positive.

CHAPTER 4

ROCK 'N' ROLL STARDOM: JOHNNY HALLYDAY

Chris Tinker

For more than forty years, Johnny Hallyday has remained one of the most prolific, enduring and visible features of popular music and the mass media in France. The sheer volume of his output, record sales and concert attendance is often cited as evidence of his popularity and commercial success: 'A thousand songs, more than a hundred hits, one hundred million records sold, concert audiences of fifteen million'.[1] What is interesting about his appeal is that it appears to cut across generational and socio-economic divisions, and several of his songs, such as 'Le Pénitencier' (The Prison, 1964) and 'Que je t'aime' (How I love you, 1969) have attained classic status in the French collective consciousness. More recently, Hallyday has achieved critical and commercial success as a film actor, particularly in *L'Homme du train* (Patrice Leconte, 2002). He also received official state recognition in 1997 when he was presented with France's highest decoration, the *Légion d'honneur*, by the President of the Republic, Jacques Chirac, who is a fan as well as a personal friend. Hallyday's special star status has been maintained through a fairly consistent stream of media coverage dedicated to his work, as well as to the ups and downs in his private life and business affairs. This coverage reached a peak during the period around his sixtieth birthday celebrations in June 2003. Indeed, in the sixty days running up to his birthday, a series of short retrospectives was broadcast every night before the main evening news bulletin on France 2, one of the main French terrestrial television channels. Hallyday's very public birthday celebrations culminated in a series of concerts in the Parc des Princes in Paris, followed by a tour of major French concert venues. Although it would appear that much of Hallyday's media representation is highly consensual, like many media personalities he is also the target of a more satirical brand of coverage. For example, television programmes such as *Les Guignols de l'info* (Canal +), the French equivalent of *Spitting Image* in the UK, have caricatured Hallyday as an inarticulate ageing rocker.

Although Johnny Hallyday is a highly significant figure within contemporary French culture, he has been largely neglected in academic accounts of popular music in France. Many of the books on Hallyday to date are biographical, if not hagiographical. Most work on the 1950s and 1960s has tended so far to focus on canonical singer-songwriters of the male-dominated French *chanson* tradition, especially Léo Ferré, Georges Brassens, and Jacques Brel (Hawkins 2000 and Tinker 2005). Although Johnny Hallyday has become increasingly involved over the years in songwriting, he still tends to be identified as the singer of other people's songs, and therefore as lacking the supposed authenticity and skill of the singer-songwriter. Academic accounts of popular music have largely neglected performers who are not the main authors of their own material, despite certain exceptions such as the work of Ginette Vincendeau and Keith Reader on Edith Piaf as a singing icon of 'suffering femininity'.[2] Thus despite Hallyday's prominence in contemporary French popular culture, to date there has been little academic discussion of his impact either in English, or, for that matter, in French. However, David Looseley has proposed a more substantial account of his cultural significance in his book *Popular Music in Contemporary France*, situating Hallyday and other singers of his generation against the backdrop of the modernisation that gripped French society and culture during the 1960s (Looseley 2003: 21–33). In the light of Looseley's work, this chapter will explore Hallyday's crucial significance as a key figure in the introduction of rock 'n' roll to France and in the development of a distinct youth culture, driven in part by commercial interests, the advent of new music technologies and the expansion of the mass media. This chapter will also consider Hallyday's passage into the

Johnny Hallyday at Le Golf Drouot club, Paris, 1962.
Photograph by kind permission of Jean-Louis Rancurel
(Rancurel Photothèque).

mainstream as well as the competing constructions of masculinity that accompanied this process.

The rock 'n' roll rebel

Hallyday played a key role in the development of popular musical forms and genres, especially the implantation of rock 'n' roll. Since the end of World War II, the authentic, traditional, homegrown French *chanson* had been the dominant form. The advent of rock 'n' roll was by no means

the first time that France had been subject to the cultural
influence of the USA. US styles had previously been exploited
by individual *chanson* artists such as Yves Montand as the
cowboy and Charles Aznavour as the archetypal American
crooner, while dance styles such as cha-cha and be-bop had
also been popularised. Prior to 1960 and the start of Hallyday's
career, rock 'n' roll had gained some initial popularity in
France with hits such as Bill Haley's 'Rock Around the Clock'
(1956).[3] However, as Ludovic Tournès argues, for rock 'n' roll to
take root successfully in France, what was really required was
'a Frenchified version of rock' ('une version francisée du rock')
(quoted in Grosdemouge 1999: 16). Indeed, adaptations of
American songs with French lyrics would be immediately more
accessible to audiences (Grosdemouge 1999: 45). French
lyricists such as Pierre Delanoë initially began adapting
American songs for French audiences. The French singer
Richard Anthony apparently listened avidly to US hits on his
radio, identifying those that he thought would be worth
adapting into French (Grosdemouge 1999: 16). However, while
French pastiches or adaptations of US songs would flourish,
recorded by artists such as Danyel Gérard and Richard
Anthony, writers like Boris Vian and performers such as Henri
Salvador (aka Henry Cording) also adopted a more parodic
mode. While rock 'n' roll was to be taken seriously by fans such
as Hallyday from the very beginning, others, as Grosdemouge
observes, saw it as something of a novelty, if not a joke, or a
'gag'.[4] These differing reactions to the arrival of rock 'n' roll in
France were perhaps an early sign of the later controversies
that would hamper its progress into the mainstream.

Becoming a rock star was not, to begin with, necessarily a
long-term or serious goal, as Grosdemouge comments, citing
the cases of Danyel Gérard, as well as Franck Jordan who gave
up his fledgling performing career to become a dentist instead
(Grosdemouge 1999: 9–10). However, Hallyday's aspirations
were less conventional. His interest as a teenager in the new
rock 'n' roll music, combined with a family background in
music and theatre, provided an impetus for the development
of his early career. Born Jean-Philippe Smet in the Malesherbes
district of Paris on 15 June 1943, Hallyday was sent at the age
of six months to live with his aunt, Hélène Mar, his father's
sister, following the separation of his parents, Huguette and
Léon. Having worked as an actress in silent films, Hélène took
Jean-Philippe on tour from an early age with her two
daughters, Desta and Menen, who were dancers in London.

Desta married an American dancer, Lee Halliday, with whom she formed a dance partnership called *Les Halliday's* (sic). Halliday had an enormous influence upon Jean-Philippe whom he called 'Johnny', a nickname which would eventually assume greater significance. It was Lee Halliday who first brought new rock 'n' roll records back to France from the USA and played them to a young, enthusiastic Jean-Philippe. His adoptive family encouraged him to learn drama, dance, guitar and singing at the beginning of the 1950s. When he was only nine, he was already performing on stage, supporting *Les Halliday's* during their tours. Jean-Philippe made his first, albeit brief, film appearance in Henri-Georges Clouzot's 1954 film *Les Diaboliques*. Although his initial ambition was to become an actor, in 1957 he saw the film *Loving You* (known in France as 'Amour frénétique'), starring his idol Elvis Presley, and, as a result, decided instead to aim for a career as a rock 'n' roll singer. The film was a typical rags-to-riches story which to some extent echoed the early lives of both Presley and Hallyday. Jean-Philippe was captivated by Presley's brand of rock 'n' roll, which blended pop, rock, country, Rhythm and Blues and gospel influences, as well as his energetic and eroticised performances, epitomised by his famous hip wiggle. Having returned to Paris in 1957, Jean-Philippe would hang out as a teenager with his friends at the famous Golf Drouot club in Paris where young rock 'n' roll fans gathered. By the age of fifteen, he was singing American numbers such as Little Richard's 'Tutti Frutti' and Elvis Presley's 'Let's Have a Party', while accompanying himself on the guitar. Adopting the stage name Johnny Halliday, he performed alongside groups and singers with similarly American-sounding pseudonyms such as *Les Chats Sauvages* (The Wild Cats) with Dick Rivers and *Les Chaussettes Noires* (The Black Socks) with Eddy Mitchell (Martin 2003: 50). It was during this period that Halliday met Christian Blondieau, alias Long Chris, who went on to write many of his songs.

The owner of the Golf Drouot club, Henri Leproux, encouraged Halliday to attend auditions which led to his first radio appearance on the programme *Paris Cocktail* (30 December 1959), performing Elvis Presley's song 'Let's Have a Party' (Grosdemouge 1999: 11). There Halliday met the lyricists Gilbert Guénet and Roger Jean Selti (better known as 'Jil et Jan') with whom he went on to collaborate extensively during the first half of the 1960s. 'Jil et Jan' also introduced Halliday to Jacques Wolfsohn, the artistic director of Vogue records and a key figure in the French music industry at the time. Signing to Vogue in 1960, Halliday released his first single, 'T'aimer follement', a French adaptation of Floyd Robinson's 'Makin' Love'. As a result of a typographical error, his name appeared on the record cover as 'Hallyday', a spelling which he subsequently adopted. Hallyday was marketed exotically as bilingual and bicultural; as the sleeve of his first single stated: 'An American with a French upbringing, he can sing equally well in English and in French' (Brierre 2003: 58).[5] In interviews, Hallyday invented a whole new history and persona for himself, recounting how he had spent his youth in the USA at his father's ranch in Oklahoma[6] and how 'Laisse les filles' (Leave the girls alone), another of the four tracks on his single, was a song about the conflicting advice which his parents had given to him as a teenager (Brierre 2003: 59). However, Hallyday's first release failed to perform well. The radio presenter Lucien Morisse dismissed his efforts, smashing the record 'Laisse les filles' on air, and promising to his listeners: 'That's the first and last time you'll listen to Johnny Hallyday' (Martin 2003: 63).[7] Such a violent reaction was perhaps not surprising, given that one of the tracks on the single 'T'aimer follement' had previously been recorded by the Egyptian singer Dalida who was already established as a successful recording artist in France and to whom Morisse was married. Although certain individuals potentially stood in the way of Hallyday's career, others would prove hugely supportive, such as Georges Leroux, who became his manager in March 1960, and the television producer Aimée Mortimer. Hallyday first appeared on French television (at the time consisting of one state-run channel) in April 1960, singing 'Laisse les filles' on Mortimer's programme *Ecole des vedettes*.

Hallyday's second single, released in June 1960, the rumba, 'Souvenirs souvenirs', was his first hit. However, his energetic brand of rock 'n' roll which involved him rolling around on the floor was still considered unacceptable to music-hall audiences, who were more used to French *chanson*. When Bruno Coquatrix, the director of the Olympia music hall, was approached about the possibility of Hallyday performing rock 'n' roll at the venue, he initially advised Leroux, 'This kind of music isn't for us, Georges. We prefer traditional French song' (Brierre 2003: 63).[8] However, in September 1960 Hallyday managed to obtain a booking for three weeks in Paris at the Alhambra music hall, as a support act to the comedian Raymond Devos. These, his first major live performances, met with a somewhat mixed reception. During the opening night on 20 September, while Hallyday's fans from the Golf Drouot cheered upstairs in the balcony, downstairs the reception was distinctly cooler. Although certain figures within the music industry such as Maurice Chevalier and Hugues Aufray were supportive, others such as Dalida and Henri Salvador were less impressed, as were the management of the Alhambra and much of the mainstream press: 'A display of bad taste' (*L'Humanité*); 'Burlesque parody' (*Le Parisien libéré*); 'A gibbering and hysterical display destined soon for the loony bin' (Brierre 2003: 72–3).[9] Claude Sarraute's disdainful comments in *Le Monde* typify the reactions of the quality press: 'On witnessing the fits, starts and raptures of this tall gangling figure, a vision of pink and blond, I confess to feeling the sort of astonishment, curiosity and enjoyment, which one experiences when looking at the chimpanzees on a visit to the zoo at Vincennes' (Grosdemouge 1999: 11).[10] Nevertheless, Hallyday attracted a loyal band of predominantly working-class followers, described by Lee Halliday as 'proletarians who felt solidarity with him, who related to his past, who hoped for a future like his, and who bemoaned their poverty' (Brierre 2003: 76).[11] Indeed, Hallyday was well received by such audiences when he toured the south of France, especially in Marseilles, Cassis and Sète.

However, Hallyday's image was still shocking to many. Just as the advent of rock 'n' roll was associated with social disturbances in the US and the UK during the 1950s, in France it was originally connected with *blousons noirs* (black jackets), groups of disaffected working-class youths, particularly from the suburbs of Paris. Hanging out with and performing for his friends at the Golf Drouot Club, Hallyday as a teenager during the late 1950s identified with the collective male bonding of *blouson noir* subculture, adopting the black-leather-jacketed look which was inspired by on-screen biker heroes such as Marlon Brando in *The Wild One* (Laslo Benedek, 1954) (Looseley 2003: 24). On 24 February 1961 he featured at the larger concert venue, Le Palais des Sports, in France's first rock festival, organised by Vogue records, playing to a packed house of around five thousand young people. The performance, which included covers of songs by Little Richard and Elvis Presley, caused an explosion of energy within the audience. Youths piled chairs in the middle of the room and several arrests were made. As a result, a law was passed insisting that seats should in future be fixed to the floor (Brierre 2003: 78–9). The police intervention was said to have been heavy-handed and something of an over-reaction, as the cameraman François Reichenbach, filming the scenes, recalls, 'I saw for the first time in France young people who were beginning to grow restless, to experience a feeling of awkward sensuality and enthusiasm ... and I felt that the police disapproved. They had erected large railings at the front of the stage, and took what was enthusiasm for aggression' (Brierre 2003: 79–80).[12] A second festival took place in June 1961 at which enthusiasm again led to violence and damage to property. As Looseley observes, this, along with the 'hyper-erotic' performances of artists such as Vincent Taylor, heightened a fear of rock 'n' roll felt by the media and parents alike. There was wide debate, with several members of the National Assembly calling for the banning of such concerts. Although the ban did not apply at national level, Hallyday was prevented from playing in cities with troubled suburbs. He was not allowed to play in Cannes, Strasbourg or Bayonne during his 1961 tour, and the Montbéliard police used tear gas to control crowds. As Looseley recounts, the press were fearful of rock 'n' roll while de Gaulle somewhat dismissively thought that French youth would be better off using their energy more constructively to build roads (Looseley 2003: 26–7). Although the kind of hysteria that rock 'n' roll music and performers caused in France was perceived as a new and worrying phenomenon, it had, to some extent, already been experienced prior to 1960. Looseley cites the examples during the 1940 and 1950s of be-pop, boogie-woogie styles, and individual singers such as the Spanish-born crooner Luis Mariano, and Gilbert Bécaud, known as 'Monsieur 100, 000 volts' (Looseley 2003: 24).

The teen idol

Rock 'n' roll provoked a good deal of anxiety, particularly amongst parents, politicians and the music industry, largely because of its associations with young, male, working-class disaffection and juvenile delinquency. Faced with this widespread disapproval, the record companies in France cleaned up their act, creating a series of inoffensive pop stars, both female (Sylvie Vartan, Sheila, France Gall, Françoise Hardy) and male (Claude François, Adamo, Frank Alamo). Their brand of popular music was known as *yéyé*, the term deriving from the word 'yeah' which often figured in the choruses of UK and US pop songs (Looseley 2003: 27, 35, n. 23). Hallyday also began to include *yéyé* songs in his repertoire. The recurring themes of *yéyé* songs, aimed primarily at a teenage audience, were love and its loss, relationships between boys, girls and their parents, as well as school life and military service. A crucial factor in Hallyday's rise to popularity is what Looseley identifies as the formation in France of a distinct teenage market. By 1964 one third of the French population was made up of under-20s. The growth of this market was assisted by factors such as the baby boom, a later school-leaving age, the expansion of higher education and the transition of the French economy into one dependent on consumer goods. Teenagers had more time on their hands and more money for items such as clothes, records and magazines; rock 'n' roll from the USA became the 'hub' of this 'distinct youth culture' in France (Looseley 2003: 23). The French popular music industry was given a further boost by technological modernisation during the 1950s. The electric guitar (e.g. Leo Fender's Broadcaster and the Precision bass) went on sale to would-be rock musicians. The early 1950s also saw the introduction of the transistor radio and the portable record player, along with the American 45 rpm single and 33 rpm long-play vinyl disc which replaced the old 78 rpm records in France. The first record-pressing plant in France was built in 1957. Such developments meant that teenagers would be able to enjoy music individually and autonomously in their own bedrooms rather than be restricted to listening as part of the family unit. By 1966, with teenagers representing nearly 40 percent of the population, 40 percent of them owned a transistor radio while 27 percent owned their own record player. The record became something of a fetishised cultural artefact, all the more attractive to teenagers when new record sleeves printed in colour and featuring images of their favourite artists were introduced in 1958.[13]

Teenagers, a new lucrative market in France, could listen to records, not only at home on portable record players, but also on jukeboxes in cafés. Moreover, the audiovisual version of the jukebox, the Scopitone player, was introduced in French cafés at the start of the 1960s.[14] Customers who paid one franc per song could listen to and watch performances on a 54cm screen. The machine, which could usually store around thirty-six songs on 16 mm film, would play prerecorded performance films of individual songs in colour. A monthly hit parade was produced, and café owners would receive a magazine which would announce which four new songs were to be added to machines the following month. The Scopitones could not be broadcast on television since the copyright was held by the production and distribution company, *Compagnie d'Applications Mécaniques à l'Électronique, au Cinéma et à l'Atomistique* (CAMECA). In any case, television viewers would not have been able to view the Scopitones in colour, as French television was still being broadcast in black and white. Hallyday, along with other artists, made a series of Scopitones during the 1960s, starting in 1962 with his hit single 'Idole des jeunes' (an adaptation of Ricky Nelson's song 'Teenage Idol'). This generally low-budget and relatively unexplored art form, the forerunner of the video promo/clip, exploited the hand-held camera, which, at the time, was a key instrument in the more avant-garde circles of New-Wave film-making in France. Indeed, several film-makers of the New Wave also produced Scopitones, including Claude Lelouch who directed Hallyday's 'L'Idole des jeunes' (1962).

Although Jacques Wolfsohn had tried to broaden Hallyday's popularity, for example making him record a cover version of Bryan Hyland's gimmicky song 'Itsy Bitsy Teeny Weeny Yellow Polka Dot Bikini' ('Itsy bitsy petit bikini', 1960), the influence of Johnny Stark, who effectively began to manage Hallyday in 1961, was to prove more crucial in his ambition to become a mainstream performer, as was Hallyday's decision to leave Vogue for the Dutch international Philips in the summer of 1961. Hallyday was certainly in demand, since another record mogul Eddie Barclay had also tried to sign him to his company. On signing to Philips, Hallyday, under the guidance of Johnny Stark, was pushed to the forefront of the *yéyé* movement, producing pop music, which was a safer, less threatening alternative to rock 'n' roll. Stark, who personally preferred *chanson* to rock 'n' roll, kept a tight rein on Hallyday in a bid to make him more respectable – a strategy used by Elvis Presley's manager Colonel Parker (Brierre 2003: 93). A fan club for Hallyday was set up with a handful of groupies/fans looking after his mail.[15] Hallyday's image on stage and on record covers became more clean-cut, ranging from a casual look (jeans, T-shirt, short-sleeved shirt) through to black dinner-suits, designed to appeal to a broad audience. Hallyday's more wholesome look contrasted strongly with rock 'n' roll artists like Vince Taylor who embodied 'hard, violent, "demonic" rock' ('rock dur, violent, "diabolique"'). As Brierre comments on the differences between the record sleeves of Hallyday and Taylor, 'Johnny, with his tanned face, and short well-combed hair is a picture of health, dressed in white trousers, white moccasins and a white open-necked shirt. Vince Taylor, dressed entirely in black leather, projects an entirely different image: dark, disturbing, almost unhealthy' (Brierre 2003: 95–6).[16] According to Brierre, Hallyday was conscious of growing competition on the scene from, for example, Les Chaussettes noires, Les Chats sauvages and Vince Taylor, and so set about making changes to his line-up of musicians (renamed The Golden Stars), and to his songwriters, collaborating, for instance, with more mainstream *chanson* artists such as Charles Aznavour (Brierre 2003: 97). While Hallyday attempted to remain faithful to his roots in rock (recording Jerry-Lee Lewis's 'High School Confidential'), his repertoire became broader and more inclusive, including sentimental ballads such as 'Douce violence' (Sweet violence) and 'Toi qui regrettes' (Regretful you). As a result, Coquatrix, who had previously dismissed the possibility of Hallyday performing at the Olympia, changed his mind a year later. Performing at the venue from 20 September until 9 October 1961, Hallyday, dressed in a dinner suit like a *chanson* artist, launched the latest trans-Atlantic dance craze, the Twist, following this up in the autumn with a single in French and English, 'Viens danser le Twist' (an adaptation of Chubby Checker's 'Let's Twist Again'), thus achieving his first gold disc. Later Hallyday admitted that he was ashamed of the Twist, describing it as 'the supreme betrayal of rock 'n' roll' ('la haute trahison du rock 'n' roll'). However, the Twist, while commercialised, was potentially progressive as a style, since it signalled a shift in emphasis from the couple towards the single dancer.[17]

From 25 October until 12 November 1962, Hallyday undertook his second season at Olympia, which further developed his dancing skills. While launching another gimmicky dance, the Mashed Potato, he also took part in a choreographed brawl with other dancers in a ballet at the end of the song 'La Bagarre' (The Fight – originally Elvis Presley's song 'Trouble'). Although his performance seems on the face of it to glamorise violence, it was rather more inspired by the recent US musical film *West Side Story* (1961) in which the representations of aggression are largely stylised and sanitised. Hallyday's ambitions as an actor were also cultivated during his concerts at the Olympia. In performances of the song 'I got a woman', Hallyday would lay his guitar down on the stage and cover it with his dinner jacket in the same way that Jim Stark, James Dean's character in *Rebel*

Without a Cause, places his red blouson jacket over the dead
body of his friend Plato. Like Elvis Presley in the USA and Cliff
Richard in the UK, Hallyday went on to develop his acting skills
further in a series of feature films in which he played the
character of a singer, e.g. *D'où viens-tu Johnny?* (Where are you
from Johnny?, Noël Howard, 1963) and *Cherchez l'idole* (The
Chase, Michel Boisrond, 1964). These functioned essentially as
marketing devices for his records. It was only in 1970 that he
finally appeared in a film playing a role that was not that of a
singer, in Sergio Corbucci's spaghetti-western *Le Specialiste,* in
which he played a cowboy in the style of Lee Van Cleef and
Clint Eastwood.[18]

Although Hallyday's more clean-cut image as a *yéyé* artist
may have reassured parents, cultural commentators were less
impressed, dismissing *yéyé* as 'moronic' and 'trash'. In
particular, Jacques Charpentreau 'stoutly defended the virtues
of the "intellectual" and "literary" tradition of French song',
and 'campaigned for forms of pop music that encouraged
ethical awareness and civic responsibility' (Rigby 1991: 164).
Musically, *yéyé* songs were often formulaic, using a standard
set of chord progressions (Grosdemouge 1999: 39). In terms of
lyrics, they were compared less favourably with the more
literary and intellectual tradition of French *chanson. Yéyé* was
very a much a 'safe' alternative to rock 'n' roll; as Michel
Winock comments, 'the lyrics sung by *yéyé* singers blend a
general niceness with petit bourgeois ideals and safe eroticism'
(quoted in Grosdemouge 1999: 15).[19] As a major figure of the
yéyé generation, Hallyday and his music were singled out for
particular criticism, often dismissed as 'stupide, nul, vide de
tout sens' ('stupid, trashy, meaningless'), as one of his best-
known songwriters Philippe Labro later recounted.[20]

Although much criticism was heaped upon *yéyé,* more
constructive views came from the intellectual and artistic
world. Edgar Morin published two articles in *Le Monde* shortly
after a free, open-air concert was organised, on 22 June 1963
at the Place de la Nation in Paris, to mark the first anniversary
of the youth magazine *Salut les copains* (Hi mates). Featuring
Hallyday and other *yéyé* performers such as Sylvie Vartan and
Richard Anthony, the event on Place de la Nation was a
modernised version of a concert which took place every year to
celebrate the Tour de France. Thirty thousand fans were
expected to attend but around 150,000 people actually turned
up. The newspapers contained a great deal of antiyouth
propaganda, reporting that the tough *blousons noirs* from the

difficult neighbourhood of Belleville had committed acts of violence, rape, theft and vandalism. For example, *Paris Press* ran the headline 'Salut les voyous' ('Hi yobbos') (Looseley 2003: 29). However, such accounts were challenged by young people and their parents who wrote to the letters pages of *Salut les copains*. It was argued that Hallyday had to be taken away in a police van simply because he had entered the crowd and risked having his shirt ripped off (Grosdemouge 1999: 33–4). Although Morin agreed that *yéyé* exploited teenagers economically, preparing them to become 'docile consumers', he was fascinated by a 'new form of class consciousness based not on socio-economic status but age' (Looseley 2003: 87). He was particularly intrigued by the scenes of 'gratuitous frenzy' ('frénésie à vide') witnessed at the Place de la Nation event. For Morin, *yéyé* contained the seeds of a revolt against 'an adult world from which seeps bureaucratic boredom, repetition, deceit, death' (Morin in Looseley 2003: 87–8). The potential for youth rebellion at the heart of the seemingly bland musical form, *yéyé*, was also recognised in contemporary French literary circles by the writer Elsa Triolet who, speaking in 1964, identified with Hallyday's youthful energy and idealism: 'How can you resent the health, happiness and youth of this fine boy? His fury reminds me of my own when they tried to bring Mayakovsky down'.[21] As the comments of Morin and Triolet attest, Hallyday can be credited at the very least for his contribution to the development of a distinctive and vigorous youth culture in France.

Although Hallyday incorporated *yéyé* songs into his repertoire, by 1964 he nonetheless wished to reaffirm his US musical credentials, having visited the home of country and western music, Nashville, in 1962. There he recorded his album *Johnny Hallyday Sings America's Rockin' Hits* with Shelby Singleton, Presley's musical director. As Brierre observes, Hallyday wished to avoid the path of Elvis Presley who, since leaving the army, had become more of a family entertainer, popular across the generations. Hallyday also continued optimistically to express a visceral attachment to rock 'n' roll which he believed would inspire and appeal to the young at a fundamental level:

> I am sure that the youngest fans, those between the ages of 8 and 12, will soon have the same thirst for rock that my generation felt. This is perfectly normal, not only because its rhythm, consisting of alternating strong and weak beats,

physically resembles human sounds such as a heartbeat or
footsteps, but also because rock 'n' roll music is the most
suitable musical form for expressing young people's dynamism
and their yearning for a free existence ...[22]

Hallyday also needed to leave a lasting, memorable image of
himself as a rock star before he would disappear from the
stage for military service. His third six-week run at the
Olympia from 15 February until 30 March 1964, accompanied
by Joey (Gréco) et les Showmen, featured blues numbers
('Excuse-moi partenaire') and rhythm and blues ('Shout'),
eliciting a favourable reaction from audiences. Hallyday also
recorded an album in 1964, *Les Rocks les plus terribles*, in which
he paid tribute to Elvis Presley, Chuck Berry, Little Richard and
Gene Vincent. However, while wishing to affirm his
authenticity as a rock 'n' roll artist, Hallyday would still need
to move and adapt to new trends in France as well as the
reaffirmation of the French poetic *chanson* tradition. By 1963,
the decline of *yéyé* had already begun, while the world of
French *chanson* received a boost with the blossoming careers of
artists such as Brel and Brassens (Brierre 2003: 110–11). While
Hallyday was away on military service, new groups such as
The Beatles, The Rolling Stones and The Animals were also
coming to the fore in France. Furthermore, the folk-song
tradition was being revived in France by Bob Dylan and
Hugues Aufray, influencing a new generation of artists such as
Antoine, Jacques Dutronc and Michel Polnareff who had not
taken American-sounding pseudonyms (Grosdemouge 1999:
76–7). As Looseley observes, by 1968, musical definitions were
no longer watertight, and *yéyé* was no longer homogenous, if
indeed it ever was (Looseley 2003: 32).

A civilian once more, Hallyday returned to the Olympia from
18 November until 26 December 1965, although the run was
not as successful as expected. At the end of the year the album
Johnny chante Hallyday was released, an album of original
songs, rather than adaptations, which saw disappointing sales.
In 1966, Hallyday reverted to recording more adaptations of US
hits. Brierre comments that Hallyday, somewhat in disarray,
was unsure how he fitted into the popular music landscape, as
his fans had moved on to new musical styles. Hallyday was no
longer the emblem of French youth, who by now were more
concerned by personal and social issues as diverse as Vietnam,
the Cold War, the nuclear threat, drugs, racism and sexuality
(Brierre 2003: 125–30). Hallyday was even mocked by Antoine,

an anticonformist singer famous for his hippy style, who joked about putting 'Johnny in a circus cage' in his song 'Les Elucubrations' ('Rantings'). The object of ridicule retaliated by releasing the single 'Cheveux longs, idées courtes' (Long hair, short on ideas). Hallyday entered something of a downward spiral as the sensational end of the press reported his excesses in drink and drugs, his depression, declining record sales, a growing tax bill and domestic problems.[23] This culminated on 10 September 1966 in a suicide attempt which provoked a sense of outrage from critics who viewed Hallyday as victim of a system that saw youngsters queuing up outside record-company offices for auditions, that emphasised profit and that contributed to bringing such a young man to the edge of self-destruction (Grosdemouge 1999: 41, 62–3).

Within a month, however, in October 1966, Hallyday was back on stage at the Olympia supported by Jimi Hendrix who was relatively unknown at the time. A fly-on-the-wall television documentary produced during the period represents Hallyday as a resurrected messianic figure. One particular sequence filmed in the dressing room sees Hallyday congratulated on his come-back by Coquatrix and the Director of the radio station Europe no. 1.[24] Hallyday also continued to try out new musical styles and images influenced by West Coast hippy and psychedelic fashions ('San Francisco', 1967) (Brierre 2003: 139–43). Indeed, his concerts emphasised the spectacular in terms of bright costumes and decor and his own dazzling performances. For example, the concerts at the Olympia from 15 March until 16 April 1967 featured eighteen costume changes.[25] He also began to play large-scale venues such as the Palais des Sports with audiences of six thousand. Hallyday was often described as a 'bête de scène', a charismatic showman who gives his all, to the point of smashing his guitar on stage. In his 1969 megashow the stage was transformed into a boxing ring, and Hallyday into a boxer, somewhat reminiscent of Elvis Presley's role in the film *Kid Galahad* (1962). As the end of the 1960s approached, Hallyday also continued to reassert his rock 'n' roll roots in terms of music and clothing. In 1968, both he and his idol Elvis Presley revived the black-leather biker look which had been associated with angry young men such as Marlon Brando (Hallyday in the film *A tout casser*; Presley in his US television comeback). Hallyday also continued to work with British and American musicians who would add to his image as an authentic rock 'n' roller, for example Micky Jones (guitar) and Tommy Brown (drums) from the Blackbirds, who both featured in a series of concerts at the Palais des Sports in Paris from 26 April until 4 May 1969.

Hallyday's central role in promoting *yéyé* brought to the surface the beginnings of a conflict between his personal beliefs and professional ambition. While *yéyé* brought him mainstream success, this inevitably compromised his image as an authentic rock 'n' roll singer. Nevertheless, he continued over the years to reaffirm his rock 'n' roll image. When the popularity of the *yéyé* fashion began to wane in the mid-1960s, Hallyday faced the challenge of maintaining his popularity as a mainstream artist, particularly since he had just returned to his career full time, following a less visible period away on military service. While the early 1960s saw him at the heart of major innovations in popular music, the later years of that decade viewed him more as a follower than a setter of musical fashions. As the main incarnation of rock 'n' roll in France, Hallyday illustrates the growing influence of the USA, represents a break from the dominant indigenous *chanson* tradition, and also underlines the importance of attempting to create a new national popular music. Moreover, he exemplifies the paradox that sees French rock 'n' roll both as an oppositional expression of young, male, working-class disaffection and as a recuperable and marketable commodity of youth culture.

The media icon: *Salut les copains*

While Hallyday's trajectory within the French music industry during the 1960s partly accounts for his significance, our discussion also requires further consideration of the role of the mass media, which were evolving at a rapid pace. A crucial factor in Hallyday's rise to prominence as a youth icon was his promotion, particularly in television, radio and glossy youth magazines. Although few people, relatively speaking, owned television sets at the beginning of the 1960s, the popularity of the small screen would increase as the decade progressed. In April 1960, a somewhat shy-looking Hallyday appeared for the first time on French television on the programme *Ecole des vedettes*, where he sang 'Laisse les filles'. Although television at this time was still much less developed than radio, Hallyday's lively performance nonetheless made a positive impression and a refreshing change as Brierre recounts: 'Young television viewers, used to more starchy-looking singers filmed from the same fixed camera angle, associated him with a lively and modern vision of the new decade' (Brierre 2003: 60).[26] Much of Hallyday's early coverage tended to cast him as an 'ordinary', young, up-and-coming artist who had begun to acquire 'special' star status.[27] While taking centre stage in his performances, he was often interviewed sitting amongst the audience, identifying with its members who were a just few years younger than himself.[28] This image of the *copain* or older brother would be taken up and developed further by radio and magazines. By the time Hallyday attained mainstream success as the emblematic figure of *yéyé*, his television coverage had shifted to a greater emphasis on his special star status. Hallyday appeared on television displaying his wealth through material possessions such as clothes, jewellery and a yacht. An archetypal 'special', jet-set star, he was often filmed at airports and appeared regularly at star-studded occasions such as the Venice and Cannes[29] film festivals, and at charity events.[30] Images of leisure also featured prominently, for example on the beach in St Tropez[31] or in Rio.[32] Hallyday's representation as a young, free and single playboy was somewhat at odds with his other image as the steady boyfriend of the *yéyé* singer Sylvie Vartan whom he was to marry in April 1965.

Radio, unlike television, was already well established in France at the start of the 1960s and its transistorised version, a new form of portable entertainment, was as significant as the personal stereo would become in the 1980s. Hallyday was, in particular, heavily promoted on the independent *radios péripheriques*, notably Europe no.1 which started broadcasting in 1955 from the Sarre region. Such independent stations were not subject to the sometimes heavy-handed interference of the French state, which saw radio as a tool of propaganda. Europe no.1 developed innovative, youth-oriented, music-based programming such as the famous *Salut les copains* (Hi mates), often referred to as *SLC*, which began broadcasting weekly in the early evening after school in the summer of 1959 and daily in October. The title of the programme, taken from the title of a song by Gilbert Bécaud and Pierre Delanoë, was reminiscent of the friendly catchphrases of British DJs such as Jimmy Saville ('Hi there guys and gals') and Alan Freeman ('Hello pop-pickers'). Its hosts, Frank Ténot and Daniel Filipacchi, already established as jazz presenters on Europe no. 1, adopted a relaxed, informal tone and style which, for teenage listeners, was a refreshing change from the rather old-fashioned text-reading announcer whose approach tended to be rather *bien pensant* (right-minded) and *scout* (well-meaning). The role of Ténot and Filipacchi was that of a *meneur de jeu* (compère). Presenters at Europe no.1 were even given a rule book, *Le Petit Manuel du parfait meneur de jeu*, which gave guidance on presentation style. For example, they would use the familiar *tu* form rather than the more formal *vous*. The spirit of the programme was very much that of 'out with the old and in with the new', as it included, for example, a section known as *le musée* (the museum), featuring tracks from recent years or even months. The innovative style of *SLC* featured jingles which helped to create a slick, seamless join between the music played and the presenters, who would often talk over a song's introduction. It was the first time that radio directly addressed a specifically teenage audience who were given an opportunity to express themselves in programmes, for example in the section entitled 'Autour du magnétophone' (Around the tape recorder). The programme also featured a great deal of advertising, given that teenagers, who had plenty of disposable income, represented a lucrative market. Although some conservative critics, the adult press and politicians such as de Gaulle's successor Georges Pompidou inevitably viewed *SLC* as distracting drivel, it was to become highly influential.[33]

In July 1962, the programme produced the first issue of a spin-off weekly magazine with the same title, one of the new, glossy, colourful, youth-oriented magazines, again aimed at the teenage market. The magazine and radio versions of *SLC* would promote each other. Soon selling over a million copies monthly, the magazine featured an innovative mix of news on record releases and concerts, a hit parade, song lyrics, biographical information and anecdotes on artists, fashion advice, photo spreads (particularly the work of Jean-Marie Perier), humour and cartoon characters (including 'Chouchou', the magazine's mascot). A favourite with readers were the pull-out posters of artists which readers could stick on to their bedroom walls. Filipacchi was the magazine's editor and again cultivated the image of a friend, mate (*copain*) or older brother – in 1962 he was 34.[34] In 1963, his reader's page 'Cher Daniel' received up to 500,000 letters. The magazine created a virtual community for readers which even included its own youth argot. A *Dictionnaire des copains* was produced in 1964. Indeed, as Looseley summarises, the 'philosophy' of the magazine was that 'all pop fans were *copains*, mates. The term spoke of wholesome friendships between boys and girls and an apolitical culture of classless youths passionate about a music that advocated nothing more than harmless vigorous fun' (Looseley 2003: 28).

Hallyday was initially the main star of *SLC*, followed by Vartan, Hardy, Sheila and Mitchell, Anthony, and Claude François. Indeed, Hallyday appeared repeatedly on the front cover and is particularly prominent in one of the most famous images in *SLC*, a photo taken on 12 April 1966 of many stars of the *yéyé* generation whose average age was 22–23, just a few years older than their fans. Hallyday's standing was also confirmed in an annual 'referendum' run by the magazine to establish who were the most popular male and female artists. Although Hallyday came first in the 1963, 1964, 1965, 1968 and 1969 polls, he came second in 1966 and 1967, a relatively difficult period following the completion of military service which culminated in his suicide attempt. He also appeared in the advertising sections, promoting youth-oriented goods ranging from electric guitars to Playboy-brand shirts. A regular feature of *SLC* was Hallyday's column 'La Lettre de Johnny', an open letter written (or ghost written) to his fans. To start with, he reviewed records, including his own, in what Pires regards as something of a departure from the norms of review journalism. Eventually, however, his column gave way to more on his own 'activities, circumstances and opinions'.[35] The column allowed him to maintain a link with his fans during his period of military service when he was unable to perform live.[36] He also adopted a strongly informal, oral, colloquial style in the same way as the radio programme. His letter produced what Pires regards as 'a sense of equality between the reviewer and the readership – an informal, chatty atmosphere'. However, the magazine also reflected a move in interest from rock 'n' roll groups towards personality cults. Pires observes that 'Hallyday's privileged position is often pointed up in photos of him with the stars, and in anecdotes about what he has got up to with them'.[37]

Although *SLC* was the most popular youth magazine, there were others which also dedicated significant amounts of coverage to Hallyday. However, these failed to challenge the prominence of *SLC* until the growth of more serious music reviews such as *Rock and Folk* (1966–). *Age tendre et tête de bois* (Young and headstrong),[38] which started off like *SLC* with an assertion of a distinct youth culture in the opening issue in January 1963, soon became a teenage girls' magazine, *Mademoiselle Age Tendre*, edited by Daniel Filipacchi who marketed it as the little sister of *SLC*. This was reflected in the content, which concentrated less on pop music and more on stereotypically feminine pursuits such as beauty, fashion and cookery. Affairs of the heart were also discussed, with the first issue published in November 1964 featuring an interview with Hallyday's girlfriend, Sylvie Vartan, entitled 'Sylvie – pourquoi j'aime Johnny' (pp.16–18).

While the French Catholic youth press (e.g. *J2 Jeunesse* for boys and *J2 Magazine* for girls) took little interest in *yéyé*, the PCF presented an alternative reading of Hallyday and his persona in its own youth magazine *Nous les garçons et les filles* (*NGF*). For example, the following review emphasises his physical strength and sincerity of character:

> Hallyday's concerts cannot be dismissed as a series of sentimental songs accompanied by a few lively dance moves. As soon as he appears, a tall muscular figure, he owns the stage. Whether you like or dislike what he sings or the way he acts, you cannot deny his determination to make sincerity the basis of his particular brand of *chanson*.[39]

Although Hallyday's work was not particularly appreciated by readers of *NGF* (in 1964 Hallyday came just tenth in the ranking of readers' preferred artists), he was credited with being a *'talent extraordinaire'*.[40] However, by 1965 *NGF* was asking explicitly, 'Is Johnny old-fashioned?' ('Johnny est-il démodé?').[41] Hallyday would appear less and less as the magazine placed more emphasis on French and world political issues in the run up to the turbulent social and political events of 1968. Whereas *SLC* was reluctant to expose Hallyday's life warts and all, *NGF* viewed Hallyday as a victim of the music industry and the mass media, arguing against the simplistic approach of the popular press (e.g. *France Dimanche, Ici Paris*). It was often assumed that Hallyday and his on-stage persona were one and the same in songs such as 'Noir c'est noir' ('Black is black'), released shortly after his attempted suicide and widely viewed as a sign of his inner turmoil. *NGF* highlights the difficulties of being a teenage idol as well as the intrusive role of the media: 'It's difficult today to be the real Johnny Hallyday and Sylvie Vartan ... They are stifled and engulfed by the characters that the press and radio have created for them'.[42] In particular, the writer Claude Lecomte is struck by Hallyday's 'solitude at the heart of his fame' ('cet aspect de solitude au milieu de la gloire').[43]

The masculine role model

While Hallyday was identified at the start of his career with a hard, macho, rebellious image of masculinity that was sexual rather than romantic, this was tempered during the 1960s by the addition of other masculine prototypes, notably the patriotic French conscript and the adoring husband. Hallyday's apparently contradictory persona is represented in the October 1965 edition of the youth magazine *Salut les copains*, which features a photo montage of Hallyday with his favourite things: an army beret, a helicopter blade, a Harley Davidson motorcycle, a guitar, a saddle, a film projector to watch westerns, a bottle of coca cola, a picture of James Dean and a bridal bouquet. Hallyday attempted to maintain his initially rebellious image off as well as on stage, particularly his love of action and adventure. In 1967, Hallyday, sharing a love of fast sports cars with his screen hero James Dean,[44] took part in the Monte Carlo Rally which was extensively covered by *SLC* and by television.[45] While cultivating a daredevil image, intended to appeal to teenage boys, Hallyday also developed a softer, romantic persona aimed at teenage girls. Accordingly, his 1963 film, *D'où viens-tu Johnny?*, features him not only as the action hero, riding a horse and performing the kind of stunts found in the western film genre, but also as something of a heart-throb.

Two episodes in Hallyday's life were particularly significant in terms of his recuperation by the mainstream media: his military service and his much publicised wedding to the *yéyé* singer Sylvie Vartan.[46] On 8 May 1964, when young men had already been drafted as conscripts to serve in the Algerian War, Hallyday, along with other singers of his generation such as Danyel Gérard and Eddy Mitchell, was called up, echoing Elvis Presley's earlier period of military service. Stationed with the Forty-third Infantry Regiment at Offenburg in Germany, Hallyday was not authorised to perform but he was allowed to record on the proviso that any publicity photos and record sleeves featured him in army uniform.[47] Although he had dual nationality (French/Belgian), he felt that he should undertake military service as he had been born in France (Brierre 2003: 115). While frustrated by his absence from the limelight, he continued to make hit records such as 'Le Pénitencier' (originally 'The House of the Rising Sun'), a song which alluded to his real-life incarceration, and which featured him on the cover dressed in uniform. Much of the coverage of Hallyday's period of military service represents him as the star-as-ordinary, fulfilling his social duty like most French men. However, the media coverage of this 'ordinary' soldier served effectively to underline his distinct, special status. Readers and viewers soon learned that Hallyday would not be confined to the barracks, and that he would still be allowed to visit the studio to make recordings.[48] His experience as a conscript not only provided the French military with a useful propaganda tool, but also cast him as a physically and psychologically healthy youth role model, an exemplary citizen of the French Republic. It was reported, for example, on the main evening television news bulletin that Hallyday had received a 'certificate for good behaviour' ('certificat de bonne conduite').[49] Hallyday speaks at length in his *SLC* column about what he has learnt from his military service, taking a strong moral stance against youth violence, using the battles between mods and rockers in the UK as an example, and argues rather paternalistically in favour of social cohesion rather than disintegration: 'Military life has made me realise more than ever that in a mixed society made up of people who haven't chosen to live together, all people can get along as long as they don't isolate themselves from others'.[50] His discourse even takes on an overtly patriotic Gaullist, independentist tone. Although a fan of the USA, his enthusiasm is not unquestioning: 'I really like the Americans, but that doesn't mean I agree with everything they do, for example, in Vietnam'.[51]

As a successful *yéyé* artist, Hallyday developed an increasingly idealised, wholesome, family image, epitomised by his relationship with Sylvie Vartan which effectively replayed the story of Elvis Presley and Priscilla Beaulieu. The celebrity relationship of Hallyday and Vartan culminated in a traditional, Catholic church wedding in April 1965 in Loconville,[52] followed in 1966 by the birth of their son David.[53] *SLC* featured a wedding album dubbed 'the wedding of the century' ('le mariage du siècle').[54] In a subsequent issue, Hallyday announced the setting up of *Le Club Sylvie–Johnny* which would provide readers with a membership card, photos of their wedding, a magazine, news, and discounts for 'typical youth-oriented' ('typiquement jeunes') products such as clothes and records.[55] A competition to win a stay with them on tour was held. Magazines carried photo spreads of the couple living a life of domestic bliss, Sylvie cooking in the kitchen and extolling the joys of marriage.[56] Although there were to be difficulties in Hallyday's marriage as well as in his professional life by Autumn 1966, these were not covered in *SLC* or at most, they were alluded to euphemistically as 'the difficult times that I've lived through' ('les heures difficiles que j'ai vécues').[57] The magazine, protective of its main attraction, led a campaign against the 'gutter press' ('journaux à scandale') which predicted the end of Hallyday's marriage and career.[58] Hallyday and Vartan joined the ranks of other high-profile couples, including the writers Jean-Paul Sartre and Simone de Beauvoir, the political couple Pierre and Yvette Poujade, the journalists Jean-Jacques Servan-Schreiber and Françoise Giroud, and the film stars Yves Montand and Simone Signoret. In France, the 'couple' assumed a particular significance during the 1950s and 1960s, as Kristin Ross observes: 'French happiness was immortalised in the number of boy-meets-girl films of the era and in the public images of various prominent couples'. According to Ross, the 'couple' effectively became the 'standard bearer of the state-led modernisation efforts and bearer of all affective values'. Not only would it provide France with the next generation of workers, as well as consumers, but it was also presented as a means to bring to the French the kind of 'happiness' that US and Soviet models could not provide (Ross 1995: 121–33). Together, Hallyday and Vartan embodied a certain notion of *le couple* as both traditional and incorporating modernity. While upholding the traditional French nuclear family, they contributed as a celebrity couple to the commodification of youth culture and popular music within the developing consumer society. Certain commentators asked whether Hallyday had effectively betrayed his rock 'n' roll credentials, becoming instead a mainstream *variétés* artist who had fallen prey to the bourgeois institution of marriage. Indeed, in a piece in *L'Express* humorously entitled 'Adieu les copains', Danièle Heymann asked, 'Won't their fans feel betrayed and abandoned, given the way in which this romance has been made to conform to bourgeois standards?' (Grosdemouge 1999: 66).[59]

While Hallyday indeed cultivated a rebellious rock 'n' roll image at the start of his career, inspired by his screen heroes Marlon Brando and James Dean, once he achieved mainstream success as a recording artist and media star his persona incorporated more conventional role models, such as the adoring husband and the patriotic and dutiful soldier, images strongly reminiscent of Elvis Presley. In a sense, his fate mirrors that of the heroes of *The Wild One* and, in particular, *Rebel Without a Cause* who both, to some extent, outgrow their rebelliousness as they discover the opposite sex. Hallyday's media representation tends to maintain patriarchal norms, which went largely unchallenged until the late 1960s and early 1970s,[60] and which insisted especially on the stereotypes of *l'homme viril* (virile man) and *la femme féminine* (feminine woman), fetishised the male-female *couple*,[61] and served generally to uphold *le pouvoir marital* (marital power).

Since the early to mid-1960s, Hallyday's place on the French music scene has been that of a consensual, mainstream artist who has posed few challenges particularly to traditional gender stereotypes. Although he found himself entirely out of step with the youth protest movements of May 1968, through elements of style and performance he has nonetheless attempted to remain faithful to an idealised, romanticised prototype of the rock 'n' roll rebel. Moreover, during the first half of the 1960s he certainly made a key contribution to the development of a distinct mass youth culture, as well as to the mobilisation of youth identities in France.

Acknowledgments

I wish to thank the Carnegie Trust for the Universities of Scotland for awarding me a personal research grant which funded archival research in Paris. I am also particularly grateful to the staff of the Institut National de l'Audiovisuel for their assistance, as well as to Jean-Marc Grosdemouge, editor of m-la-music.net, for his help and useful insights.

Notes

1. 'Mille chansons, plus de cent tubes, cent millions de disques vendus, quinze millions de spectateurs en tournée' (Martin 2003: 9).
2. See, for example, Keith Reader's chapter on Piaf in Dauncey and Cannon 2003: 205–24.
3. For further details of the Americanisation of popular music in France prior to the 1960s, see Looseley 2003: 22–3.
4. See Looseley 2003: 23, and Grosdemouge 1999: 9.
5. 'Américain de culture française, il chante aussi bien en anglais que français'.
6. See Brierre 2003: 58 and also Hallyday's appearance on the television programme *Discorama* produced by Denise Glaser, 6 June 1961.
7. 'C'est la première et dernière fois que vous entendez ce Johnny Hallyday'.
8. 'Ce genre de musique, ce n'est pas pour nous, Georges. Nous, c'est la chanson française traditionnelle'.

9. 'Exhibition de mauvais goût'; 'Parodie burlesque'; 'Une exhibition baragouinante et hystérique promise à brève échéance au cabanon'.
10. 'J'avoue avoir pris, aux soubresauts, aux convulsions, aux ecstases de ce grand flandrin rose et blond le plaisir fait d'étonnement et d'intérêt mêlés que procure une visite aux chimpanzés du zoo de Vincennes'.
11. 'Prolétaires qui se sentaient solidaires de lui, qui reliaient leur passé au sien, qui espéraient un avenir comme le sien, qui criaient la misère'.
12. 'Je découvrais pour la première fois en France une jeunesse qui commençait à s'agiter un peu, qui avait une certaine sensualité dégingandée, un enthousiasme. Et je pensais bien que la police était contre. Elle avait mis de grandes grilles devant la scène, et elle a pris pour de la bagarre ce qui n'était que de l'enthousiasme'.
13. For further discussion of technological developments, see Looseley: 21–5; Grosdemouge 1999: 8–9.
14. For further discussion on Scopitones, see http://scopitone.free.fr/.
15. *Johnny Hallyday, parfum des fans*, France 3, 14 October 2001.
16. 'Pantalon blanc, moccasins blancs, chemise blanche, col ouvert, visage bronzé, cheveu court et bien peigné: Johnny respire la santé. Vince Taylor, entièrement vêtu de cuir noir, donne une tout autre image – sombre, inquiétante, presque malsaine'.
17. For further discussion of dance crazes in France, see *Du Twist au jerk*, Canal +, 7 July 2000.
18. For further cowboy representations, see *Age tendre et tête de bois*, 1963a and 1963b. The Scopitone 'Je ne danserai plus jamais' also features Hallyday alone riding on horseback.
19. 'Les paroles des chanteurs "yéyés" sont confondantes de gentillesse, d'idéal petit-bourgeois, d'érotisme inoffensif'.
20. See *Johnny Hallyday, parfum des fans*, France 3, 14 October 2001.
21. 'De quoi lui en veut-on à ce splendide garçon, la santé, la gaieté, la jeunesse mêmes? Je reconnais en moi cette colère qui me prenait au temps où l'on essayait d'abbattre Maïakovski' (*Télérama hors serie*, 9). In 1939 Triolet, who was herself of Russian origin and a member of the French Communist Party (PCF), published a memoir, *Maiakovski poète russe*, in admiration of Vladimir Mayakovsky. A major poet of the Russian Revolution and early Soviet era, Mayakovsky became increasingly alienated from the Soviet regime, was attacked by critics and was thwarted in love before committing suicide in 1930.
22. 'je suis convaincu que les plus jeunes copains, ceux de 8 à 12 ans, éprouveront bien vite cette grande soif de rock que ma génération a connue. Elle est en effet naturelle: non seulement parce que le rythme de cette musique, avec son temps fort et son temps faible, correspond matériellement à des phénomènes de la vie comme les battements du coeur ou la démarche de l'homme, mais parce que le rock est la meilleure forme musicale qu'on ait encore jamais trouvée pour exprimer le dynamisme des jeunes et leur élan vers une existence libre ...' Hallyday also often asserted his attachment to rock 'n' roll in his regular column 'La Lettre de Johnny' in the youth magazine *Salut les copains*. See, for example, the March 1965 issue, 54–5.
23. *Telerama hors série*, 18.
24. *Le Retour de Johnny*, Canal Jimmy, Office National de Radiodiffusion et Télévision, 1967.
25. See *Salut les copains*, May 1967, 36.

26. 'Les jeunes téléspectateurs, habitués à des chanteurs raides comme des piquets, figés dans des cadrages sans surprises, trouvent en lui l'image vivante, moderne de la décennie naissante'.

27. Richard Dyer's work on film stardom identifies the need for a star to appear at once 'ordinary' and 'special'. See Dyer 1979: 49.

28. See, for example, Hallyday sitting amongst his audience in two editions of the television programme *Age tendre et tête de bois*, 27 October 1962 and 22 January 1964.

29. See *Festival de Cannes* broadcast on 12 May 1965.

30. See, for example, the televised *Palmarès de l'espoir*, ORTF, 18 December 1968, a gala in aid of the French charity La Ligue Contre le Cancer.

31. See, for example, the television programme *Le Temps des loisirs*, ORTF, 25 September 1965, which contains various images of Hallyday at leisure (dressed in swimming trunks; travelling by helicopter and by yacht; singing on a café terrace).

32. See 'La Tournee tropicale et agitée de Johnny', *Salut les copains*, April 1967, 92. The article contains a photo spread of Hallyday in swimming shorts on holiday in Rio de Janeiro.

33. For further discussion of the radio programme *Salut les copains*, see Grosdemouge 1999: 2–5, 26–9, 69 and 72, and Pires 2003: 87.

34. For further discussion of the magazine *Salut les copains*, see Grosdemouge 1999: 13, 21, 26, 46 and 51.

35. For further discussion of Hallyday's contribution to the magazine *Salut les copains*, see Pires 2003: 88–9.

36. See, for example, *Salut les copains*, August 1964, 58.

37. Pires 2003: 88–9.

38. A title lifted, like *Salut les copains*, from a Gilbert Bécaud song, 'Tête de bois' (1961). See Looseley 2003: 29.

39. *Nous les garçons et les filles*, February 1964, 43: 'son tour de chant n'est en rien une succession de "guimauves" enveloppées de pas de danse plus au moins sautillants. Dès qu'il entre la scène lui appartient, c'est un paquet de muscles montés sur un mètre quatre-vingt-cinq. Chacun peut aimer ou non ce qu'il chante et ce qu'il fait, mais on ne peut nier le tempérament du personnage et sa volonté de tenir dans la chanson une place où tout doit dépendre de la sincérité'.

40. *Nous les garçons et les filles*, April 1964.

41. *Nous les garçons et les filles*, November 1965, 32.

42. *Nous les garçons et les filles*, February 1967 43: 'Il est difficile aujourd'hui d'être véritablement Johnny Hallyday et Sylvie Vartan … Les personnages créés par la presse et la radio les étouffent et les débordent'.

43. Hallyday's feelings of isolation and *ennui*, following his attempted suicide, were also highlighted by the more serious, current-affairs end of French television, in a fly-on-the-wall documentary, broadcast on 4 November 1966, which formed part of the well known series *Cinq Colonnes à la une*.

44. *Guitar Collector's hors série, Johnny Hallyday*, 11.

45. See *Salut les copains*, March 1967, 26: 'Le rallye de Johnny'. See also *Journal National*, 24 January 1967 (television news). Hallyday leaves for the Monte Carlo Rally following a goodbye kiss from Sylvie Vartan.

46. See *Réveillon chez Johnny Hallyday*, 24 December 1964. Hallyday, dressed in soldiers uniform, serenades Sylvie Vartan with the song 'Je ne t'oublierai jamais'.

47. See, for example, Hallyday adopting a military pose, on the front cover of the magazine *Salut les copains*, May 1964, as well as a photo spread in the July 1964 issue, 62–71.

48. See, for example, the fly-on-the-wall documentary *La Journée du soldat Smet*, ORTF, 25 September 1964.

49. See *Journal télévisé de 20 heures; Edition spéciale*, ORTF, 25 August 1965.

50. *Salut les copains*, November 1964, 89: 'la vie militaire me fait mesurer, plus que jamais, que dans une société très mélangée dont tous les membres sont réunis sans l'avoir voulu, n'importe qui peut s'entendre avec n'importe qui à condition de ne pas commencer par s'isoler'.

51. *Salut les copains*, May 1965, 137: 'J'aime beaucoup les Américains, mais ça n'est pas pour cela que je réponds "amen" à tout ce qu'ils font, par exemple, au Vietnam'.

52. 'Le Mariage des Copains: Sylvie Vartan devient Madame Smet', *Les Actualités Françaises*, 14 April 1965.

53. *Le fils de Johnny Hallyday*, 15 August 1966. Coverage of the birth of David Hallyday.

54. *Salut les copains*, May 1965, 75.

55. *Salut les copains*, November 1965, 44–7.

56. See *Télérama hors série*, 31.

57. *Salut les copains*, October 1966, 40–1.

58. *Salut les copains*, August 1969, 32.

59. 'Leurs fans vont-ils voir dans la régularisation bourgeoise d'une idylle romanesque une trahison, une défection?'

60. For further discussion of the challenge to the patriarchal order, particularly in France, see Badinter 1986: 199–251.

61. Terms used by Badinter 1986: 315, 321.

CHAPTER 5

STARDOM ON WHEELS: RAYMOND POULIDOR

Philip Dine

Introduction: *le premier des Français*

The cycle road-racer Raymond Poulidor was France's pre-eminent sports star of the 1960s and early 1970s. Not widely known outside his homeland, either at the height of his career or subsequently, Poulidor was, on the face of it, an unlikely figure for elevation to sporting stardom. At a time when France was beginning to make a significant impact in international sport, many other champions were perceived as distinctly more glamorous than him: from Olympic athletes like Guy Drut and Colette Besson, to dashing skiers and sailors such as Jean-Claude Killy and Eric Tabarly, and even a swimmer turned cover-girl, in the person of Christine 'Kiki' Caron. In terms of their relative exposure in such style-conscious magazines as *Paris Match*, cycling in general and Poulidor in particular were rarely, if ever, mentioned.[1] Yet, the man affectionately known for the past forty-odd years as 'Poupou' was by far the biggest sports star of his generation. A poll carried out by the Institut Français d'Opinion Publique for the Ministry of Youth and Sport in 1977 showed that Poulidor was the most famous of all modern French sporting champions, with an unprecedented popularity rating of 48 percent, well ahead of all other sports stars of the postwar period (Pagnoud 1977: 5). The novelist

Poulidor, the eternal runner-up, completes the 1964 Tour de France, alongside his habitual nemesis, Jacques Anquetil.
Photograph by permission of Getty Images.

Antoine Blondin, who was additionally one of the most authoritative commentators on French sport at this time, described Poulidor in 1973 as among 'the half-dozen French citizens that are the most admired and the best loved' ('la demi-douzaine de citoyens français les plus admirés et les mieux aimés') (Blondin 2001: 667). The following year, at the end of the 1974 Tour de France, in which Poulidor finished as runner-

up, newly elected President of the Republic Valéry Giscard-
d'Estaing sent the rider a personal telegram which stated: 'If the
French public had been asked to vote for the real winner of the
demanding competition that you have just completed, there is
not the slightest doubt that, from the very first round, they
would have unanimously voted for you'.[2] Leading journalist
Robert Escarpit went one better in his front-page column for *Le
Monde* – the famously sober national daily – telling his readers
that 'There's no doubt about it, the next time, if I have to
choose, I'll vote for Poulidor' ('Décidément, s'il faut choisir, la
prochaine fois, je voterai Poulidor') (Pagnoud 1977: 77).

How can we explain the phenomenal popular enthusiasm
that this sportsman generated? Part of the answer is to be found
in the particular spell cast on the French nation by the
unforgiving sport in which Poulidor excelled: cycle road-racing.
To this basic ingredient, we need to add the following essential
items: the rider's emergence from a background of genuine
hardship; his regularly displayed courage, dedication and
tenacity; his almost equally recurrent, and frequently
spectacular, misfortune; and, most of all, his series of heroic
defeats in an extended and highly mediatised duel with his
fellow-countryman and great sporting adversary, Jacques
Anquetil. As we shall see, 'Poupou' successfully combined in his
public persona the traditional virtues of the French peasantry
with the media-awareness of an authentically modern sporting
entrepreneur. This innovative amalgam was particularly
appreciated by an armchair audience seeking cultural
reassurance in the face of the major societal changes of the
1960s. In consequence, the Poulidor 'product' sold well, to the
clear benefit not only of the star himself, but also of the mass
media, including particularly the emerging force of television,
as well as serving to promote a wide variety of commercial
interests. This particular rise from rags to riches thus tells us at
least as much about the receptiveness of the French society of
the day to preferred images of cultural continuity as it does
about the frequently harsh mechanics of sporting stardom.

Central to both processes in Poulidor's case was the
quintessentially French sporting spectacle of cycle road-racing.
France's first truly indigenous sport, cycling has for over a
century been the country's most socially significant and
culturally invested sporting discipline. This is particularly true
as regards the cycling season's annual climax in the Tour de
France, which has been the world's greatest stage race since its
launch in 1903. Run over three weeks in high summer, it has

become firmly established as part of both the national
calendar and the national heritage, retaining its unique
appeal despite its regular trials and tribulations, particularly
involving a string of drug-abuse scandals. As such, cycling has
been, and continues to be, a powerful generator of sporting
heroism and sporting heroes, as well as, more mundanely,
sports stars. After previous high points for such popular homegrown competitors as Antonin Magne, André Leducq, and
Georges Speicher in the 1930s, and the equally celebrated Jean
Robic and Louison Bobet in the late 1940s and early 1950s, the
1960s and the early 1970s were to be a golden age in French
road-racing. Poulidor's performances over these two decades
would be of central importance both to the sporting outcomes
of the relevant races, and, even more obviously, to the media
representations and public perceptions of France's principal
sport at this time of rapid and radical social transformation.

Raymond Poulidor's variety of sporting stardom thus
conforms to a historic pattern of durable public identification
with a select band of iconic athletic performers. In the French
context, these range from the tennis player Suzanne Lenglen,
who established herself as the country's first international
sports star (even 'superstar') either side of World War I,
challenging established gender roles in the process, to boxers
like Georges Carpentier and Marcel Cerdan, who, in their
different ways, offered altogether more reassuring images of
French masculinity against the backdrop of the two World
Wars. The Casablanca-born Cerdan attained European and
world prominence both through his exertions in the ring and,
more revealingly, through the media's depiction of his
'doomed' love affair with the singing star Edith Piaf.[3] In later
decades, the figure of the immigrant as footballing hero would
regularly appeal as a characteristically French variety of
sporting stardom, as exemplified by Raymond Kopa (of Polish
descent) in the 1950s, Michel Platini (of Italian descent) in the
1980s, and, most striking of all, Zinedine Zidane (of Algerian
descent), the uncontested star of the historic French World Cup
triumph in 1998. Yet, in sharp contrast to the celebrity of these
and other French sports stars, Poulidor's enormous and
abiding popularity was predicated less on his genuine
successes, than on his intensely mediatised failures. For this
phenomenally talented athlete was destined to be cast as
l'éternel second, the continually unlucky loser, the perpetual
'nearly-man' of French sport. His successes were always
modest (at least in relative terms) and, on many occasions,

particularly later in his career, his greatest achievement was not to be the best in any given event, and especially the Tour de France, but rather the strongest of the home-based competitors, and thus *le meilleur des Français* (the best of the French). As we shall see, the overwhelmingly traditionalist audience that followed French cycling in the press, on the radio and, increasingly and especially, on television in the 1960s and early 1970s came to identify in an unprecedentedly personal fashion with Poulidor, sharing vicariously in the occasional triumphs and altogether more regular disasters that made up the rider's career. This fundamental paradox is all the more remarkable in a cultural sphere characterised by its extended celebration of victors and its generally instant forgetting of the vanquished, and thus provides the central focus of the analysis that follows.

From farmboy to race-rider

Raymond Poulidor was born on 15 April 1936, the youngest of four sons, to Maria and Martial Poulidor, who were tenant-farmers in the Creuse *département* of central France. Theirs was a life of authentic rural poverty, yet Raymond spent a happy childhood in a strong and supportive family, firmly rooted in the traditional agricultural environment that he would always enjoy. At school he was a good pupil, and had no difficulty passing his *Certificat d'Etudes* (the junior school-leaving certificate) in 1950, when he was fourteen years old. He would have liked to have stayed on at school, but was obliged to leave in order to work on the family farm and to bring in whatever income he could. Already remarkable for his strength and athleticism, the youngest Poulidor became interested in cycling, like his three brothers before him, and took to the country byways on his mother's heavy, old bike. However, such was his ability that local competitive success soon followed, which encouraged both the young man's own dreams of a career in the sport, and the necessary investment of time and money by the rest of his family to allow him to develop his obvious talents (Ollivier 1994: 5–9).

A major break in this pattern of development occurred when Poulidor was called up for military service in August 1956. The young man was typical of his generation, in that he was required to spend a total of twenty-eight months in the army, including over a year in an Algeria ravaged by the *Front de*

Libération Nationale (*FLN*)'s war of independence against French colonial rule. Between the ages of twenty and twenty-two, at the peak of his physical fitness, and just as he was breaking onto the national cycling scene, Poulidor was thus subjected to an experience that would leave its mark indelibly on what Xavier Grall has memorably termed *la génération du djebel* (the lost generation of the Algerian mountains) (Grall 1962). In contrast to the usual experience (or, at least, assumption) that military service promotes physical fitness, the already honed young road-racer actually gained twelve kilograms in excess weight during his time in the forces. More seriously, Poulidor would, like many others who had the misfortune to *Avoir vingt ans dans les Aurès* ('be twenty years old in the Aurès mountains of Algeria' [Vautier 1972]), be psychologically disturbed by his experiences. As he put it himself some four decades later, using the (French) present tense to underline the undiminished immediacy of the memories generated by the Algerian war:

> To say I was traumatised is putting it mildly. In fourteen months, I aged ten years. I felt a complete stranger in my own body ... I felt ill at ease in my own skin. The things that had mattered hugely to me in the past now just bored me. It seemed to me that I had left a big part of myself on the other side of the Mediterranean, that I had become divided in myself, and that I urgently needed to find myself again (Ollivier 1994: 17–18).[4]

Like many before and after him, Poulidor would return to a France and a home life that, while seemingly unchanged, had been rendered alien by his experiences of combat in North Africa. His path to personal redemption would be provided by cycling, and his spiritual guide would be none other than Antonin Magne, the double winner of the Tour de France from the 1930s, who spotted Poulidor's talent and persuaded him to turn professional (Ollivier 1994: 21–2).

It was doubly appropriate that 'Tonin' Magne should have been the one to identify Poulidor's potential and to channel his efforts throughout his career. In addition to being a great competitor, Magne came from a comparable background and was temperamentally very similar to Poulidor. Born in a village in the Auvergne (although his family later moved to the Parisian *banlieue*), 'Tonin' was regularly seen smiling and was depicted as, above all, 'modest and stalwart' ('*valeureux*' [Rearick 1997: 146]). As Charles Rearick notes, '"Tonin" was not a great talker, but the press made him known to masses of fans as a devoted friend and team player, and he became the favourite of many' (Rearick 1997: 147). Under Magne's guidance, Poulidor would make rapid progress, and thereby came to the attention of the national sporting press. In the 25 April 1960 edition of *But et club*, the periodical's special correspondent, Roger Bastide, recounted a visit to Poulidor's family home, thus setting the pattern for subsequent representations of the rising star. Insisting on the cyclist's rootedness in the traditional rural community, he goes on to quote his ageing parents:

> 'Raymond is a good boy', his parents assure the special correspondent from Paris ... 'Perhaps, thanks to him, we will one day be able to buy our own farm. For we are tenant farmers, and it is not easy to work every day for other people' (Ollivier 1994: 26).[5]

As we shall see, this reassuring image of the country boy who remains faithful to his family and his roots was to prove an exceptionally attractive one in the rapidly urbanising and industrialising France of the early 1960s. The ethic of decency, responsibility and, above all, hard, physical work that underpinned this representation of the cyclist would remain central to his public persona throughout his long competitive career; as would a certain rural fatalism and a capacity for self-sacrifice, both of which are similarly implicit here. The question of Poulidor's belief (or lack of it) in his capacity to influence his own destiny is also hinted at here and would be central to the rider's evolution as a professional. More specifically, the rider's often proven ability to work for the good of the group rather than himself is of special interest here. For it was Poulidor's willingness, like Antonin Magne before him, and which he now demonstrated in his first professional team events, to protect better placed colleagues at the expense of his own final placing, that first endeared him to the hardened professionals around him (Ollivier 1994: 27–8). Such work as a *domestique* (servant), in the lucid vernacular of professional cycling, is an essential rite of passage for young riders who aspire to greater things, but few are able to impose themselves as team leaders in their own right. Poulidor would rapidly go on to do so, yet even from the earliest stages he would worry his manager by his tendency to combine ill-considered displays of bravado with an underlying passivity (Ollivier 1994: 49–50 and 54). These are themes to which this chapter will return.

Following commendable performances in prestigious events such as the Paris-Nice and the Milan-San Remo, Poulidor would come to real national prominence in his first Tour de France in 1962. Wearing a plaster-cast on his arm for over half the race, his determination and *panache* – particularly demonstrated in audacious, if rarely successful, breakaways – brought him national acclaim, while his third place overall revealed him to be a worthy opponent to that year's winner, and the dominant force in French and European cycling, Jacques Anquetil. This overall performance was also the start of Poulidor's extraordinary popularity, which was to transform his existence. It brought with it thousands of letters and many offers of contracts (Ollivier 1994: 58). Thus began a love affair between Poulidor, the French public and, crucially, France's most emblematic sporting event that would last the better part of two decades.

The Tour de France: *la gloire sans maillot jaune*

As a variety of cultural commentators from Roland Barthes to Julian Barnes have observed, the Tour de France is much more than a bicycle race (Barthes 1957b; Barnes 2002). Georges Vigarello, in his contribution to Pierre Nora's monumental survey of French *lieux de mémoire* (sites of remembrance), has underlined the event's paradoxical ability to celebrate national unity through the spectacle of regional diversity, combining geography and history to powerful symbolic effect in an annual reappropriation of the land and its past (Vigarello 1992). However, as Vigarello goes on to explain, the Tour has additionally established its own memory and, crucially, its own mythology, which together go well beyond the bare statistics of winners and losers, of times, speeds, and distances. Indeed, such has been the intensity of the commemorative investment in the event since 1903 that the objective circumstances of any given Tour have, to a large extent, become indissociable from the collective representations to which the race as a whole has given rise. Thus, previous editions of the Tour together constitute an interpretative grid within which each new race is situated and comprehended. As Philippe Delerm has aptly put it: 'one does not watch a single Tour de France, one watches *all* the Tours de France' ('on ne regarde pas le Tour de France. On regarde les Tours de France' [Delerm 1997: 39]).[6] At the deepest level, as Vigarello himself explains, the Tour de France is a long-running narrative, rather than an event, and one uniquely appealing to *la France profonde* (deep or 'real' France). His incisive analysis of the Tour's characteristic narrative mode is worthy of quotation at some length, as it provides the necessary conceptual framework within which to begin to make sense of Raymond Poulidor's rise to sporting stardom:

> The Tour promotes sport as a popular serial or soap opera, an approach that is certainly encouraged by the tactics of cycling: the riders break away, they catch each other up ..., they help one another, they do the unexpected. All of which provides an anecdotal framework. The invention, in 1919, of the yellow jersey, to identify the overall leader, was to produce a permanently visible emblem, irrespective of the ups and downs of the race, which has added to its daily narrative. From this point of view, the Tour is a model of its kind. But it is also a paradigm of memory. More obviously than in other sporting competitions, the event relies for its continued existence on storytelling. It needs its past, and it needs to remember it. No doubt this is because the Tour is told, first and foremost, rather than observed from the side of the road. It lives in the telling. It nourishes itself on this narrative, with a very fine attention to changes of fortune and to their chronology. Its descriptive style draws on the art of the storyteller. Which explains the seductiveness of linking narratives, comparing stories and playing odd games with time. It also explains the temptation to create a whole culture out of the event. The Tour's memory is an integral part of the race (Vigarello 1992: 915).[7]

The race, in short, is a mobile and constantly renewed celebration not only of the nation, but also of itself. This characteristic self-referentiality should be borne in mind as we now explore Raymond Poulidor's personal contribution to the Tour's *légende*.

Poulidor is generally regarded as the finest cyclist never to have won the Tour de France, nor ever to have worn the race leader's coveted yellow jersey (*le maillot jaune*). This bittersweet variety of national celebrity – *la gloire sans maillot jaune*, as it is often summed up – was (and still is) central to the rider's paradoxical variety of sporting stardom. For Poulidor was never one of the Tour's pantheon of celebrated champions, which reserves a special place for multiple victors. To win the Tour once is the undoubted high point of any 'normal' rider's career, while to triumph in more than one edition of the race marks a cyclist out as particularly favoured by the sporting gods. Louison Bobet became the first French rider to achieve three victories and, moreover, in succession, between 1953 and 1955, to huge public acclaim. Yet, even this would be topped by the achievements of a new elite of almost superhuman victors, each completely dominating the event for the period of their reign as the uncontested champion of their sport. Five men (two Frenchmen, a Belgian, a Spaniard, and an American) have thus recorded five victories in the Tour de France: Jacques Anquetil (1956 and 1961–1964), Eddy Merckx (1969–1972 and 1974), Bernard Hinault (1978–1979, 1981–1982 and 1985), Miguel Indurain (1991–1995), and Lance Armstrong (1999–2003). In 2004 and 2005, Lance Armstrong did even better, achieving record sixth and then seventh successive victories in the Tour, before retiring triumphantly from competitive cycling.

In comparison, Raymond Poulidor's record appears modest, although it is undoubtedly remarkable both for the rider's consistency and longevity. Poulidor competed in the Tour on no less than fourteen occasions between 1962 and 1976 (the fourth longest participation in the event), abandoning only twice a competition that nearly half of all entrants have failed to complete. Such was his constancy that he came third in both his first Tour and his last, fourteen years later, collecting a further three third places, together with three second places, along the way. He also recorded stage wins in 1962, 1964, 1965 (twice), 1966 and 1967. Yet he never once led, still less won, the country's most prestigious sporting event. However, even today, Poulidor is still more positively regarded by the French sporting public than any of those great champions, including even the French stars, Jacques Anquetil and Bernard Hinault. Indeed, Poulidor's great rivalry with Anquetil was to be a central aspect of the construction of his sporting stardom, as, to a lesser extent, was his later battle with the Belgian champion, Eddy Merckx. What was beyond doubt, even if he did not win, was that Poulidor was, like them, *un géant de la route* (a giant of the road) and, as such, an integral part of both the Tour's history and, crucially, its *légende* or mythic pantheon.

This paradoxical centrality was underlined by the 2004 edition of the Tour de France, which included a stage that not only started at Poulidor's tiny hometown of St Léonard de Noblat, in the rural Creuse *département*, but also looped back on itself to finish in the same part of what Tour historian Alistair Fotheringham evocatively describes as 'deepest central France', in what was a double first in the event's 101–year history. As Fotheringham explains, this stage was 'a 164km leg apparently more designed to write off ... the Tour's historical debts than to have any impact on the general classification' (Fotheringham 2004: 57). To understand the nature of the event's peculiar indebtedness to Raymond Poulidor, we need to analyse the events of 12 July 1964, exactly forty years and one day before the 2004 Tour stage that started and ended in his native Creuse. To do this, we also need to discuss the media's representation of the rider, and particularly his long-running rivalry with that other great force in French cycling in the 1960s, Jacques Anquetil.

The writer and the rider: Blondin on Poulidor

If, as Vigarello persuasively argues, the Tour de France depends for its existence on *la chronique*, then it is only fitting that the event should have drawn some of the most talented and devoted of sporting chroniclers. Foremost among these was the major literary figure, Antoine Blondin, who, in 524 daily pieces for *L'Equipe*, followed the Tour's progress from 1954 to 1982. He was thus uniquely well placed to witness, and comment upon, the rise to prominence of Raymond Poulidor and the evolution of his subsequent career. The young rider's first stage win, at Aix-les-Bains in 1962, marked him out as a competitor capable of success at the very highest level, yet, intriguingly, Blondin's *chronique* for that particular day does not even mention Poulidor or his victory. In contrast, earlier in the Tour, Blondin had devoted his account of the Herentals (Belgium)-Amiens stage to an extended reflection on the impression produced by Poulidor as he vainly attempted to get the better of the eventual stage winner, the veteran André Darrigade. By foregrounding Poulidor as the plucky loser, and then ignoring him when he actually went on to win, Blondin may well have set a precedent for subsequent media representations of the competitor.

Moreover, Blondin's first depiction of the young racer provides us with an object lesson in the journalistic art of inscribing sporting contests within a preferred set of cultural parameters. This technique serves to make readily understandable a constantly changing cast of characters by means of systematic reference to a pre-existing interpretative grid. In this case, a bicycle race is 'read' like a literary narrative, specifically *Manon Lescaut* (1731), the *Abbé* Prévost's classic novel of love and betrayal, in which the tragic heroine comes to an untimely end in the then French colony of

Louisiana. As suggested by its characteristically punning title, 'Manon de l'Escaut' (after the major river of the Franco-Belgian border country), the article in question is a witty pastiche that neatly ends the sporting action where Prévost had begun his own cautionary tale, in the northern French city of Amiens. By this conceit, Blondin transposes the *département* of the Somme for Louisiana, while André Darrigade, as the actual winner of the Herentals-Amiens stage, takes on the character of the fictional hero-villain Des Grieux. Most dramatically, Poulidor himself becomes the ill-fated heroine, the eponymous Manon Lescaut, whom we follow on an ultimately futile desert crossing that reveals him, like her, to be the epitome of doomed youthful ambition.

Interestingly, Darrigade competed on fourteen successive occasions in the Tour de France, between 1953 and 1966, the same number as Poulidor, but he only abandoned on a single occasion, as compared with Poulidor's two failures to complete. He was thus the Tour's third most regular participant. He also achieved a total of twenty-two stage wins (the fourth-highest total), and wore the leader's *maillot jaune* in six different editions of the great race. However, his highest final placing was only sixteenth (albeit on no less than three occasions), and he never achieved the popularity with the French public that his outstanding record deserved.[8] While Darrigade may have gone on to win the stage, it is the atmosphere of pathos associated with the fate of Prévost's tragic heroine, and thus, by association, with Poulidor's first major public failure, that is significant. For, in spite of his humorous rendering of the novel's *dénouement*, Blondin nevertheless stresses the inevitability of the young cyclist's defeat by the combined forces of a hostile environment, regularly defective equipment and, ultimately, a tragic destiny. The narrator here is an imaginary 'Chevalier Mercier-Bépé', that is to say a member of Poulidor's support staff from the Mercier-BP professional cycling team:

> ... We kept going for as long as the courage of Poulidor held out, that is to say, thirty leagues or so; for this incomparable nature constantly refused to stop before then. Overtaken finally with weariness, he [NB *'elle'* ('she') in the original, referring to 'cette nature incomparable'] set his foot down upon the earth, although not without first uttering, to the wilderness, a feeble sound that I took at first for a sigh. 'I think that I'm worn out' [or 'that I've got a puncture', the French is intentionally – and amusingly – ambiguous], the sublime child from Masbaraud-Mérigna[t] timidly said to me (Blondin 2001: 269–70).[9]

Here, for the first time, but remarkably clearly, we see the outline of the persona that would be developed by Poulidor (or would be developed around him) throughout his competitive career. The wholly unexpected feminisation of the rider in Blondin's pastiche serves subtly to underline both his youth and his inexperience – in this archetypal sporting universe of 'real men' – while elsewhere in the piece the writer alludes to the fact that Poulidor was, as will be recalled, already carrying an injury.

For all its undoubted comedic value, this striking image of the racer as the victim of (multiple) circumstances beyond his control was one that would be constantly repeated by other commentators, and thus became fixed in the popular imagination. As a direct result, the concluding comment by Blondin's imaginary *suiveur* (literally 'follower', a member of the racing team's technical staff) – to the effect that 'I received from this indomitable creature the greatest and the most exhausting of examples' ('Je reçus de cette indomptable créature les plus grands exemples et les plus épuisants' [Blondin 2001: 270]) – could have been repeated by any one of Poulidor's devoted army of fans at virtually any point in the cyclist's competitive career, and, *a fortiori*, at its end. Blondin was thus among the first, and certainly among the most incisive, observers of the young Poulidor, and contributed significantly to what would become the casting of this hugely talented rider in the role of permanently unlucky loser. Indeed, this process of 'victimisation' would be a constant of Poulidor's representation by both the print and broadcast media from 1962 onwards. Central to that process would be his long-running rivalry with Jacques Anquetil, the undisputed master of French and European cycling in the late 1950s and early 1960s, and, as such, the almost complete antithesis of Poulidor, the eternally plucky runner-up.

Anquetil and Poulidor:
the aristocrat versus the labourer

Few subjects have received more attention in the voluminous literature of the Tour de France than the relationship between Jacques Anquetil and Raymond Poulidor. Articles, chapters, even whole books have been devoted to their rivalry. It was also the subject of a film produced in 2001 (Hennegrave 2001). As the two leading lights in French cycling at this time, it was probably inevitable that there should have been some competitive and media linkage between the professional – and personal – development of the two riders. However, the public fervour that rapidly grew up around their encounters was out of all proportion to their objective circumstances. Anquetil was quite simply the outstanding cyclist of his generation, as his record five victories in the Tour de France made clear. To his Tour *palmarès*, which included sixteen stage wins, can be added particularly the world one-hour record, which he took from Fausto Coppi in Milan in 1956, and his achievement of the most difficult double in professional cycling, namely victories in the Giro d'Italia and the Tour de France in the same year (1964), only the second man to do so, once again after the great Coppi. Other achievements verged on the superhuman, as John Goodbody notes with regard to the 1965 season: 'when he competed in the eight-day Dauphiné Libéré, he finished at 5pm and flew across France to take part against fresh cyclists in the now obsolete Bordeaux to Paris motor-paced event. This began at 2a.m. the next day but Anquetil still won' (Goodbody 2003: 10).

Yet, for all his competitive success, Anquetil was not particularly appreciated by the French public. This was partly the result of his competitive style, which tended to rely on his mastery of time-trials, which he used to build up unassailable margins over his rivals, rather than on exuberant performances in breakaways across the plains or in attacks up the mountains. Although highly effective, this approach was perceived to lack *panache*, to be clinical and calculating, rather than conforming to the 'true' spirit of the sport. As for the man himself, he was seen as cold and aloof, as his nickname, 'Maître Jacques', suggested.[10] No one doubted his innate ability, still less his technical competence, but, in a sporting *habitus* historically characterised by its popular – and even populist – ethos, Anquetil's elegant variety of sporting aristocracy was not well received. Antoine Blondin, although never able to get any closer to the resolutely independent competitor than other cycling correspondents, was nevertheless a determined defender of Anquetil in the face of the public's hostility. He summed up the champion memorably in 1963:

> The essentially chronometric character of his performances, a somewhat glacial manner of winning that left no room for compromise, and a polite but suspicious disdain for external shows of familiarity might, taken together, lead one to think that

he thought of his job in the narrowest and most limited of ways:
the outlook of a man who had no time for a friendly word with
his neighbour, once the day's work was done. A cool customer, if
not actually a cold-blooded animal, Anquetil secreted himself
under the slippery skin of an amphibian or a reptile. We never
knew the taste of his tears or the price of his smile. He used to
race alongside his persona (Blondin 2001: 335).[11]

Anquetil's jealous guarding of his privacy further alienated
the sporting media and their public, in an age when increased
access to the personal lives of stars of all kinds was becoming
the norm. In Anquetil's case, this desire to keep his distance
had the paradoxical result that his periodic displays of
independence of spirit were often portrayed as betrayals of
sporting tradition. This was notably the case when, during the
1964 Tour, he used a 'rest' day in Andorra not to stay in shape
– by means of the long training rides that professional cyclists
typically complete on their days 'off' – but rather to attend a
social event organised by the local radio station, where he was
reported to have overindulged in champagne, supposedly his
favourite drink. Although such hedonism did not generally
seem to have too much of an impact on his performances on
the road, on this occasion the other members of the *peloton*
(main pack of riders) made him suffer in the following day's
stage in the Pyrenean mountains. Poulidor was to the fore in
pushing Anquetil hard on the arduous climb up to the Col
d'Envalira, in what many perceived to be a riposte to
Anquetil's perceived slight to himself, his fellow professionals
and, above all, the hallowed event in which they were all
competing (Ollivier 1994: 84).[12] If Anquetil's periodic breaking
of the unwritten rules of the race did not commend the
champion to his colleagues,[13] still less did it endear him to the
traditionalist followers of the Tour de France. When Anquetil
also admitted in 1968 to having used performance-enhancing
drugs throughout his racing career – a practice undoubtedly as
widespread then as it is today – his honesty not only sparked
a major controversy but also established another reason for
the French public to compare him unfavourably with the
famously drug-free Poulidor.[14]

In order to make sense of the specifics of the two riders'
sporting rivalry, it is necessary to begin even before Poulidor's
Tour de France *début* in 1962. For in 1961, when the Tour was
still organised on the basis of national teams rather than the
commercially sponsored outfits that were to become the norm,

concerns regarding the possible negative impact on the rising star's commercial value of playing second-fiddle to Jacques Anquetil in the French side had led Poulidor's management team to persuade him to refrain from entering that year's event (Reed 2003: 112). It was only when commercial squads were introduced the following year that Poulidor was able to join the Mercier-BP Tour line-up as a team-leader in his own right. Endearing himself to the public through his valiant efforts in the 1962 Tour, in which he finished third, Poulidor became hugely popular and was widely expected to go on to victory in the 1963 edition of the event. As Jean-Paul Ollivier puts it: 'At the start ... Poulidor was clearly in the lead on the "clapometer". He gave a reassuring impression of quiet strength' ('Au départ ... Poulidor est le premier à l'applaudimètre. Il donne une impression de force tranquille qui rassure' [Ollivier 1994: 63]). Indeed, such was the popular confidence in Poulidor, in what was still only his second season at the top level, that the rider was actually whistled by the disappointed crowd at the Parc de Princes when he eventually managed to finish no higher than in eighth place. In the light of subsequent developments, this overreaction may be read as a variety of *dépit amoureux* (lovers' quarrel), with the love affair between Poulidor and the French public destined to go from strength to strength in subsequent editions of the Tour de France. For his part, Jacques Anquetil, as victor of the 1963 event, was accorded a rare ovation by a public that seemed, at last, to have appreciated his outstanding achievements, even if it was still not wholly convinced of his heroic virtues.

By the 1964 season, both riders were at the height of their powers. Anquetil was attempting to add a fifth Tour victory to what was already a record four wins, and had recently triumphed in the Giro d'Italia, while Poulidor had already won that year's Tour of Spain, and appeared to be in the best form of his life. The editor of the 2001 collected edition of Blondin's cycling *chroniques*, Stéphanie Rysman, sums up the mood of the 1964 Tour as follows:

> This Tour was dominated by the memorable duel between Anquetil and Poulidor. The passion generated matched the heights of their combined talents. The whole of France was divided between the 'Anquetilists' and the 'Poulidorists' (Blondin 2001: 337).[15]

In fact, popular interest in the contest between the two men would be heavily weighted in favour of Poulidor, just as it had been in the two previous editions of the race, irrespective of their actual outcomes. This had already been remarked upon by Anquetil early in the 1964 season, when he commented to his manager, the former top-class racer Raphaël Géminiani, that in the event organised by the *Provençal* regional newspaper he had done his best to remain 'neutral' in the race, in order specifically to prevent accusations that he was adopting tactics intended to prevent Poulidor from winning. Yet, as he pointedly remarked, Poulidor had lost just the same, and could have no hope of winning the Tour de France if he continued to commit basic tactical errors (Ollivier 1994: 75). This private prediction would be publicly borne out in what has become known as the greatest set-piece contest in the long history of the Tour de France.

The Duel on the Volcano: 12 July 1964

The 1964 Tour was, as predicted, dominated by the rivalry between Anquetil and Poulidor. Also true to form, Poulidor's race was marked by a run of bad luck, such as the punctured tyre that prevented him winning the time-trial between Peyrchorade and Bayonne. A puncture was also to blame in the stage between Andorra – visited for the first time, and the scene of Anquetil's rest-day partying – and Toulouse, which also included the first ascent of the very demanding Port d'Envalira mountain pass. Having outpaced his hung-over rival on the climb, Poulidor then established a significant lead on an eighty-kilometre breakaway through the valleys. However, the puncture that brought him to a halt was compounded by a fall when he remounted, which together lost him over two-and-a-half minutes and thus his advantage over Anquetil. Yet, unperturbed, and to his great credit, Poulidor put his misfortunes behind him in the following day's Pyrenean stage, which he won in Luchon. However, the 1964 Tour was then to be the setting for an altogether more serious drama on the stage between Bordeaux and Brive on 11 July, when a supply lorry travelling ahead of the riders collided with waiting spectators on a bridge in the village of Port-de-Couze. The accident left nine dead, including a little girl, as well as a number of injured, some of whom needed to be rescued from the canal below (Bastide 2003; cf. Blondin 2001: 364–5). Arriving barely a quarter of an hour later, the shocked *peloton* naturally halted but could only look on ineffectually, before restarting and carrying on to Brive at a respectfully slow speed. Such was the combination of high excitement and deep tragedy that immediately preceded the events that Tour commentators now refer to as the 'duel on the volcano'.

As Georges Vigarello has accurately observed, mountains are of central importance in the mythology of the Tour de France, and represent one of its dominant images: 'The mountains play a particular role, in this respect: they constitute a barrier that must always be confronted. They are a place of exhaustion, of falls, and of dramas. They are unnerving ...' (Vigarello 1992: 892).[16] In this case, the mountain selected as the finish of the 237.5-kilometre twentieth stage of the 1964 Tour, contested between Brive and Clermont-Ferrand on Sunday 12 July, was nothing less than the Puy-de-Dôme. A dormant volcano towering 4,800 feet above the industrial city best known as the headquarters of the Michelin tyre company, the Puy-de-Dôme not only gives its name to the surrounding *département*, but offers views of another ten from its summit. On that hot summer Sunday, its slopes attracted over half a million spectators to witness what was to prove a unique event in the history of the Tour de France, as Jean-Paul Ollivier, one of the race's most authoritative chroniclers, makes clear: 'Never in the history of the Tour have the two highest-placed riders in the overall classification been obliged to engage in such a closely fought battle. Nor has a race ever taken place in such an atmosphere of passion' (Ollivier 2000: 104).[17] By the time the race reached the foot of the mountain, Anquetil was just 56 seconds ahead of Poulidor in the overall classification. The two men then set off, side by side, on what was to be the decisive section of the whole 1964 Tour: Anquetil, blond (with a quiff that meant he was often likened to Johnny Hallyday), fine-featured and naturally elegant; Poulidor, swarthy and stocky, an honest journeyman wholly in the Tour tradition of *les forçats de la route.*[18]

In his literary revisiting of these dramatic events, *Duel sur le volcan* (1998), Christian Laborde captures the essence of the two riders' battle on the mountainside, with each refusing to give the slightest ground on the tortuous ascent:

> Still parallel, still on the same line, then, little by little, as if the road was shrinking, as if it was losing, on the rock-face side and on the ravine side, absolutely identical sections of asphalt, the two monsters come closer together, almost touching. The space separating them, separating their handlebars, the white tags

on their black cycling shorts, the cut-off straps of their toe clips,
is no wider than a box of matches. Then the matchbox breaks,
and the buffer of air between the two falls away: Jacques's
shoulder touches Raymond's, and becomes glued to it, as if they
were Siamese twins (Laborde 1998: 53–4).[19]

Add to this the masses of excited spectators, several rows deep
on each side of the road, shouting and whistling, jostling for
their own positions, and only restrained with difficulty by the
local *gendarmerie*, and the pressure on the strictly limited space
available to the competitors becomes even more apparent. Yet
the two riders remained virtually conjoined until around a
kilometre-and-a-half from the summit, when Anquetil was the
first to show signs of weakening. He lost a metre, then another,
which spurred Poulidor to attack, which he did all the way to
the line, leaving the great champion labouring in his wake.
The exhausted Anquetil finished looking alarmingly pale and
seemingly on the verge of collapse, and it seemed to Poulidor's
cheering supporters that the rider would finally get to wear the
race leader's yellow jersey. Yet with reporters and cameramen
flocking around the anticipated recipient of *le maillot jaune*, it
was announced that Poulidor had only clawed back forty-two
seconds of Anquetil's lead, leaving the reigning champion
with a slender fourteen-second advantage. Two days later, in
the final stage, a time-trial between Versailles and Paris,
Anquetil characteristically went on to push his lead back out
to fifty-five seconds.

From a purely competitive angle, the riders' epic 'duel on
the volcano' might as well never have happened. Yet, the
pair's rivalry had now entered the Tour's *légende*, and Anquetil
and Poulidor were thus effectively 'immortalised' (Vigarello
1992: 914). The significance of the 1964 clash was underlined
by subsequent events, in that this was to be Anquetil's last
victory in the Tour de France. Absent in 1965, he would be
forced to abandon in 1966, in his last ever Tour, although not
before he had helped his team mate, Lucien Aimar, in his own
successful battle against Poulidor, who, once again, was
destined to come off second best. For his own part, Poulidor
would never get nearer to his ultimate goal than the fourteen
seconds that he was in arrears to Anquetil at the top of the
Puy-de-Dôme in 1964, despite another twelve years of trying.
In consequence, the rider's whole career would retrospectively
be equated – for good or for ill[20] – with his heroic failure on the
volcano. In short, the two riders would forever be linked, and

permanently fixed in the collective memory of the Tour de France: Anquetil, triumphant, as the event's first ever five-time winner; and 'Poulidor in his role as the eternal runner-up, although his popularity was at an all-time high' ('Poulidor dans son rôle d'éternel second avec, néanmoins, une popularité qui grimpe au zénith' [Ollivier 2000: 107]).

The Poulidor phenomenon: marketing '*la poupoularité*'

Why should defeat have so become Raymond Poulidor? More to the point, why should his regularly displayed inability to impose himself at crucial times have been so eminently marketable? For, in a new era of affluence, and in an event dominated since its origins by commercial considerations, the Poulidor 'product' sold well. Crucially, this period was one that saw a significant shift in the nature of the media's relationship with, and representation of, the Tour de France. Having been intimately connected with the popular press since its launch by *L'Auto* in 1903, the Tour was transformed by the advent of radio coverage in the 1930s. In the postwar period, television reports were initially limited to film recordings made by cameramen carried on motorcycles, which then had to be sent to Paris by train and edited, ready for transmission in the following day's lunchtime news bulletin. Live television coverage by the state-run *Office de Radiodiffusion-Télévision Française* (ORTF) did not begin until 1958 with a transmission from the top of the notorious Col de l'Aubisque in the Pyrenees. Mountain settings were again privileged the following year – as they would be in all subsequent Tours – with live coverage of the time-trial on the Puy-de-Dôme and then of the passing of the 2,770-metre Col de l'Iseran, in the Alps. This 1959 coverage necessitated a major commitment of staff and equipment, including, notably, the first use of a helicopter for broadcasting purposes. It was the beginning of a process of investment in the Tour de France by French television that has continued to this day, becoming ever more intensive, and revolutionising the event in the process.

In 1962, wireless cameras were mounted on motorcycles for the first time, and the continuous live feed of images of the Tour's progress – now so integral a part of the race's annual representation and reception – was thus made possible (Morice 2003: 38–41). Thanks to the new medium, the race

became an altogether more immediately accessible version of
the armchair excursion that it had been since 1903. In the
estimation of Hervé Le Roux, film director and former
contributor to the influential *Cahiers du Cinéma*, television
gave 'everything' to the Tour de France in the early 1960s, and
is still central to its popular appeal:

> [I]t essentially involves crossing 'deep' France, or the France of
> the 'lower orders', if you prefer. It thus entails a change of
> scenery, among other things. When you travel by car or TGV
> [high-speed train], it all goes too quickly. With the Tour, you
> cross the country with enough time to take in the sights, and to
> notice the people who line the route. It is the last television
> adventure (Morice 2003: 40).[21]

It is significant that Raymond Poulidor's first participation in
the Tour de France, in 1962, should have coincided with this
new epoch in sports broadcasting. Eric Reed has analysed the
crucial role played by the media, and especially the
expanding television network, in the construction of Poulidor's
public persona, specifically as the foundation of the rider's
marketing power. As he explains: 'Television allowed cycling
fans to see and hear Poulidor's provincial mannerisms, which
served to underline his "peasant" identity and popular
appeal' (Reed 2003: 116). The fact that professional cycling
had for so long been associated with peasant (and proletarian)
practitioners, and the popular values that they were held to
embody, meant that Poulidor's 'everyman' character was
reassuringly familiar from the outset of his career. He was
recognised as the spiritual descendant of such celebrated
peasant heroes of the prewar Tour de France as the Pélissier
brothers in the 1920s, and his own manager, 'Tonin' Magne,
in the 1930s. As a consequence, the rider did not threaten the
preconceptions of the Tour's traditionalist audience, rather he
reinforced them in ways that were to prove highly profitable
both for himself and for his various employers.

The peculiar nickname attached to Poulidor from the
earliest days of his professional career provides a clue to the
psychological mechanisms that were mobilised to permit this
successful marketing of the rider. For while Anquetil may have
been the distant and apparently disdainful 'Maître Jacques',
and his later rival Merckx was the all-consuming and suitably
fearsome 'Cannibale', Poulidor was no more nor less than
'Poupou'. This homely, even 'cuddly', pet name is reputed to

have been first used in 1964 by Emile Besson, the cycling correspondent of the Communist daily *L'Humanité*, and also a contributor to the specialist publication, *Miroir du Cyclisme* (Beaurenaut 1996). Even to a French audience, this apparently trivialising sobriquet requires some unpacking, as Jean-Paul Ollivier explains:

> 'Come on Poupou!' Censorious types would see derision and a condescending attitude in this childish pet name. But is it not rather a question of the growth of an emotional attachment? At the beginning, we adopted him instinctively and without knowing him, this shy and self-conscious farm boy, who has now become a star of the cycling world, almost in spite of himself, it seems. His name sounded right and tripped easily off the tongue. Nowadays, hundreds of broadcast interviews have revealed an individual who is undoubtedly 'one of us': an honest and hardworking countryman, a good son, a good father and a good husband, and above all an unpretentious character. Thus has this idol become our pal (Ollivier 1994: 134–5).[22]

Rural rootedness and media-friendliness, modesty and conformity, honesty and humility, these are what combined to make 'Poupou' the putative 'pal' of very many followers of the Tour de France. Such was the extraordinary esteem in which the rider was held that a new term – '*la poupoularité*' – was coined to describe this adulation, and even entered popular parlance in the mid-1960s (Reed 2003: 115).

Among the most striking expressions of the Poulidor phenomenon was the so-called 'Tour de Poupoularité', that saw the rider cover sections of the Tour de France route alone in 1971, after an attack of shingles had prevented him from starting as planned with the official competitors. When he had recovered, Poulidor was employed by the Luxembourg-based independent broadcaster RTL to set off each day one stage ahead of the racers, covering the ground at racing speed, and reporting on his experiences for the benefit of radio listeners and television viewers. Such was the rider's appeal that crowds flocked to see him all along the route, and in numbers that often obliged him to stop and accept handshakes and embraces, as well as the traditionally symbolic gifts of food and drink. Recalling this solitary tour as one of his fondest memories, Poulidor describes spending as much as three hours on some evenings signing autographs. On his arrival in Strasbourg, more than ten thousand spectators were waiting to greet him, causing the local police unanticipated crowd-control problems a full day ahead of the official Tour (Rigoulet 2003: 53).

These fervent supporters were the same die-hard *poulidoristes* who annually made the rider's name the most frequently shouted and, especially, the most often written on banners lining the route, and also painted on the very tarmac that their hero and every other Tour competitor had to cover. The spare time of many race followers was thus spent in preparing what one account of Poulidor's racing career terms 'a carpet of affection' ('un tapis de tendresse'): 'the road becomes covered with enormous inscriptions in white paint, the gigantic labour of love of rural summer nights …' ('la chaussée se couvre d'inscriptions énormes à la peinture blanche, oeuvre amoureuse gigantesque des nuits d'été rurales …'[Poulidor 1967: 5]). Writing in 1967, Antoine Blondin commented on the birth of a craze that has continued to this day:

> (W)e witnessed yesterday the birth of a new literary genre: the supporter's banner. Let us note the following example:
>
> > Come on Poulidor
> > If we love you
> > It's because you are certainly
> > The best
> > And a team-member worth your weight in gold
> > > (Blondin 2001: 476).[23]

By the same token, it was this passionate public support that explained the over forty thousand letters received by the sports daily *L'Equipe*, when it invited its readers to send the star a personal message on his fortieth birthday on 15 April 1976, a few months before his final Tour de France. These included notably one correspondent's statement that Poulidor was 'the greatest Frenchman in History (with de Gaulle and B.B. [Brigitte Bardot])' ('le plus grand français [*sic*] de l'Histoire (avec de Gaulle et B.B.)' [Piel with Terbeen 1976: 233–40]). Rather more objectively, perhaps, Paul Giannoli wrote in 1974 that Poulidor had firmly established himself in the popular tradition of such celebrities as the singers Edith Piaf, Charles Aznavour and Maurice Chevalier, and the comic actor Louis de Funès: apparently 'ordinary' stars, essentially created by the mass media and venerated by average French people (*'les Français moyens'*) (Pagnoud 1977: 76). Without doubt, very many French people felt that the Poulidor presented to them by the print and broadcast media, the 'little guy from the sticks' who had risen to stardom was, indeed, 'one of us' (*'bien de chez nous'*). As Blondin, with typically trenchant irony, summed up the rider's popular appeal: 'Poulidor is a product created for mass consumption ..., but at least he's a local product' ('Poulidor est un produit de consommation ..., mais c'est un produit local' [Blondin 2001: 548]).

Not surprisingly, a variety of French companies were attracted by the possibility of associating Poulidor's hugely positive image with their own goods and services. To the fore was the Groupe des Assurances Nationales (GAN), a major insurance company that, as Eric Reed explains, had been looking to associate itself with a top cyclist for several years, and in 1971 embarked on sponsorship of the Mercier racing team, led by Raymond Poulidor. What exactly were GAN getting for their investment? Reed takes up the story:

> In 1972, Claude Sudres, GAN-Mercier's public relations agent, pointed out that after only a year of team sponsorship the firm's name had become synonymous with Poulidor. 'When spectators see a GAN car drive by [during a race], they think, "That's Poulidor's team", and they applaud spontaneously.' Sudres concluded that Poulidor's celebrity was so valuable that it would be 'inconceivable' for GAN to allow Poulidor to join another team before his retirement. When ... Poulidor announced that the 1976 Tour de France would be his last, and that he would retire from cycling the following year, GAN ended its sponsorship of the team (Reed 2003: 116).

Like his great rival, Jacques Anquetil, Poulidor had become a household name, and was duly rewarded for his achievement. His first significant cash prize had come in August 1956, when a second-place finish in a modest one-day event brought him 80,000 (old) francs, more than he had earned in six years of labour on the family farm (Poulidor 1977 [1968]: 44; cf. Rigoulet 2003: 55). His wages when he joined Mercier in 1961, the year before his first Tour de France, were 25,000 (old) francs per month. This had rocketed to 350,000 (old) francs by 1964, a fourteenfold increase (Pagnoud 1977: 38). By 1966, in the rider's own estimation, the value of Poulidor's contracts were virtually the same as those paid to the five-time Tour winner Anquetil (Piel 1976: 104), while, by 1968, his earnings had risen again to forty times what they had been when he started his professional career.

Yet, this exponential rise in the rider's income was never allowed to detract from his unassuming public persona. More specifically, the financial reality that both Anquetil and Poulidor had profited substantially from their cycling stardom was less important than the popular perception of the former as having become *bourgeois* and *nouveau riche* in the process – he was often pictured in front of his characteristically elegant *château* in Normandy, for instance – while the latter was felt to have remained faithful to his popular origins, and particularly his peasant roots. Where Anquetil's remarkable success was associated with conspicuous consumption, Poulidor's more modest achievements had seemingly been reflected in a correspondingly down-to-earth lifestyle. Indeed, even Poulidor's legendary meanness with tips – his nickname among the other members of the *peloton* was, Blondin suggests, 'Léonard de vingt sous' (Blondin 2001: 548)[24] – was positively received, as further confirmation of his durable attachment to the stereotypically tight-fisted peasantry from which he had sprung. This less than glamorous characteristic of 'Poupou' was thus regarded approvingly by his adoring public, who vicariously encouraged the star to take good care of his hard-earned cash.

Poulidor accordingly managed to navigate the commercial twists and turns of modern sporting stardom to considerable effect, using the paradoxical prestige of his original rural poverty to cloak great financial success. This was a pattern that continued as he switched to a broader range of enterprises in the later stages of his racing career, and particularly after his retirement from competition in 1977. These undertakings have included broadcasting work and a variety of promotional activities, particularly in connection with the Tour de France, which Poulidor has followed for the past thirty years as part of the commercial *caravane* that annually accompanies the Tour in its circuit of the nation. In addition, the former rider has had his own cycle sales company since 1978, which markets machines all over the country. While the star himself is, perhaps understandably, reticent as regards the size of his personal fortune, Poulidor is reputed to be a millionaire several times over, and to have made extensive acquisitions of property in Limoges, the principal city of his native region (Rigoulet 2003: 55). As Laurent Rigoulet tellingly put it in a retrospective piece on the star, as part of *L'Equipe*'s coverage of the Tour de France in 2003: 'Poulidor has a reputation for getting beaten, but he is the most loved and the best paid' ('Poulidor a la réputation de se faire battre mais il est le plus aimé et le mieux payé' [Rigoulet 2003: 53]).

From this point of view, the fact that Poulidor never achieved victory in the Tour de France may be considered as relatively unimportant. Indeed, although the Tour is generally perceived as the ultimate goal of all French competitive cyclists, one plausible reading of this very special rider's career is that he was never a loser in any real sense. Rather, he became, and was to remain, an objective winner from the day he left the undoubted hardships of his rural origins behind him by signing up as a professional (Laborde 1998: 51–2). More than this, in Poulidor's case, failure – or at least his permanently anticipated but constantly deferred victory – actually sold better than success. Jean-Paul Ollivier is firm in his assertion that journalists following the Tour actually preferred the rider to be beaten, because it made for better copy (Ollivier 1994: 142). The psychological mechanism at work here is shrewdly assessed by Georges Dirand and Pierre Joly, the ghost-writers for Poulidor's autobiography, *La Gloire sans maillot jaune* (1968). As this title suggests, and as noted above, not winning the Tour de France, despite sixteen years of trying, is central to Poulidor's peculiar variety of sporting stardom. More specifically, his continued failure is precisely what renders possible the fan's 'absolute identification' with an otherwise untouchable, elite performer: 'The civil servant, the businessman, the tradesman, or the farmer, when they take a cool and clear-headed look at their own careers, will be obliged to admit that in the race of life they have more often been runners-up or in tenth place than winners' (Poulidor 1977 [1968]: 6).[25] For all such *Français moyens*, or even *Français vaincus* (defeated or downtrodden French people), it is very much easier to associate oneself with the heroic failure of Poulidor than the phenomenal, almost superhuman, invincibility of Jacques Anquetil: 'Between Anquetil and the crowd, there was always the barrier of his enormous talent. ... Between Poulidor and the crowd, there was no such barrier' ('Entre Anquetil et la foule s'interposa l'écran des dons. ... Entre Poulidor et la foule, cet écran n'existe pas' [Poulidor 1977 [1968]: 7]). Indeed, where Anquetil's dominance alienated audiences, Poulidor's hard-luck stories allowed his followers to dream: 'He remains the epitome of missed opportunities and, when he did overcome misfortune, of the revenge of the eternally downtrodden, the daily dream of the bullied and the defeated' (Poulidor 1977 [1968]: 8).[26] In short, the dazzling performances of 'Maître Jacques' were fundamentally inimical to the popular audience of the Tour de France, whether assembled by the roadside, around the television set, or at the bar of the local *bistrot*. What Poulidor's public wanted was not prodigious ability, but (relatively) modest achievement on the basis of honest toil: 'Anquetil, at fifteen or sixteen years of age, was already like a young Mozart, whereas "Poupou" was an apprentice accordionist, full of good will, but barely more talented than the average person. His supporters are grateful to him for having become a virtuoso through hard work' (Poulidor 1977 [1968]: 8).[27] Good, but not too good, and, above all, reassuringly familiar; these were the qualities that together underpinned Raymond Poulidor's appeal in the France of the 1960s and early 1970s.

Conclusion: making sense of *le cas Poulidor*

In one of the most incisive recent analyses of French cycling heroes, Hugh Dauncey has characterised Raymond Poulidor as an 'anti-star' (Dauncey 2003: 184), in so far as the rider's enormous popularity was based not upon competitive success, the usual prerequisite of the sports star, but rather on repeated failure. He goes on to explore the Anquetil–Poulidor 'tandem' as a 'symbiotic pairing of sporting stars', which functioned very profitably not only for the two riders, but also for the media and associated commercial interests (Dauncey 2003: 199). For Dauncey, the pair's much analysed rivalry was thus essentially 'confected', or artificially generated, by the media's obsessive attention. However, while the tension between the pair may well have been more or less consciously created, it was also undeniably creative, to the extent that it did not simply derive from the two riders' obvious differences in approach, attitude and style. Rather, the duo offered newspaper readers, radio listeners and, above all, television viewers contrasting images of Frenchness: 'as French society began to feel the stresses of modernisation, these two riders began to represent different social and cultural values, as well as their sporting meaning' (Dauncey 2003: 199). Thus, events played out annually on the route of the Tour de France took on a deeper, symbolic importance. Drawing on the cultural historian, Michel Winock, in his 1987 analysis of '*Le Complexe de Poulidor*' ('The Poulidor Complex'), Dauncey explains the linkage between the racers' extended duel and the evolution of the French society of the day:

> [Anquetil's] technical mastery of the time-trial ('man against machine') reflected French society's technocratic and technological

modernization under the later Fourth Republic and under de Gaulle. Poulidor, in contrast, ... represented much less the new confident France of the Fifth Republic advancing towards technological and sociopolitical modernity under the guidance of national planning and a new constitution, than '*la France profonde*' of Poupou's native and still archaic Limousin. This interpretation portrays Poulidor as the anachronistic representative – still loved as the underdog, like Astérix, Vercingétorix, Roland, Joan of Arc and Charles de Gaulle – of the France of the Fourth Republic's uncertainties and weaknesses, and casts Anquetil as the embodiment of Gaullist '*grandeur*' and as the harbinger of '*la France qui gagne*' (victorious France) (Dauncey 2003: 195; cf. Winock 1986 and 1987).

This reading of the Poulidor phenomenon is particularly persuasive in that it foregrounds the appeal to nostalgia intrinsic to both the Tour de France and the rider's variety of stardom, together with the centrality of heroic narrative in the evolution of the event and the 'Poupou' persona alike. For if the followers of the event continued to look back to the glories of the past, the increasingly mediatised and, crucially, televised Tour of the 1960s had an insatiable appetite for daily doses of new triumphs and disasters. Poulidor's constant trials and tribulations – his hard-luck stories, his near-misses, his accidents, thrills and spills – together provided ample material for all those involved in (re)constructing the Tour's *légende*, which, under the influence of the omnipresent media, began to resemble nothing so much as soap opera, albeit on a grand scale. The advent of live television coverage in the early 1960s turned the Tour de France into a qualitatively new spectacle, one which, as Hervé Le Roux has pointed out, has elements of the road-movie, the western, the war film, the thriller and even, on occasion, knockabout comedy (Morice 2003: 40–1). However, the dominant narrative form of the Tour's three-week-long travelling shot remains *le feuilleton* (the serial) or, more accurately perhaps, *le mélo à épisodes* (the soap opera), with its recurrent characters and storylines: 'Every day, we meet up again with the riders, some of whom we know already, while new ones also appear, and we know that So-and-so is ill and So-and-so is raring to go' ('Tous les jours, on retrouve les coureurs, on en connaît certains, de nouveaux apparaissent, on sait qu'Untel ou Untel est malade ou gonflé à bloc, etc.' [Morice 2003: 41]). Poulidor's habitual misfortunes were a godsend for journalists and related commentators, ever more anxious to provide the French public with suitably poignant tales of this most demanding of sporting competitions.

In the event, it was not Poulidor but Anquetil who was to provide an appropriately melodramatic epilogue to their competitive rivalry. Having been sworn enemies on the roads of France, with no love lost in personal life either – at least as far as their public images were concerned – the two riders became close friends in the mid-1970s (Rigoulet 2003: 54), and remained so right up to Anquetil's premature death from stomach cancer in 1987. It was this reconciliation that allowed Anquetil to have the final, and distinctly bitter, satisfaction of telephoning Poulidor from his deathbed to announce that, one last time, he was going to beat his old opponent to the finish-line. Having never made any secret of his admiration for Anquetil as a rider, even at the height of their public rivalry, 'Poupou' thus joined Eddy Merckx, Lucien Aimar and Luis Ocaña – who together had won the Tour de France seven times – in carrying Anquetil's coffin on the great rider's final journey (Beaurenaut 1996). Poulidor may never have beaten Anquetil in the Tour, but he survived him not only in life but also in the affections of the French sporting public. Always the bridesmaid, never the bride, the star became the centre of a nostalgia industry that was particularly marked in *L'Equipe*'s 2003 celebration of the centenary of the Tour de France. For many observers, the man quite simply became synonymous with the event. As the leading *bande dessinée* (comic book) artists Dupuy and Berberian show in their illustrated contribution to this celebration of one hundred years of Tour history, even not quite seeing the man himself was enough to convince one patiently waiting child of the awe-inspiring nature of the nation's great bike race: 'One day, I nearly saw Poulidor. ... That's how I was touched by the magic of the Tour' ('Un jour, j'ai failli voir Poulidor. ... Voilà comment j'ai été touché par la magie du Tour' [Dupuy and Berberian 2003: 71]).

Notes

1. These comments are based on a survey of *Paris Match* for 1968, selected as a midpoint in Poulidor's career, as well as an obvious political and cultural watershed.
2. 'Si les Français avaient eu à désigner, par un vote, le vrai vainqueur de la dure épreuve à laquelle vous venez de participer, nul doute que, dès le premier tour, leurs suffrages unanimes vous auraient porté à la première place' (Ollivier 1994: 189).
3. Cerdan's premature death in an air crash in 1949 was the inspiration for Piaf's hit recording 'Hymne à l'amour', in a striking interaction of

     mediatised sport, show-business and the music industry – half a century before 'Posh and Becks'.

4. 'Il est peu de dire que je me suis traumatisé. En quatorze mois, j'ai vieilli de dix ans. Je me sens complètement étranger dans mon propre corps. ... Je me sens mal dans ma peau. Ce qui me passionnait hier m'ennuie désormais. Il me semble que j'ai laissé beaucoup de moi outre-Méditerranée, que je me suis dispersé et qu'il faut à tout prix que je me retrouve.'

5. 'Raymond est un brave petit, assurent les parents à l'envoyé spécial parisien ... Peut-être grâce à lui pourrons-nous un jour acheter une ferme. Car nous sommes métayers et ce n'est pas drôle de travailler tous les jours pour les autres.'

6. Delerm mentions only three riders from the Tour's past by way of illustration: Jacques Anquetil, Roger Rivière and Raymond Poulidor.

7. Le Tour promeut le sport en feuilleton populaire, favorisé, à coup sûr, par les tactiques du cyclisme: les coureurs se détachent, se rattrapent ..., ils s'entraident, créent de l'inattendu. Autant d'actions permettant une trame anecdotique. L'invention du maillot jaune, en 1919, désignant le premier du classement, emblème toujours visible malgré les aléas de la course, ajoute au récit quotidien. A cet égard, le Tour est un modèle du genre. Mais un modèle de mémoire aussi. Plus qu'ailleurs, l'épreuve vit de chronique. Il lui faut un passé; il lui faut de l'évocation. Sans doute parce que le Tour se raconte, plus encore qu'il ne s'observe du bord des routes. Il vit dans la narration. Il s'en nourrit, avec cette attention toute particulière aux rebondissements et à leur chronologie. Sa description tient à l'art du conteur. D'où cette séduction d'entrecroiser les récits, de les comparer, ce jeu très particulier avec le temps. D'où cette tentation de créer une culture. La mémoire du Tour fait partie de la course.

8. It is revealing that the recent, and authoritative, study of the Tour de France, edited by Dauncey and Hare (2003), should devote no less than thirteen pages in whole or in part to Raymond Poulidor, but makes no reference to André Darrigade.

9. 'Nous marchâmes aussi longtemps que le courage de Poulidor put le soutenir, c'est-à-dire environ une trentaine de lieues; car cette nature incomparable refusa constamment de s'arrêter plus tôt. Accablée enfin de lassitude, elle mit pied à terre, non sans avoir adressé à l'écho un faible son que je pris d'abord pour un soupir. "Je crois que je suis crevé", me dit timidement l'enfant sublime de Masbaraud-Mérignan [*sic*, more accurately Masbaraud-Mérignat, the actual hamlet in the Creuse where Poulidor was born]'.

10. The French noun 'maître' is usually translated as 'master', but it is also the title habitually associated with lawyers, for which there is no direct English equivalent. It additionally has similar connotations to the Italian '*maestro*', although used ironically here.

11. Le caractère essentiellement chronométrique de ses performances, une façon assez polaire de triompher sans un effort d'accommodement, un mépris ombrageux et poli à l'endroit des manifestations extérieures de la sympathie pouvaient donner à penser qu'il concevait son métier sous l'angle le plus aigu et le plus étriqué: celui d'un homme qui ne traîne point sur le pas de sa porte, une fois la journée finie. Être de sang-froid, sinon animal à sang froid, Anquetil se dérobait sous l'écorce fuyante du batracien ou du reptile. On ne connaissait ni la saveur de ses larmes ni le prix de son sourire. Il courait à côté de son personnage.

12. Ollivier not only confirms the story, but also suggests that Anquetil engaged in a sangria-drinking competition with his manager.

13. Dauncey cites Jacques Calvet, who argues that, contrary to both mediatic representations and public perceptions, 'Poulidor was in reality disliked by the peloton for his ill-humour and selfish tactics, whereas Anquetil was appreciated for his fair-play and courtesy' (Dauncey 2003: 194).

14. An unusual show of solidarity between the two riders occurred during the 1966 Tour, when an unannounced drugs test in Bordeaux, in the presence of a court bailiff, with Poulidor selected as the first to be sampled, prompted a strike by the rest of the riders, led by Anquetil. See Augendre 1991.

15. 'Ce Tour est animé par le duel mémorable entre Anquetil et Poulidor. La passion est à la hauteur du talent. La France entière est partagée entre les "anquetilistes" et les "poulidoristes".'

16. 'La montagne joue, à cet égard, un rôle particulier: barrière qu'il faut toujours affronter. Elle est lieu d'épuisements, de chutes, de drames. Elle inquiète …'.

17. 'A aucun moment dans l'histoire du Tour, les deux premiers du classement général n'avaient eu à se livrer une bataille aussi serrée. Jamais non plus une course ne s'était déroulée dans un tel climat de passion'.

18. This term, meaning literally the galley slaves (or convicts) of the road, dates back to the investigative reporting on the Tour de France conducted in the 1920s by the celebrated journalist, Albert Londres, and since republished in various editions, including *Les Forçats de la route* (Londres 1996).

19. Toujours parallèles, toujours sur la même ligne, puis, peu à peu, comme si la route rétrécissait, qu'elle perdait, côté roche et côté ravin, des parcelles d'une superficie absolument semblable de macadam, les deux monstres se rapprochent, se frôlent. L'espace qui les sépare, sépare leurs guidons, les tags blancs sur leurs cuissards noirs, les courroies coupées de leur cale-pieds, n'est pas plus large qu'une boîte d'allumettes. Et la boîte d'allumettes se brise, les cales d'air chutent sur la chaussée: l'épaule de Jacques touche l'épaule de Raymond, épaules maintenant collées, siamoises.

20. A notable critique of Poulidor's essential passivity, even at this critical moment, is provided by Anquetil's racing manager, Raphaël Géminiani, in the television documentary *Anquetil, champion de légende* (Dries 1996), a companion piece to *Poulidor, coeur d'or* (Beaurenaut 1996). The titles of the two films accurately reflect the treatment of each cyclist, as does the classical music chosen to accompany archive footage of Anquetil and the accordion similarly selected for Poulidor.

21. [C]'est une traversée de la France profonde, ou d'en bas si l'on veut. Il y a là une part de dépaysement. Quand on se déplace en voiture ou en TGV, cela va trop vite. Dans le Tour, on traverse en ayant le temps de voir le décor, les gens sur le bord de la route. C'est la dernière aventure télévisuelle.

22. 'Vas-y Poupou!' Des censeurs voient une dérision, une intention condescendante dans le diminutif puéril. Ne s'agit-il pas plutôt d'une évolution affective? Au début, l'on avait adopté d'instinct et sans le connaître ce petit rural timide et gauche devenu vedette du cyclisme, presque à son corps défendant, semblait-il. Son nom sonore galopait sur

la langue. Aujourd'hui, des centaines d'interviews au micro ont fait apparaître un personnage bien de chez nous. Paysan travailleur et honnête, bon fils, bon père, bon époux et surtout pas prétentieux. Ainsi cette idole est devenue un copain.

23. [N]ous avons assisté hier à l'éclosion d'un nouveau genre littéraire: la banderole. [...] Notons:

> Vas-y Poulidor
> Si on t'aime
> C'est que t'es quand même
> Le plus fort
> Et un équipier en or

24. This is a play on 'Leonardo da Vinci', with the term 'vingt sous' having the approximate sense of 'tuppence'.

25. 'Le fonctionnaire, l'industriel, le commerçant, l'exploitant agricole, qui jettent un regard froid et lucide sur leurs carrières, sont bien obligés d'admettre que dans la course de la vie ils ont été plus souvent deuxièmes ou dixièmes que premiers'.

26. 'Il demeure la vivante illustration des occasions manquées et, au delà de la malchance surmontée, de la revanche des éternels battus, le rêve quotidien des brimés et des vaincus'.

27. 'Anquetil, à quinze ou seize ans, était déjà une sorte de Mozart enfant, "Poupou", un apprenti accordéoniste, plein de bonne volonté, mais à peine plus doué que la moyenne. Ses supporters lui sont reconnaissants d'être devenu laborieusement un virtuose'. The Mozart tag was often applied to Anquetil. See also above, note 9, regarding the two films associating the riders with classical music and the tradition of the *bal musette*, respectively.

CHAPTER 6

THE AUTEUR AS STAR: JEAN-LUC GODARD

Alison Smith

To talk about a film director in the context of stardom clearly has different connotations to discussion of performer-stars such as Hallyday or Bardot. The audience involved is undoubtedly smaller, and its interests undoubtedly different: the ways in which the star image is conveyed may also be expected to be different. The preliminary question of whether it is appropriate to talk about stardom at all in this context therefore needs to be posed, and so the chapter will start by considering the justification for including Jean-Luc Godard in a discussion of stardom through an assessment of the status of the film director in the public experience of the cinema. Having laid out a basis for considering a film director's stardom, I will then look at the ways in which Godard, particularly, established his status as star in the context of the *Nouvelle Vague* group from which he emerged, first through the differentiation of that group in relation to the rest of French cinema, and subsequently through the differentiation of Godard himself with respect to the rest of the group. Godard's star status was also created through various strategies, by which particular qualities and values, both cinematic and extracinematic, were incarnated. These strategies will be considered in relation both to the early establishment of his status (in the period 1959–1965), and to

The Director as Star.
© Elizabeth Catalano.

its subsequent consolidation and development in the later stages of his career (in the late 1960s and after).

Can a director be a star?

The following questions arise in a consideration of how stardom can be convincingly attributed to a film director: what functions can a director fulfil *qua* star? When might a famous director qualify for 'stardom'? In theory, a film-maker's potential audience, among which his or her stardom will be created and propagated, comprises the whole of the film-going public, as it does for a star actor or actress. In practice, the sphere of interest in or fascination with a director tends to be much smaller. If this sphere consists entirely of *cinéphiles* in the narrowest sense – those who read the film reviews, buy the specialist press, or make a particular effort to see all the new films critically considered important – then the proportion of the population concerned is too small to speak convincingly of stardom. On the other hand, there are directors who have made names in a much wider field, approximating to the entire (international) film-going public, without at the same time achieving stardom. Steven Spielberg would be an example: everyone knows his name and can list some or even all of his films, but stardom seems an inappropriate term perhaps because the name is not accompanied by an easily accessible personal image. Spielberg, one might say, *is* his films as far as most of the public is concerned: his own appearance is only vaguely known, his habits, tastes, private life even less – and there seems little demand for information about these.

In practice, then, in order to speak of stardom in connection with a film director two considerations would seem to be important. One is that he (there has never yet been a female director to qualify, in any country) excites an interest which extends outside the narrow circle of those 'in the know'. The other is that this interest must hinge at least to some degree on the man, rather than the films he makes.

Within the highly film-literate culture of France in the 1960s and 1970s, the conditions for the elevation of a director to such a status were undoubtedly favourable. I would argue that during the early to mid-1960s, two French directors enjoyed a reputation and a level of public interest sufficient to give them potential for stardom, these being François Truffaut and Jean-Luc Godard. A combination of factors made Godard, finally, a more convincing 'star' than Truffaut: some perhaps fortuitous, some a result of careful management, and these will be discussed in the course of this chapter. Among these factors, however, it is important to note that the films themselves play a relatively minor role. Even among *cinéphiles*, Godard gained a reputation for being difficult very early. Not only were the films he made complex, fragmented and designed to startle and jab the spectator, but even in the early 1960s it was recognised that, with the exception of the first, *A bout de souffle*, they were not often seen.

Since the issue of Godard's 'audience' will become important later on, I will give a broad outline here of its structure and of the different expectations which the various elements of it had of Godard. To adopt a description based on the model of 'concentric circles' as used elsewhere in this book, one could say that the inner circle, apart from those involved in cinema for whom Godard rapidly became a reference, would be made up of a specific group of *cinéphiles* classing themselves as principally young and intellectual. Outside these come the broader, cinema-going public who were interested and inspired by the Nouvelle Vague, and outside these again the readers of the popular weeklies and the television audiences who were concerned to have a general idea of the cultural landscape, to 'know what was going on'. In the very outer circle would be those who had heard a few well known names almost despite themselves, to whom most film-makers' names would mean precisely nothing, but to whom the syllables 'Jean-Luc Godard' might stand as a shorthand for something – 'the contemporary cinema' or, later, 'political intellectuals'. It will be seen that the actual content of the association (what Godard signifies or incarnates) changed over time. The devotion of these audiences to Godard tended to decrease in intensity as one moves outward, so that while the student audience provided a fan-base passionate enough to amaze the film-critics, the wider audience probably felt mere curiosity mixed with irritation or respect.

In considering how Godard attained his relative stardom, I would like to begin by considering one factor which is relevant for both Truffaut and Godard: that is the nature of the Nouvelle Vague movement of which they were the most high-profile representatives. The Nouvelle Vague brought to French cinema a number of elements that meant that it was very clearly differentiated from the films and the directors that preceded it (even when the directors were still making films). It presented itself as young and radical, in opposition to traditional structures and to established personalities – the new generation of French cinema. In its radicalness, however, it adopted positions particularly calculated to increase the potential of directors to become stars – that is, it founded its movement for the renovation of the cinema on a *'politique des auteurs'*, promulgated and defended in the critical writings of its principal exponents. The nucleus of the Nouvelle Vague, a tightly knit group of friends working on the same, new magazine, *Cahiers du cinéma*, adopted as models and ideals of cinema a number of directors who themselves had very sharply defined personalities and public profiles (Renoir, Welles and Hitchcock), and these examples influenced them in ways that we will return to later. In more general terms, the 'politique des auteurs' attributed cinematic significance to the director as a personality. By highlighting the role of the film director as creative individual, it gave importance to his (or her) mental structures of the world, and therefore his (or her) life. For the readership of *Cahiers* in the first instance, and later for a more general public, although probably always limited to those who read about films, the concept of the *auteur* served two purposes:

(1) It provided reasons for taking an interest in the director's personality as revealed by sources other than his films, as

his life might throw some light on his personality and his personality on his films. This is, of course, a very cinephilic standpoint (assuming that the *ultimate* interest is in the films) but, as this approach trickled from the specialist press into more general acceptance, the availability of interviews, articles, even gossip about strong personalities in certain cases might lead to them taking on an interest for their own sake;

(2) It guaranteed the elevation of the director as a creative individual (who had a certain authority over the glamorous star-actors). Rumours about a relationship between a director and a glamorous star, of course, tended to attribute some reflected lustre to the director quite apart from his status as auteur. More people knew Roger Vadim's name because of his relationship with Brigitte Bardot than would normally have taken an interest in the creator of *Et Dieu créa la femme*, even though Vadim was, initially at least, considered part of the auteur-oriented Nouvelle Vague. Roberto Rossellini's fame was undoubtedly impelled beyond the admirers of neorealism by his connection with Ingrid Bergman. However, the valorising of the creative potential of the director could only contribute to this; Rossellini, again, was no doubt given brighter and more durable amplitude by the awareness, even the vague awareness, of his critical reputation as a film-maker and of the role which his skill might be presumed to have in his success with Bergman.

The philosophy of the Nouvelle Vague critics, then, contributed to the creation of a climate where the director's importance was enhanced and his personality highlighted. When Dyer considers the auteur theory (1979), however, he does not appear to consider it as a factor which might potentially elevate directors to stardom. Indeed, he largely discounts it for two reasons. First, summarising several later critiques of it, he tends to reduce the creative personality to the status of a textual construct, responsible for the particular style of the films perhaps but unconnected to any extracinematic person or even persona – a view which would seem to rule out any possibility of the formation of star image from the position of director. Secondly, he considers the possibility that the actor may be the dominant creative personality in a film to the extent that s/he may be considered its principal auteur, i.e. the star may become an auteur but the auteur can never attain the public visibility indispensable to the creation of stardom.

In as far as the role of auteur does depend almost entirely on the analysis of texts, this argument seems clear and convincing. However, there are a number of directors whose public visibility has transcended their film-texts, borne by a variety of media other than those texts themselves. In the case of Truffaut and Godard, their deep attachment to the auteur theory which so privileged the directorial position is clearly not wholly unconnected to their status. Nonetheless, we are faced with a phenomenon which is not completely explained either by the spread of the auteur theory and of interest in their films (especially not in Godard's case) or by interest in their private lives, and this despite the fact that Truffaut's colourful past did retrospectively become a part of his image.

If for the *Cahiers du cinéma* critics the auteur theory represented a way of talking about cinema in an analytical context similar to that used for 'intellectual' art – and this was very important to them and to other *cinéphiles* who wanted to claim for their interest some genuine intellectual justification – for the majority of the population this aim was almost certainly irrelevant. If the concept of the director became influential enough in the world of French cinema audiences for the director's name to begin to feature prominently on film announcements, it was not so much because of what Truffaut, Godard, Rohmer etc. wrote in *Cahiers du cinéma*, but because the films that they made, which were enormously successful, were marketed largely on their own personalities. This was to some extent due to their philosophy, and no doubt to their egotism, to some extent a result of necessity: to begin with, the Nouvelle Vague could not rely on the box-office power of their stars, as the young directors could not afford stars, nor on scriptwriters or literary originals, since they wrote their scripts themselves. Publicity then hinged on the film-makers themselves, their youth, their innovation, their rejection of the dominant values of the French cinema of the period, polemically dubbed by Truffaut 'Dad's cinema' ('*cinéma de papa*'). Furthermore, Truffaut's first full-length feature film, *Les 400 Coups*, exploited its autobiographical aspect for marketing purposes, and its popularity was thus linked to Truffaut's off-screen personality. The real-life friendship between the main core of Nouvelle Vague film-makers was widely known, and some of their ideas began to take on the aura of association, creating a self-reinforcing process where widely known directors' ideas about the important cinematic role of the director made the public re-evaluate their interest in directors in general and also become more convinced that these directors in particular were strong personalities. The Nouvelle Vague by the early 1960s had become a collection not of films but of names, some names recurring in first place and at all times, to such an extent that in 1964 Robert Lapoujade complained that for a beginner there was no chance of entering mainstream cinema: 'no one will have faith in me, unless I'm called Truffaut' ('Personne ne me fera confiance, à moins de s'appeler Truffaut' [Various 1974: 83]).

The Nouvelle Vague thus introduced to a wide French audience the habit of thinking of films in terms of their directors, to some extent by their writings but most of all by their example. To a degree, however, they were doing no more than pick up on a trend which had already begun in the USA. It can be no coincidence that the most striking examples of independent US director-stars, such as Alfred Hitchcock or Orson Welles, were singled out by the *Cahiers* critics for special auteur status. Their films were discussed in the magazine in a strictly cinephilic context, of course, but the public profiles of these men already stretched beyond their films, and it is worth looking at the elements which contributed to their immense celebrity, not least because these were the Nouvelle Vague's cultural heroes, and the French directors might be expected to model themselves on them, consciously or unconsciously, when it came to forging their own image. Many of the factors which established the stardom of the US directors will be found to have parallels in the careers of both Truffaut and Godard.

Despite the undoubted brilliance of Welles or Hitchcock, it is clear that their reputation was based on many factors other than their simple directorial skill. Both men had widely publicised personality clashes with other branches of the industry because of their insistent declarations of independence and creative personality. This tended to anchor them in the public mind as individuals, and led to assumptions about the individuality of their films which did not necessarily require first-hand verification. The fact that their creative claims were frequently confirmed, and practically never denied, by the critics who had seen the films would be enough to consolidate this idea. Orson Welles's creative individuality was further reinforced by a determined belief in his youth and 'appearance from nowhere'. In fact, as Penelope Houston points out (1980: 1056), twenty-five was not that young for a first-time Hollywood director of the period, and he was already quite firmly established in theatre, but the fact that she has to state this underlines the persistence of the myth. The parallel with the Nouvelle Vague's relative youth, their eschewal of the traditional entries into film-making (they never worked as assistants on anyone else's sets), and their determined self-publicity as creative individuals is clear.

A second parallel can be drawn: the creative reputation of both Hitchcock and Welles was certainly helped by knowledge of the effects of the film-maker's work even among a public who had never experienced any such effects. Hitchcock's name quickly became synonymous with suspense and with the thriller, but also, and this especially after the appearance of *Psycho* and the reputation of the Shower Scene, with an atmosphere which is probably most easily described as weirdness. Welles, of course, could claim to have single-handedly, or single-voicedly, caused panic in New York, no doubt much exaggerated, but contributing to his reputation as a powerful commander of audience reaction.[1] In this regard, we shall see later how Godard, in particular, succeeded in associating his name with particular characteristics and thus began to acquire a superficial reputation for incarnating them.

Thirdly, and especially in the case of Hitchcock, this reputation was propagated not only through the cinema but through other media, notably through television. The immense boost to Hitchcock's already established reputation which came from his *Alfred Hitchcock presents ...* series can hardly be exaggerated. Within the series, Hitchcock took very deliberate measures to cultivate his own, simplified and exaggerated image, a decision which John Russell Taylor attributes in part to his belief that television was a medium which dealt in stereotypes, and which therefore needed them in order to function (Taylor 1981: 209). Through the series, which ran for ten years and has since been frequently repeated, Hitch's famous silhouette became, quite literally, a trademark. His reputation for weirdness, mentioned above, could be personally verified not only by his – admittedly large – cinema audience, but by the ever-growing number of households equipped with a television. Welles also occasionally used television, although it probably contributed little to his star status. His radio work, however, undoubtedly had an enormous effect on his stormy reputation. The Nouvelle Vague directors did not perhaps use the creative possibilities of television so fully, at least not in the early years (public exposure to TV was, besides, much more limited in France), but they did make appearances in the popular press and increasingly on television discussion programmes.

A fourth parallel exists. Along with Welles's and Hitchcock's reputation for combative independence went insistent and titillating stories about their respective private lives. Less important for the Nouvelle Vague directors, this factor was nevertheless not entirely absent; rumours did circulate, and their weddings – and, later, separations – were matters of public interest.

A fifth and final parallel was the director's *appearance* in films, and the propagation both within and outside the films of a recognisable image. Welles, of course, was an actor as much as a director. Hitchcock on the other hand limited his appearances to a fleeting glimpse per film, and thus he created a schematic image based on the salient features of his physique (portly, bald, slightly sardonic). His habit became so well known that first viewers of a Hitchcock film began to watch for him, actively seeking out that typed appearance which they thus had to internalise. The Hitchcock-figure became a managed exercise in brand awareness, with his silhouette as his own logo, even before he adopted that same logo, further reduced into a cartoon caricature (of his own device) as a regular signature for his television programmes. A picture of Hitchcock off his guard, when the 'trade-mark' features are not accentuated, can in fact be surprising, or even hard to recognise. Of the Nouvelle Vague directors, it was Godard who paid the most attention to the cultivation of a trade-mark image or silhouette. The significance of this should not be underplayed, as it was one of the key ways in which he began to differentiate himself from other directors in the group. It is with an examination of Godard's carefully cultivated image that we will therefore commence a more particular consideration of Jean-Luc Godard, the auteur as star.

The case of Jean-Luc Godard

The Nouvelle Vague, of course, was differentiated from the beginning by creative tension with the French film establishment, and by the demand for recognition of the directors' individuality. In the early days, however, no one director was identified individually with a particular effect produced on the audience – this tended to be located in the bloc. Neither were their private lives the subject of much scandal or speculation. If Truffaut and Godard were early singled out from the group, relevant factors would seem to be, in Truffaut's case, the relatively great interest accorded to his biography, and, in both cases, their visibility – in films, their own and other people's, in photo-calls, at round tables and festivals and on television.

Truffaut and Godard both appeared in their films, although Truffaut did not do so in the early days of the Nouvelle Vague. However, he used actors with physical resemblance, narratives with biographical resemblance, characters with (presumed) psychological resemblance to himself, tricks which, more or less consciously, created a typed persona. Godard's rather different approach to public visibility was equally a factor from early days in establishing his public profile. If by 1990 Alain Bergala, in a *Cahiers du cinéma* special issue devoted to him, could refer to 'this man whose image everyone knows – even those who have never seen any of his films' ('cet homme dont tout le monde connaît l'image – même des gens qui n'ont jamais vu aucun de ses films' [Bergala 1990: 28]) this familiarity was the result of a cumulative process of photographic repetition which began with the early days of Godard's filmic career.

The physical appearance which has become the Godard trademark was, from the start, strongly typed. The dark glasses, the cigarette and the high, balding forehead are insisted on very early. Photographs without the accessories are practically nonexistent. This is clearly a case of a carefully selected public profile (even if there was a good medical reason for the dark glasses, as several friends have confirmed), and it is certainly not fortuitous. That Godard was conversant with the process of moulding one's own image is visible in his first film, *A bout de souffle*, where the central character is obsessed with recreating himself in the image of Humphrey Bogart, the star who has made himself or been made into the archetype of a gangster. Michel Poiccard's careful choice of accessories and mannerisms, among them those which Bogart had made his own, illustrate the film-maker's consciousness of the factors which make up a star-image.

However, the image that Godard created for himself also offers many major advantages which may not be immediately obvious. It is at once more transient and more strongly stereotyped than Truffaut's. You do not need to gaze long at a photograph, even a small and distant one, to recognise the figure with the dark glasses and the high forehead. On the other hand, if he removes the glasses, or covers the forehead with a hat, the image changes totally. The Godard image, then, by its basis in removable or easily hideable traits, remains very much in the control of its owner. It is also an image more concealing than revealing: the dark glasses and the semipermanent presence of a cigarette – hardly ever removed except when it is replaced by a microphone – obviate the need for any very well-defined facial expression. Further, it is an image which survives the process of ageing. When Godard first adopted it he was in his late twenties. A few photographs of this period – mostly stills from other people's films – show him without his glasses, with his receding hair not emphasised, and in them we see a conventionally attractive young man, who bears a more than passing resemblance to Buster Keaton in Agnès Varda's short sketch *Les Fiancés du pont MacDonald* from her 1961 film *Cléo de 5 à 7*. To deliberately hide what could well have been perceived as good looks, and to emphasise features which prematurely aged him – notably the receding hairline – seems a contrary strategy for one seeking celebrity in a visual medium, but it has resulted in an amazingly durable persona, who in 2007, at the age of 77, is still recognisable as the young man approaching thirty who appears, looking up from behind a newspaper, in a brief shot of *A bout de souffle*.

   With this we come to the strategy of cameo appearances in his own films, which Godard, probably following the Hitchcock model, adopted from early days. He also occasionally appeared for other members of his immediate circle, always in small and obscure roles. Although Godard's adherence to this habit was not quite as unfailing as Hitchcock's, it was nonetheless known, and to his own audience was an element to be watched for. It ensured that those who watched Godard's films knew how to recognise the director, although Godard's audience was never large enough to constitute fuel for stardom properly speaking. However, the figure also appeared in other contexts. At festivals and film conferences, he was already more than prepared to be photographed as he talked about cinema: his own cinema, other people's cinema, the cinema in society, the cinema as an art form. Apart from his appearances in films, most of the photographs of him that appeared in the early 1960s show him behind a microphone. He also appeared increasingly on television, to begin with as an expert on film, but, increasingly, in other contexts. There is in this context a very revealing episode of the lively cultural programme *Dim Dam Dom*, made in 1965 and devoted to Scott Fitzgerald. The programme, made by Guy Seligmann, mostly takes the form of a short film purporting to show Fitzgerald and Zelda in Paris, which exhibits all the mannerisms of the Nouvelle Vague to the extent of being close at times to a pastiche of the Godard of

Vivre sa vie. Interspersed with this 'film' are commentaries on the significance of Fitzgerald, sometimes by Françoise Sagan but principally by Godard. He is thus presented as an expert in literature; the desk he stands behind bears a very visible typewriter and a disordered mass of papers, the paraphernalia of a writer rather than a film-maker. Although his 'take' on Fitzgerald is to see in him a precursor of the Nouvelle Vague in general, and the Godard of *Pierrot le fou* in particular, he also mentions Chagall in this connection and his qualification as presenter of this particular programme is clearly not simply his cinematic celebrity. Rather, he is becoming recognisable as someone who talks with authority about culture generally, and we should not perhaps be surprised that in that same year, 1965, *Lettres françaises* published an article by the doyen of left-wing Communist-tending culture, Louis Aragon, entitled 'Qu'est-ce que l'art, M. Godard?'. The title was ironic, but it is still revealing. Godard the film-maker is someone of whom a *general* question can be asked – no longer 'what is cinema?' but 'what is art?' – by a very established member of the politicised intelligentsia.

In his later films (from *Loin de Vietnam*), Godard increasingly appears in a more substantial role, no longer in front of a microphone or a pile of papers, but next to a camera or to editing or projecting equipment, if he is not, as in *Soigne ta droite*, shown stumbling under the weight of piles of cans of film. This firm identification with his work as film-maker extends to still photographs, such as the cover of the 1985 edition of *JLG par JLG*, the monumental collection of his essays and interviews which *Cahiers* first published in 1968, and have regularly updated and reissued ever since. The increasing importance in the development of the Godard persona of the idea of the 'expert' in the audiovisual medium belongs largely to a later period than the one under discussion, but its foundations are laid in the 1960s with his establishment as a general, cultural commentator. Arguably it is only after having attained that status that his position within the film world could have reached the paradoxical grandeur that characterises it today, that of the film-maker whose current films are practically unseen but who is an inevitable reference in even the briefest article on the possibilities of the film medium in France. It is perhaps thanks to Godard's notoriety, more than any other, that film-makers in general came to be considered part of that nebulous and questionable, but still surprisingly important, French confraternity called 'intellectuals'.

We now come to the ways in which Godard's growing reputation was mediated by the press, and especially to the ways in which his 'natural' constituency, the *cinéphile* community of film magazines, reacted to it. These magazines soon found Godard's 'stardom' singular and therefore began to contribute analyses of it, while not always being immune from the reactions and representations which defined it. In considering Godard's treatment in the film magazines, I am largely concentrating on those neutral publications which considered the Nouvelle Vague neither as the 'home team' (as *Cahiers du cinéma* of course did) nor as immediate and deadly rivals, as did *Positif* at this period. Although the loud and lively polemic between these two undoubtedly raised the profile of the movement as a whole, their *parti pris* (biased positions) make them less informative as to the genuine status of Jean-Luc Godard in the world of French cinema than some other possible sources which will be looked at here.

It was not, of course, only or even principally the specialist press which established Godard's profile. René Prédal in *Jeune Cinéma* (Prédal 1965: 30–2) notes that Godard's reputation is being boosted mostly by the popular weeklies such as *Paris Match* and *Le Petit Echo du monde* (not to speak of *Les Lettres françaises*). Verification of this in Julia Lesage's invaluable bibliography (Lesage 1979) shows indeed an impressive rise in press interest. The simple volume of articles appearing in these years is revealing. From a total of four in 1959, the number of pieces devoted to Godard internationally rises as detailed in Table 6.1[2]:

Table 6:1: French press articles devoted to Jean-Luc Godard, 1960–68.

Year	Number of articles
1960	40
1961	61
1962	75
1963	100
1964	119
1965	169
1966	156
1967	217
1968	241

When these are looked at in more detail, it is noticeable that although *Paris Match* figures relatively rarely, *L'Express*, another 'lifestyle bible' of the early 1960s, very quickly took interest in Godard, and published an extended interview in 1961. The general intellectual magazines also took an early interest in his work. In 1961, *Les Temps Modernes* devoted a nine-page article to him, and they continued to publish work about him in following years. *Esprit* adopted a negative stance to Godard's work, but felt it necessary to explain it at relative length, devoting five pages to *Vivre sa vie* in 1962. It is also interesting that among the discussion of his work, interest in his private life was not absent, a telling symptom of incipient stardom. An early indication of this was an anonymous article which appeared in *Time* in 1961 (Anon 1961), when *A bout de souffle* had just arrived in the US and *Une femme est une femme* was announced. The author goes to considerable, cheerful trouble to make the most of Jean-Luc's rather minor adolescent misbehaviour, raking up stories of class-skipping, petty thieving from his father and from *Cahiers*, and even 'a half-hearted pass at safe cracking', all in the interests of supporting his film habit. The general tenor of these anecdotes suggests that the author is trying to rival Truffaut's colourful and film-obsessed youth: the themes are almost identical.

Within the cinematic press, the irresistible rise of Jean-Luc Godard is remarked on and analysed notably in two articles which appeared in *Jeune cinéma* in May and June 1965, and in a different way, by the dossier which *Cinéma* devoted to him in the same year (*Cinéma 65* 1965). We will now consider these two testimonies to 'le PHÉNOMÈNE GODARD', as René Prédal puts it in the second *Jeune cinéma* article (Prédal 1965: 30).

The articles in *Jeune cinéma* by Jean Delmas (Delmas 1965) and René Prédal (Prédal 1965) provide a critical assessment of the phenomenon. Both, but particularly Delmas, are at best ambivalent regarding the films, but their major interest is the way in which the reputation of the film-maker has outstripped any possible merits that the films may conceivably have. They cite various symptoms of this, for example the retrospective of Godard's work currently showing in Paris, an honour which, Delmas notes, celebrities like Bergman, Visconti or Antonioni had hardly achieved in twelve or fifteen years, while Godard had done so in six. They also note the extensive coverage in the nonspecialist press.

Having established the extent and the nature of the Godard phenomenon, and their own very qualified appreciation of it, the authors go on to consider possible reasons for Godard's phenomenal success. The reasons they suggest are of obvious relevance to this study. Delmas, in the first article, notes what we have already noted in general terms, which is that the public in the cinemas for screenings of Godard's films was not numerous enough to bear the weight of his incipient stardom. The key to it must therefore lie in his reputation, spreading among those who do not appreciate or even necessarily attend the films. Having rejected one or two possible keys to Godard's appeal, such as eroticism – 'Eroticism? Sexiness? Frankly no' ('l'érotisme? le sexy? Vraiment non') – and the 'short-cut culture' appeal of his numerous quotations, Delmas's conclusion finds the key in a general cultural malaise. Godard, somehow, serves as a guide to modern life for an uncertain public, whose confusion he seems to share and to express:

> So one wonders if Godard's current prestige does not spring from his role as a medium for our uncertainty, our present demotivation. Some recognise in him their mental confusion, their acquiescence in nonresponsibility, their satisfaction with staying shut up in themselves as if in a prison ... But if the function of Godard's work is to bear witness for the prosecution – very innocently be it said – against us and our time, it remains to be seen why we take pleasure in and make a success out of that witness (Delmas 1965: 79).[3]

Prédal, perhaps more critical even than Delmas, contributes a further explanation: social peer pressure. Like Delmas, he notes that Godard's public is limited, but very sharply defined. His films are aimed at, and a success with, the movie-mad students and teenagers of the *Quartier Latin*:

> A clique-ish cinema meant for initiates only, his films are principally aimed at students – more exactly at overgrown schoolkids – who recognise in the outrageous provocation of his works their taste for organised heckling and prep-school practical jokes (Prédal 1965: 302).[4]

From the students, Prédal contends, Godard's reputation has spread to their elders, the previous generation of intellectuals who wish to avoid appearing 'old-fashioned' ('*rétrogrades*') in the eyes of their potential successors, and from them to a whole class of 'rich and middle bourgeoisie' with intellectual pretensions (Prédal 1965: 302). Godard's fame and universal acclaim in the weekly press, then, owes at least something to a 'vast movement of snobbery'. Although a rather jaundiced assessment, as the rest of the article further exemplifies, the analysis of the make-up of Godard's audience is highly convincing.

The dossier which *Cinéma* allocated to Godard in 1965 also deserves further attention. *Cinéma* is interesting anyway in relation to Godard: from a relatively early date it entertains a love-hate relationship which appears in the letters page as much as in the articles, and which it relates to a similar split among its readership. Many of its critics lose no opportunity to criticise, and there is an interesting account of a retrospective at Annecy which relays – while carefully attributing them to others – a series of insults ('Nobody came to accuse Godard of the boorishness, the impertinence, the sentimentality (!), the constant provocation, the bad puns, the stuffing, which his detractors systematically discover in each of his films' [Anon 1965a: 17, their exclamation mark]).[5] This and a negative review of *Une femme mariée* brought two letters published in the March issue, of which the second particularly deserves quoting. From a M. Daubanney at Sarcelles, it reads in part 'It is true now that M. Godard is a God (and he moves your hearts!!) and you want to make us believe ... that you never thought otherwise, and that you never frequented the Godard-phobes' (Anon 1965b: 87).[6]

This echoes the description of the audience at the Annecy meeting, which apparently ran 'from the most friendly Godard-phile to the most virulent Godard-phobe' ('du Godard-phile le plus aimable au Godard-phobe le plus virulent' [Anon 1965a: 17]). The editorial note to the letters observes that many unpublished letters were received 'to cover him with flowers or insults' ('pour le couvrir de fleurs et d'injures' [Anon 1965b: 88]). The magazine's posture, carefully maintained, is of mildly astonished neutrality: 'you must try to understand something very difficult for minds contaminated by the *politique des auteurs*, that is that we have no definitive opinion about him (any more than about any of his colleagues) ... Jean-Luc Godard is neither a genius, nor a loser' (Anon 1965b: 88).[7] The dossier devoted to him in the same issue opens – semi-apologetically – 'so here is a file on JLG. All those readers who hate or who adore Godard will be astonished ... We know that in their case "criticism", if so it can be called, is merged with emotional reactions which have nothing to do with culture.' (*Cinéma 65* 1965: 48).[8]

The policy of *Cinéma*, then, as of *Jeune cinéma* and the rest of the specialist press, seems to have been to stand a little apart from the phenomenon which they watched with a certain sophisticated horror as it swept the cinema-going – and even the noncinema-going – public. However, the title-page of the *Cinéma* dossier is an astonishing image. A double-page spread, it writes the name 'Godard' in a variety of ornamental fonts, diagonally across the pages as backdrop to a full-length figure of the man himself, complete with dark glasses and a microphone on a pedestal, before which he stands, with an expansive gesture towards a notional public. Despite his suit he could equally well be a rock star as a film-maker or an intellectual. It is probably the most convincing image of Godard as star to be found anywhere.

Godard was clearly fast becoming a public star, at least in the opinion of those within the world of cinema who had never seen anything like it before. One can read in the ironic disavowal of the film magazines the degree to which such status accorded to a film-maker was novel and disorientating. The critics find it hard to credit that the reaction to any director's work can be so clearly emotive, and *Jeune cinéma* compares it to 'a jazz star's fans breaking chairs the day that the idol is "revealed"' ('les fans d'une vedette de jazz cassant les chaises au jour où se "révèle" l'idole.' [Delmas 1965: 7]). But the critical establishment, despite its wariness, found itself impelled, or perhaps constrained, to pay homage to the phenomenon. The *Cinéma* dossier is already entitled 'Godard par Godard' (three years before *Cahiers* published the first edition of its book) and consists in large part of a collection of his own comments. In 1967, Godard merited a number of the review *Etudes Cinématographiques*, the first contemporary, French film-maker to be considered in this prestigious series (Estève 1967).

By the end of the 1960s, then, the name of Godard was beginning to acquire a significance separate from the actual activity of Jean-Luc Godard. For the critics, he became the inevitable term of comparison in certain, well defined contexts. Any fragmented or collage-type formal structure, or comment on society in the course of a film, is apt to call forth a reference to 'the influence of Godard', or to an attempt to 'go beyond Godard'. On the other hand, when foreign film-makers are asked to comment on contemporary French cinema, Godard is the instant (although not always the positive) reference. The fact that this reaction occurs even when the film-maker in question is about to declare that he dislikes Godard indicates the importance that Godard had gained in the landscape of the French and even of the European cinema of the 1960s. If, in the early 1960s, he is quoted in conjunction with Truffaut, by the end of the decade the names are more cosmopolitan, more typed in the region of the 'all-round intellectual' in the French tradition – Pasolini, for example. Godard has become *the* name in French cinema among film-goers and film-makers, who have mostly seen his films. Outside that narrow circle, his reputation, if not his work, was perhaps even clearer.

'Godard has been, for men of my generation, I think, at least for me … *cinema*: that's all' ('Godard a été, pour les hommes de ma génération, je crois, en tout cas pour moi … *le cinéma*: c'est tout' [Desbarats and Gorce 1989: 122]). The Italian poet Edoardo Sanguineti, the same age as Godard, contributed this comment to a book published by the Cinémathèque de Toulouse in the late 1980s with the promising title of *L'Effet Godard*, which aimed specifically to examine Godard's image. Part of the book consists of the questioning of a certain number of celebrities, although the question ('What influence has Godard had on your work?') was perhaps not well chosen, since several answers claim no influence while admitting admiration or respect. Sanguineti's comment is interesting because it is not the response of a *cinéphile*: it implies no deep engagement with Godard's work, as some of the others do; it is, rather, a symbolic response. Godard becomes a kind of *Monsieur Cinéma*. This reputation has passed also through a small number of sayings, constantly repeated for their pithy summing-up of the effect which cinema can have: 'Cinema is truth 24 times a second' (actually said by a character in *Le Petit Soldat*, although always attributed unquestioningly to the film-maker); 'a tracking shot is a moral question'; 'it's not the only possible image, it's only a possible image'. ('Le cinéma c'est la vérité 24 fois par seconde' ; 'un travelling c'est une affaire de morale' ; 'ce n'est pas l'image juste, c'est juste une image').

So, what does Godard represent, and how far would we concur with the analysis of his star status offered by Delmas and Prédal in 1965? *L'Effet Godard* describes his films as 'work that is little known and poorly understood, despite its author's notoriety' ('une oeuvre mal et peu connue, malgré la notoriété de son auteur' [Desbarats and Gorce 1989: 122]). The description can be compared with that given by Bergala in 1990 and quoted above. Even at the end of the 1960s it summed up the situation well. At this point in Godard's career, as perhaps still in the early 1990s, that notoriety was based on the reputation, or the rumour, of the effect of Godard's films, fanned by media interest and media presence in an 'intellectual' context. A reputation for difficulty, or lack of concession, for fragmentation and for cryptic comment on a variety of subjects was perhaps not one that would encourage the average cinema-goer in search of entertainment to seek out his films, but it was all-pervading and any films with which his name was linked became branded with it. This led to a considerable degree of interest in the combination of Godard's name with those of other stars. Since Godard's reputation was for unconventionality and spiky individualism, what would he do confronted with personalities such as Bardot, of whom the public expected many specific things, some at least of which seemed contrary to much that Godard stood for? Throughout the 1960s Godard worked with several actors who would qualify as stars, at least within French culture and in some cases internationally: Jean-Paul Belmondo (*A bout de souffle*, *Pierrot le fou*), Brigitte Bardot (*Le Mépris*), and even the Rolling Stones (*One + One*), Yves Montand and Jane Fonda (*Tout va bien*, in the 1970s). Such collaborations were seen as an event at the time. The filming of *Le Mépris*, especially, occasioned great interest, such as might be expected from the encounter of two great icons of cinema. Personality clashes were half-expected, but they seem not to have taken place. When Marina Vlady worked with Godard on *Deux ou trois choses*, their collaboration was the subject of another episode of *Dim Dam Dom*, in which Vlady is lavish in her praise of the director. Godard was a little less fulsome with regard to Vlady. She seems to have recruited herself – or to have been recruited – to the cause of furthering his stardom.

The cases mentioned above are admittedly not entirely comparable. Godard worked with Belmondo *before* the actor had acceded to his full glory, and the stardom of both was launched with the same film. Bardot, the Stones, Fonda and Montand, and to a rather lesser extent Vlady, were already there. However, the director's personality is here in conflict with that of very major star names for 'possession' of the films, both in terms of influence over their making, and the determination of audience expectations as they go in to see them. In the case of *Le Mépris*, Godard, still in the process of establishing himself, seems to have been very aware of this and to have felt the need to affirm his ownership with more than ordinary emphasis. To that end the credit 'A film by Jean-

Luc Godard' ('un film de Jean-Luc Godard') is not written but spoken, and the unusual procedure draws attention to the words. Of course in the case of *Le Mépris*, Godard was dealing with another very eminent film-maker, Fritz Lang, as well as with Bardot and with an American male star (Jack Palance), who by all accounts was highly self-assertive, so that his need to place himself firmly in authorial control is not surprising. Although it would be difficult without audience analysis of these films to prove the contention, I would suggest that, certainly by now, and probably even at the moment of their making, they are watched as Godard films primarily, as part of the corpus of the stars only secondarily. They mostly stand out against the actors' other appearances – *Le Mépris* famously covered Bardot's blonde mane with a short, dark wig – while all are imprinted with the Godard manner.

Of course, working with Bardot, Vlady and so on increased Godard's attraction for the nonspecialist media. His consistent good relations with his actress stars, and his ability to successfully adapt them to his image rather than pay homage to theirs, contributed to the respect in which he was held; and also, no doubt, to his fashionable success. By the end of the 1960s the 'Godard effect' benefited, however, from a further element, one which seems very clearly prefigured by the analyses of *Jeune cinéma* in 1965. The reaction to *La Chinoise* (1967) could indeed be seen to be the logical end to a continuous process whereby Godard did become, increasingly, an exemplar and spokesperson for the movements of the times, both for 'our uncertainty and demotivation' (Delmas 1965: 79) and for 'organised heckling' (Prédal 1965: 302). With hindsight, it is very clear that the best-known elements of the Godard style (and you did not need to watch the films to know of them) coincided, and developed, with the tendencies and developments of the most innovative currents of the 1960s, currents which were remarkably high-profile in this decade of all-pervading innovation.

Thus the increasing attention given by Godard to sociopolitical problems and issues corresponded to a growing politicisation of society which had been proceeding in France since the Algerian War, along with the developing influence of a US counter-culture following in the wake of the mainstream influence of the 1940s and 1950s. The other members of the Nouvelle Vague seem not to have perceived this current, or not to have been interested in it, but Godard's increased engagement with it corresponded with the growth of political awareness among society at large, especially the young, urban middle-class (and students, middle-class or not). The unease surrounding the Vietnam War, for example, which most French intellectuals, and indeed French cinema, largely ignored throughout the 1960s, perhaps because of the uncomfortable closeness of France's own, traumatic confrontation with similar issues, appears in Godard's work in 1965 (*Pierrot le fou*). In *Le Petit Soldat* he even dared to approach the issue of Algeria, but while the ambiguous political stance of that film was interpreted as favouring the Right as often as the Left, and annoyed both sides, as the decade went on the films' stance increasingly corresponded with a radical approach, while still remaining ambiguous.

I believe it is important to this aspect of Godard's reputation that until the end of the 1960s his general interest in social issues did not translate into a definite political stance which could have attached a party label to him. An elliptical and enigmatic manner of tackling the subjects established him as a commentator rather than a polemicist, and a commentator whose comments could be taken in several different ways and therefore were widely applicable. The audience could take what it wanted. The fact that this could also work in reverse, as it did with *Le Petit Soldat* – with each side reading the film as against their interpretation – did not necessarily harm Godard's growing status. It created arguments about the films and the issues involved, which spilled gradually into the consciousness of those who did not feel obliged to watch the films themselves. The division between 'Godard-philes' and 'Godard-phobes' became a real polarisation, as noted above.

The films were also synchronised with the development of French society in their borrowings from and repeated references to popular art, comic strip (*bandes dessinées*) and adverts. Not only did everyone watch these and know them, but their increasing visibility was making them a social issue which other artists elsewhere were latching on to. In an increasingly media-dominated culture, interest was growing in the medium itself as well as the message, and not least amongst media professionals themselves, who were very willing to spread and increase the reputations of artists who took them as subject. Warhol thus increased his public profile. Godard's films were concerned with the media, and the media therefore were interested in them and in him, even if the larger part of their audience would not have great taste for the complications of the films concerned.

All this came to a head in 1967–1968. *La Chinoise* appeared in 1967 to mitigated interest, the Marxist-Leninist student groups which it took as subject objecting – with some justification – to its satire. But the events of 1968 caused the film to take on a new significance. Godard was the only film director, indeed the only mainstream creator, who had thought this a worthwhile subject.[9] *La Chinoise*, with its homage to Brechtian performance and disrupted presentation of the students' desire for disruption, suddenly appeared prophetic when its subjects and those like them burst into the headlines and the television news. Godard's wholehearted absorption in the movements of 1968 – his important role in the *Etats-Généraux du cinema*,[10] his withdrawal into a collective committed to making political films – retrospectively eliminated any suspicions over his motives in making the film. From being the representative of innovative cinema in France he became the main name associated with political cinema, or with political engagement. This reputation went beyond the world of cinema; to many insiders he represented a form of commitment possible to the artist/creator, to the wider world he became to some extent the future, radical cinema itself. Perhaps it is at this time – paradoxically when his public visibility reduced dramatically – that Godard's persona of 'Monsieur Cinéma' began to fix itself in the public mind. Truffaut wrote of him in the *Nouvel Observateur* (1968: 53) 'From May 1968 onwards, he has been the only French artist to know what was really important' ('A partir de mai 1968, ça a été le seul artiste français qui savait ce qui était réellement important').

Stardom, then, came through being seen as the spokesperson of new currents of culture. His beginnings in the Nouvelle Vague, however, remained extremely relevant to his new celebrity. The Nouvelle Vague had received very wide public enthusiasm from even a middle-of-the-road audience. Godard was certainly not the most reassuring or lovable of its exponents, but his connection with the movement gave him a cultural respectability which the younger avant-garde film-makers of the late 1960s lacked. Even if his work was known to be difficult, it did not come out of an artistic or political ghetto: his face was known; his friends were known; his origins were known. To express an interest in Godard was then to connect oneself with the fashionable cultural interests of the time, to express a degree of political and even of artistic engagement, without leaving the relatively safe shores of mainstream French culture. It is perhaps this attitude which assured that

Godard's name remained attached to connotations of culture which other film-makers were exploring sometimes more radically than he was. In the confusion of 1968 and its aftermath, it is likely too that for a number of people the new currents of thought, which could no longer be ignored, seemed alarming, and in order to explore them and make sense of them there was an actual need for established figures who seemed to be navigating without difficulty these dangerous waters. Sartre to some extent fulfilled that need, but Godard was younger and more radical, and seemed more thoroughly integrated in the new youth movement.

During the early 1970s the number of people who saw Godard's production could surely not have been more than a few hundred, those that understood it considerably less. But those who knew why they were not seeing any of Godard's production were much more numerous. Godard's 'disappearance' may in a way, have added to his stature, which became apparent when he returned to mainstream cinema in the early 1980s.Without any actual production, the connotations of the figure became fixed. These connotations still remain today. A recent discussion with a French law student, not with any great cinematic culture, revealed that, though not greatly interested in the Nouvelle Vague and never having heard of Agnès Varda, for example, she recognised Godard as 'somebody' ('quelqu'un'), and that if he appeared on television she would probably watch the programme, because, in a rather vague way, he was perceived as 'having something to say', even though she had never seen any of his films.

Godard remains a star, although for some time he was a hidden one. He himself said, in an interview with *Libération* in 1996, that by dint of having moved into the margins, he had, little by little, left the page altogether (Haizfeld 1996: 52). Throughout the 1990s, the occasional films he made were almost as invisible as the Dziga-Vertov productions.[11] And yet, although he may have left the screen, he never 'left the page'. His name was a reference, his reputation, though vague and even somewhat outdated, remained alive. He began to reposition himself as a cinematic Wise Old Man somewhere in the Swiss mountains, arranging parts for himself in several films which made that status explicit. With the monumental *Histoires du cinéma,* his reclusive position began once more to change; the series was the object of concentrated televisual attention and considerable hype. Evidence of his status can be gleaned from the advertising campaign launched in 2000 by the internet employment agency Monster: under the slogan 'Don't Waste Your Talent', a Godard lookalike was presented attempting, ineptly, to adapt to work as a shop assistant. The campaign itself – to which Godard gave his blessing – generated a certain amount of press interest, with articles in *Libération* and *Elle*.[12] And, at the start of the new millennium, Godard's international visibility once again increased. *Eloge de l'amour* (*In Praise of Love*, 2001) achieved both general theatre and DVD release in the UK and the US (paradoxically, especially given its strong criticism of US cultural imperialism, it is currently only on offer in France as an import from the United States) and aroused considerable discussion. *Notre Musique* (*Our Music*, 2004) had less immediate impact abroad, but it certainly did not pass unnoticed, and Godard's presentation of it at the Cannes film festival made headlines and provoked one journalist to observe:

> Jean-Luc Godard was indisputably the star of the day. ... The man isn't yet a myth, but he is a genius, or at least he's treated like one. There's a Godard magic, as if his films, his statements were somehow essentially different from others.[13]

The article continues with the expression of certain doubts about the position which Kontcheff identifies in the film, doubts more philosophical and political than cinematic. In fact, the Godard of the new millennium has returned to the domain which made his name at the end of the 1960s: his films of the early 2000s engage directly with contemporary political debates perceived as both urgent and complex, while preserving an enigmatic style which prohibits easy labelling. In seeming to pose more questions than they answer, and conveying a strong sense of unease, they accurately locate the changing priorities of cultural debate and the concerns of a small, but active, audience. While his Nouvelle Vague colleagues Claude Chabrol, Jacques Rivette and Eric Rohmer continue to produce films and command respect for it, and François Truffaut, *post mortem*, has become a much-loved institution, all – with the possible exception of the discreet Rivette – have become somewhat familiar presences, part of the mingled current of the French cinematic mainstream. Godard has never become familiar or integrated; he remains an exception, a challenge and, clearly, still a star.

Notes

1. In her article on Welles, Houston notes that his famous broadcast was not particularly striking; the credit, if that is the right word, should properly go to the gullibility of the audience (1980: 1056).
2. After 1968, where the data in the table ends, the number drops off. In 1974, after six years of obscurity with the Dziga-Vertov group, only thirty-five documents on Godard appeared.
3. Alors on se demande si le prestige présent de Godard ne tient pas à son rôle de médium pour notre incertitude, notre démobilisation présente. Les uns trouvent en lui leur confusion d'esprit, leur complaisance à la non-responsabilité, leur contentement à rester enfermés en eux-mêmes comme dans une prison. ... Mais si la qualité de l'œuvre de Godard est de témoigner à charge, très innocemment du reste, sur nous et notre temps, il resterait à savoir pourquoi nous prendrions plaisir et ferions un succès à ce témoignage.
4. Cinéma 'de Chapelle' pour seuls initiés, ses films s'adressent avant tout aux étudiants – aux potaches plus exactement – qui retrouvent dans les outrances provocatrices de ces œuvres leur goût pour le chahut organisé et les canulars des normaliens.
5. Personne ne vint reprocher à Godard cette muflerie, ce culot, cette mièvrerie (!), cette constante provocation, ces mauvais jeux de mots, ces scènes de remplissage que les détracteurs décèlent systématiquement dans chacun de ses films.
6. Il est vrai maintenant que M. Godard est un Dieu (et il émeut vos cœurs!!) et vous voulez nous faire croire ... que vous n'avez jamais pensé autrement, que les Godard-phobes, vous ne les fréquentez guère.
7. [I]l vous faut essayer de comprendre ce qui est fort difficile pour des esprits contaminés par la politique des auteurs, que nous n'avons sur lui (pas plus que sur ses confrères) d'opinion définitive ... Jean-Luc Godard n'est ni un génie, ni un raté.
8. Voici donc un dossier JLG. Tous ceux de nos lecteurs qui haïssent ou idolâtrent Godard s'en étonneront ... Nous savons que pour eux la 'critique', si l'on peut dire, se confond avec des mouvements passionnels qui ne relèvent plus de la culture.
9. Actually, Resnais, an eminent director on the fringes of the Nouvelle Vague, had, in *La Guerre est finie* in 1966, touched on the new face of radicalism. However, he had done it through a protagonist firmly committed to the old dispensation, through a straightforward fiction, which was not particularly innovative (indeed much less so than many of his other films), and with cultural references and apparently cultural proclivities which all tended to the world of his middle-aged militant hero.
10. *Etats-Généraux du cinéma*: the series of meetings held from 17–25 May 1968 in an attempt to reformulate the structures of French cinema. The 'Etats-Généraux' developed into a coordinating body for radical cinematic initiatives, with its headquarters in the rue St-Georges. Godard participated in the making of several documentary shorts recording street activities for the *Etats-Généraux*: he later turned to politically radical and formally experimental production with a number of young collaborators. From 1969 they went under the name of the Dziga-Vertov Group.
11. See note 10.

12. 'Monster.fr recrute l'image de Godard', *Libération* 5919, 26 May 2000; 'Pub: faux Dutronc ou vrai Delon', *Elle* 2841, 12 June 2000. Both reproduced on the agency's own website: http://www.monster.fr/presse/gpublic.stm.

13. Jean-Luc Godard est l'incontestable star du jour. ... L'homme n'est pas encore un mythe, mais il est un génie, en tout cas traité comme tel. Il y a une magie Godard, comme si ses films, comme si sa parole n'étaient pas tout à fait de la même essence que les autres.' (Christophe Kontcheff, *Politis*, 19 May 2004, http://www.politis.fr/ article967.html).

CHAPTER 7

THE INTELLECTUAL AS CELEBRITY: CLAUDE LÉVI-STRAUSS

Christopher Johnson

If there is an intellectual in France who has achieved an iconic status at least comparable to that formerly enjoyed by Jean-Paul Sartre, it is Claude Lévi-Strauss. An anthropologist by training, author of works whose technical complexity exclude all but a small group of specialists, everything would seem to confine this figure to the rarefied sphere of academic exchange. And yet Lévi-Strauss's reputation extends far beyond his own area of specialisation. In France, at the beginning of the twenty-first century, he has assumed the status of the elder of the tribe, a respected sage, a 'living national treasure' (Clément 1993: 22). Repeatedly, surveys of the French intellectual scene have designated him as France's leading thinker, and he has been the subject of countless interviews.[1]

Born in Brussels in 1908, Lévi-Strauss's original training was in philosophy, but like a number of his contemporaries he quickly became disillusioned with the subject and decided to concentrate on ethnology. After a year in secondary education he was offered a teaching post in sociology at the University of São Paulo, which enabled him to undertake a series of fieldwork expeditions into the Brazilian interior. His contacts with the indigenous inhabitants are vividly described in *Tristes tropiques* (1955), an autobiography that rapidly became a best-seller and ensured his wider celebrity. The crucial

The Intellectual as Star.
© Jerry Bauer / Opale.

experience, however, was that of the years spent teaching in New York during the war, when he met most of the leading US anthropologists of the day, and began what was to be a lifelong friendship and collaboration with the Russian phonologist Roman Jakobson. Decisively, Jakobson introduced him to the methods of structural linguistics, which he would go on to apply in his pioneering work on kinship structures and mythology. After the war Lévi-Strauss remained in the

United States as French cultural attaché in New York, returning to France at the end of the 1940s. In 1950 he was appointed to the chair in comparative religions at the *Ecole Pratique des Hautes Etudes*, and in 1960 took up the chair in social anthropology at the prestigious *Collège de France*. In 1973 he was elected to the *Académie Française*.

From the vantage point of the present, Lévi-Strauss's position as an intellectual icon seems unassailable, but obviously this was not always the case, and his elevation to this position was neither essential nor inevitable. One could easily imagine an alternative scenario in which Lévi-Strauss would have remained an eminent anthropologist, of international repute (as a number of his contemporaries indeed are), but which would not have entailed any wider celebrity. Our task, therefore, is to examine the specificity of Lévi-Strauss's case, to reconstruct the different factors contributing to his unprecedented success as an intellectual celebrity. It could be said that the principal parameters of this celebrity were more or less set by the early 1960s, and the following reconstruction will deal mainly with this first period of his career. However, this reconstruction will not simply be a genealogical one, tracing the different stages of the making of a celebrity, detailing the events and contexts that make that celebrity possible. Equally, it will be a *structural* one, to the extent that the mediation of Lévi-Strauss, of his thought and his persona, could be seen to take place on three, interrelating levels, each of which is, in a sense, the condition of possibility of the other. The first would be the intradisciplinary instance of academic specialisation and academic recognition, in view of the immense contribution Lévi-Strauss has made to the discipline of anthropology. Without this primary instance of legitimation, it is difficult to imagine Lévi-Strauss's wider influence as an intellectual figure. The second level or instance would be the interdisciplinary effect of Lévi-Strauss's thought, more precisely, the phenomenon of structuralism as it developed in the wake of his pioneering work in anthropology. Despite Lévi-Strauss's various disclaimers regarding structuralism, it granted him a visibility and notoriety beyond the confines of his own discipline, in the wider arena of intellectual debate that has traditionally been so strong in France. Finally, the third instance of mediation would be the extra-academic mediation (and mediatisation) of Lévi-Strauss as an intellectual personality. This level of mediation would have less to do with the actual *content* of Lévi-Strauss's thought than with the *values* that might be attached to the persona of the intellectual. While this persona might to some extent be an externally generated construct – the projection of the expectations and imaginations of a certain public – it cannot be said that Lévi-Strauss played an entirely passive role in the process. Crucial in this respect are his many contributions to the more public medium of the interview, though perhaps even more crucial was his abandoning of academic protocol in 1955 to write what was essentially an autobiographical text, the best-selling *Tristes tropiques*. In a very important sense, *Tristes tropiques* is the key to Lévi-Strauss's celebrity: it is arguable that had he not published this text, he would never have attained the public profile he later enjoyed. But the phenomenal success of this book, still in print some fifty years hence, should be seen as continuous with and not separate from the other instances of mediation described above. To understand the man and his influence, more generally to understand how the intellectual becomes something more than an intellectual, it is necessary to examine each of these instances of mediation in their turn. My method will therefore be to work outwards from the primary instance of mediation, what one might term the instance of academic consecration, to the outer circle of influence just described, that of the mediatisation of Lévi-Strauss as an intellectual figure.

Anthropology

In anthropology, both in France and internationally, the importance of Lévi-Strauss's work is undisputed. He can be credited with single-handedly creating a new paradigm for French anthropology and more generally with initiating new areas of debate in the discipline as a whole. As a separate academic discipline, anthropology had been established relatively late in France and, before Lévi-Strauss, had lacked a coherent theoretical framework. In part, this was due to the influence of anthropology's sister discipline, sociology, as illustrated in the work of Emile Durkheim. Earlier in the century, Durkheim had been successful in establishing sociology as an independent new discipline, with its own distinct object, methodology and theoretical approach, at the same time contesting the more established positions of disciplines such as philosophy and history. An important feature of Durkheim's later sociology was the use of ethnological data in the formulation of his theory of social cohesion: his seminal book *The Elementary Forms of Religious Life* (1912) draws extensively on studies of Australian aboriginal tribes carried out by British anthropologists. However, it was Durkheim's nephew and close collaborator, Marcel Mauss, who came to specialise in anthropology and who made a crucial contribution to its academic provision in the university. It was Mauss who taught and trained practically all of the first generation of French ethnologists. It was also Mauss who published what is still one of the most influential texts in twentieth century anthropology, his celebrated essay *The Gift* (1925). Together, Durkheim and Mauss can be credited with providing the initial framework in which French anthropology was able to develop, but this also meant, inevitably, that ethnology was viewed as an auxiliary to sociology rather than a discipline with its own independent programme.

This brief parenthesis on the history of French anthropology is necessary in order to understand the context in which Lévi-Strauss's first major works were written, the powerful intellectual tradition which he had, necessarily, to reckon with. Typically, as with all original thinkers, his attitude towards this tradition was an ambivalent one. On the one hand, he was initially hostile to Durkheim's sociology, criticising its tendency to abstraction and its lack of feel for the nuances of ethnographic fieldwork. On the other hand, he later came to recognise the extent of anthropology's debt to Durkheim's thought, despite its limitations (Lévi-Strauss 1973: 57–62; 1978a: 44–8). Doubtless Lévi-Strauss felt Durkheim to be very much his analogue, a systematic thinker and a powerful producer of ideas – hence the ambivalence. Whatever the case, the title of Lévi-Strauss's first major work, *Les structures élémentaires de la parenté* (1949, *The Elementary Structures of Kinship*,1969), is visibly an echo of Durkheim's *The Elementary Forms of Religious Life*, and is similarly ambitious in both its scale and its scope.

The Elementary Structures of Kinship was the culmination of a period of intensive research undertaken by Lévi-Strauss in the 1940s, mostly outside of France, in the United States. While much of the text is highly technical, accessible by and of interest mainly to specialists of kinship studies, it is also of enduring interest to non specialists because of the strong theoretical framing Lévi-Strauss gives to the work. At the core of the book is a philosophical premise, a theory of human relations based on Mauss's notion of reciprocity. In *The Gift*, Mauss had argued that the non utilitarian exchange of gifts in traditional societies was an important agent of social cohesion, ensuring the mutual integration of different social groups and the resolution of potential conflict between them. In the *Elementary Structures*, Lévi-Strauss suggested that the reason for the prohibition of incest, a practically universal trait of human societies, was social rather than biological. This apparently negative rule also had a positive dimension, in that the prohibition of incest also meant the prescription of exogamy, the exchange of spouses, thus ensuring integration through intermarriage with other social groups.

Apart from Lévi-Strauss's sophisticated reworking of Mauss in the *Elementary Structures*, another distinguishing feature of the book is its use of models that do not belong to the sphere of sociological theory proper. This is the case with the reference to linguistic theory which, while not as foregrounded as in some of Lévi-Strauss's later studies, visibly informs the stated methodology of the book: to reduce the diversity of observable kinship structures to a small number of invariant, elementary structures.

The *Elementary Structures* definitively established Lévi-Strauss as a leading figure in French anthropology, and indeed internationally. The bold theoretical sweep of the book, its breadth of reference, covering an impressive range of world cultures, brought to anthropology a boldness of vision and a grand synthetic manner unknown since Durkheim. While responses to the book were mixed – more empirically-minded British and US anthropologists were suspicious of its generalisations – it represented a formidable challenge to sociologists and anthropologists alike. Equally distinctive were the book's philosophical leanings, which meant that interest in Lévi-Strauss's ideas was not restricted to anthropology alone.[2]

In principle, the area of enquiry opened up by the *Elementary Structures* could have provided Lévi-Strauss with a lifetime of study and a distinguished reputation among his peers. However, his election to the *Ecole Pratique des Hautes Etudes* in 1950 also carried with it a change in his area of specialisation, from kinship studies to the anthropology of religions. From the point of view of his subsequent celebrity as an intellectual, this transition represents a crucial turning point in Lévi-Strauss's professional trajectory. In one sense, it could be seen as entirely the result of contingent and external factors – the direction of his research being dictated by the title of the new chair. In another sense, though, and perhaps more profoundly, it would seem to correspond to a psychological trait which, for want of a better term, one might call intellectual nomadism. As has been noted, the area of research opened up by *The Elementary Structures of Kinship* would potentially have provided Lévi-Strauss with a lifetime's work, but in other respects it also represented a closed horizon. Rather paradoxically, the scientific ambition of the *Elementary Structures* and the reductionism that he promotes in this work lead him to a kind of intellectual impasse. The logical end-point of the analysis pursued in the *Elementary Structures* would be the formalisation – ultimately, the mathematisation – of the basic structures of kinship alliance. However, not only is Lévi-Strauss, on his own admission, not qualified to undertake such formalisation, it also seems that he simply would not be interested in following this path (Lévi-Strauss and Eribon 1988: 78; 1991: 52; Clément and Casanova 1973: 29–30). It is as if what matters for him is the *possibility* of reduction, or more precisely, the possibility of revealing that possibility, rather than its actuality. It is as if he were more interested in the delineation and occupation of a new terrain of speculation than in the long-term cultivation of that terrain. Viewed in this light, the conjuncture of 1950, the move to the *Ecole Pratique des Hautes Etudes*, might be seen as a convenient means of exit from the intellectual closure of an increasingly technical branch of anthropology. It could be said that the area he was now moving into, the anthropology of religions, and more precisely within this specialism, the study of myth, allowed more room for the kind of speculation already apparent in *The Elementary Structures of Kinship*, the practically inexhaustible universe of mythology providing the perfect terrain for the intellectual nomad.

Immediately, in the same year, the publication of his *Introduction to the Work of Marcel Mauss* sees Lévi-Strauss imposing his personal mark on this new terrain (Lévi-Strauss 1978b). In principle an introduction to a collection of Mauss's essays, in fact this text is in many ways more like an introduction to the next phase of Lévi-Strauss's research, a statement of where he thinks anthropology could and should be going. Significantly, while he repeatedly asserts the originality and the modernity of the master, he also parts company with him (and Durkheim) on a point of interpretation, the essence of which is that Mauss has allowed subjective interpretation to take precedence over objective analysis.[3] In this sense, Lévi-Strauss consigns Mauss to a certain prehistory of French anthropology, a distinguished predecessor, certainly, but one who did not follow the implications of his thought through to their logical conclusion. Lévi-Strauss's own formulation in the *Introduction* of the elements of a structural anthropology is presented as the continuation and completion of the path initiated by Mauss, the fulfilment of the theoretical promise of the master's work. Indeed, Lévi-Strauss positions himself and his discipline, anthropology, in such a way that the only possible future of Maussian sociology appears to be its conversion into this general (structural) anthropology.

If the *Introduction to Mauss* sees the disciple daring to measure himself against the master, appropriating his legacy and inflecting it towards his own, specific programme, then in the following years Lévi-Strauss proceeds, as it were, to put the flesh on the bones of this new programme. In this respect, a landmark text is the article 'The Structural Study of Myth', first published in 1955 (Lévi-Strauss 1958: 227–56; 1977: 206–31). At the centre of the article is the now famous structural analysis of the Oedipus myth, which can be seen as the starting point and the template of all Lévi-Strauss's subsequent work in mythology. This analysis treats the myth as a kind of second-order language: following the example of structural linguistics, Lévi-Strauss suggests that we should be looking at the rules underlying the production of myth rather than the actual 'speaking' of myth. But beyond the theoretical content of the article, for our purposes what is interesting here is the *performative* aspect of Lévi-Strauss's text, how he introduces the theory and how he validates it.

The style of Lévi-Strauss's theorisation of myth could be described as a combination of demonstration and speculation. Its structure is ternary, a three-step process consisting of first the delineation of a 'problem' (articulated here through the image of disorder and chaos);[4] second, the proposition of a solution to the problem (model or hypothesis); finally, the integration of the solution by expressing it in the conditional form of 'if X then Y'. Particularly important is the transition between the second and third steps of the process, the second step consisting of an act of speculation (here, the proposal of the linguistic model), and the third acting as the point of consolidation or validation of the hypothesis. In the present example, the point of consolidation is the point at which Lévi-Strauss summarises the main elements of the proposed structural method of analysis and then writes: 'If the above three points are granted, at least as a working hypothesis, two consequences will follow' (1958: 232; 1977: 210). At first glance, this proposition seems unexceptionable, a necessary part of the demonstrative process mentioned above. However, here as elsewhere in Lévi-Strauss's work, the hypotheses he advances are closed to the extent that he does not submit them to external verification and self-validating to the extent that he does not return to them. Propositions like this therefore function as a kind of rhetorical switching point, they permit Lévi-Strauss to proceed to the next stage of his demonstration, in what is essentially a one-way process: there is rarely, if ever, any reflexive questioning or revision of the fundamentals of the theory. It could be argued that as Lévi-Strauss's career progresses, there is an increasing asymmetry between his theoretical production and possible external sources of censorship and criticism, so that his thought achieves a kind of relative autonomy, a self-sufficiency, even a certain self-referentiality, which sets him apart from his contemporaries in the field of French anthropology, and grants him a kind of academic immunity.[5]

A final qualification, when looking at the different components of Lévi-Strauss's academic legitimation, would be that in addition to the theoretical texts examined above, he also pronounces more generally on the state of his discipline – its scope, its methods and its missions. This kind of meta-commentary is most apparent in the important collection of essays and articles published in 1958, *Anthropologie structurale* (*Structural Anthropology I*, 1977). While substantial sections of the book are devoted to Lévi-Strauss's two major areas of specialisation (social organisation and anthropology of religions), the later chapters take a more synthetic view of the discipline of anthropology and its place within the human sciences. Characteristically, this overview is not just descriptive – reference to the work of contemporary anthropologists, for example, a fortiori to French anthropologists, is limited or nonexistent – but also prescriptive, concerning the general principles and orientations of the discipline. Predictably, it is strongly coloured by Lévi-Strauss's own opinions and preoccupations, and sometimes reads as simply a transposition of what has been his own programme of research up to this point. Notable in this regard is his widening of the normal definition of the discipline by substituting the term 'anthropology' for the (in France) more common 'ethnology', and distinguishing between three stages or moments of anthropological enquiry: ethnography, the preliminary collection of data in the field; ethnology, the synthesis of data provided by ethnography; and anthropology, the comparative analysis of ethnological material, leading to a general theory of human society (Lévi-Strauss 1958: 355; 1977: 388). This redefinition of the scope of anthropology meant that it was not restricted to the so-called 'primitive' societies which had traditionally been the object of ethnology; it also meant that the theoretical ambitions of the discipline, as Lévi-Strauss conceived it, extended beyond the traditional ethnographic monograph, confined to this or that culture or cultural area. The name that Lévi-Strauss gives to this general anthropology (social, or occasionally, social and cultural anthropology) shows the influence of British and US anthropology, but the modulation of 'structural' anthropology, taken as the title of the 1958 text, also signals his own, original and distinctively *French* contribution to the discipline. The epithet 'structural' is an explicit statement of the scientific aspirations of the new anthropology, and this needs to be viewed in the context of the increasing prestige of the exact sciences and by extension, the human and social sciences, in the postwar period. For Lévi-Strauss, the bridge between the exact and the human sciences is structural linguistics, as pioneered by the Swiss linguist Ferdinand de Saussure at the beginning of the century. He believes that structural linguistics has achieved a degree of scientific maturity that can serve as inspiration to the other human sciences. His own use of the linguistic model, along with the enlarged scope he envisages for anthropology, as described above, would therefore place the discipline in the avant-garde, indeed at the centre of the human sciences in France.

Inevitably, the claims Lévi-Strauss was making for (structural) anthropology during the 1950s were not without effect on other, nominally proximate disciplines in the academy, since his programme seemed to suggest a realignment of the traditional hierarchy of disciplines. The most recently established of these, sociology, as we have seen, had originally provided the seeding ground for ethnology in France, but Lévi-Strauss's extension of the field of anthropology by implication reduced the position of sociology to a subspecialism of this more comprehensive and more universal science of the human. Similarly, history (and especially the new history) is seen as a discipline with which anthropology might have more in common than its ostensibly closer cousin, sociology, but even here, the relationship is not an entirely equal and reciprocal one, since it is articulated from the perspective of a discipline with a stronger, more clearly defined theoretical framework. It is philosophy, however, that represents the most problematic protagonist in Lévi-Strauss's reconstruction of the human sciences, since the synthetic and federating role he is in effect claiming for anthropology had traditionally been that of philosophy. The interdisciplinary effects of Lévi-Strauss's renovation of French anthropology, especially with respect to philosophy, will be discussed in more detail in the next section. For the moment, it is enough to note that Lévi-Strauss's capacity for synthesis, for overview, for reflexive statement on what his discipline is about and also what it *should* be about – this prescriptive element is particularly strong in his earlier texts – could be seen as an essential characteristic of the *maître penseur*, the intellectual guide who is not simply a producer of ideas and of theories, but equally and inseparably, an influential commentator on a given (inter)disciplinary field. By the start of the 1960s, in his inaugural lecture at the *Collège de France*, Lévi-Strauss is able to ask: 'What, then, is social anthropology?', and his response – that it is a semiology – immediately defines the discipline as a structural anthropology in the image of his own programme of research in the preceding ten years (Lévi-Strauss 1973: 18; 1978a: 9). At this point and from the prestigious position he now occupies, it is apparent that Lévi-Strauss has become more than simply a distinguished specialist in his discipline, that he has become in effect the voice of French anthropology.

Structuralism and the human sciences

The different aspects and stages of Lévi-Strauss's academic legitimation, as outlined above, show him as possessing considerable intellectual capital within his own specialism, anthropology, both in France and internationally. However, this academic profile is a necessary but not sufficient condition for his role as an intellectual celebrity. For this to be the case, it is necessary that the anthropologist become an intellectual in the French sense of the term, that his work have repercussions beyond the restricted sphere of academic production, that he contribute to the ferment of ideas and ideologies characteristic of the French intellectual scene. For Lévi-Strauss, a key factor in his early promotion to the category of 'intellectual' was the phenomenon of structuralism. In most standard accounts of French intellectual history, Lévi-Strauss is recognised as the father of French structuralism, though the origins of the movement were more diffuse than this (Piaget 1971). Very quickly, as early as the mid-1950s in France, the new models of analysis Lévi-Strauss was proposing for anthropology were provoking interest in other areas of study – Marxism, psychoanalysis, history, literary and cultural studies.

Just as it is impossible to imagine existentialism without a Sartre, it is doubtful that structuralism could have existed in the form that it did without the animating presence of Lévi-Strauss. His choice of the linguistic model is particularly important in this respect, since it gave the elements of a scientific method of analysis in a relatively assimilable form. Saussure's theory of language rested on a few basic distinctions and principles which, following Saussure's own suggestion for a more general science of signs, or semiology, could be applied to a whole range of cultural formations. While Lévi-Strauss's own practice of structural analysis is conceptually more complex, also drawing on other disciplines such as information theory and cybernetics, it seems that he foregrounds the linguistic model as the more 'user-friendly' of the various possible models of conceptualisation. To say that myth is like a language is intuitively simpler – and also aesthetically more attractive – than saying it is like, for example, an information processing system. So Lévi-Strauss's decisive role, in a period when many were turning to the human and social sciences for more rigorous tools of analysis, was to focus on an object that was essentially transcultural (a collective representation, i.e. myth) and provide a reproducible method of analysis appropriate to that object.

However, the phenomenon of structuralism is not reducible simply to the mediation – however skilful – of a technique of analysis imported from linguistics and other new sciences. It could be argued that, whatever its claims to scientific status, the whole enterprise of structuralism rests on foundations that are, in essence, philosophical. For it seems that Lévi-Strauss is never content simply to operate on the level of analysis, but that for that analysis to have validity, it must always be shown to be grounded in a more fundamental level of reality. Already, the opening chapter of *The Elementary Structures of Kinship*, which focuses on the 'problem' of the prohibition of incest, sets the philosophical tenor of the book, and the application of Mauss's theory of reciprocity in subsequent chapters is accompanied by an (in principle, unnecessary) attempt to demonstrate the deep-level determination of the principle of reciprocity as an essential component of the human mind. Similarly, for the structural analysis of myth to work, it is necessary that there exist a universal 'language' of

myth; that at a certain, unconscious level, the human mind
work always in the same way, regardless of cultural variations.
The mental unconscious that Lévi-Strauss proposes, analogous
to the deep-level structures of language revealed by structural
linguistics, would therefore be the transcendental ground
which guarantees the ultimate intelligibility of systems of
representation radically different from our own.[6]

Though Lévi-Strauss has tended to play down the importance
of the philosophical component of his work, in the context of the
French intellectual scene of the 1950s and 1960s the
philosophical implications of structuralism were not neutral in
their effect. Indeed, it would be appropriate to speak here of a
context of differentiation, if one takes into account that feature
of French intellectual life which demands the dialectic and
supercession of 'schools' or 'movements'. Because the
phenomenal success of structuralism in France in the 1960s is
almost impossible to conceive without the previous hegemony of
existentialism, of which it appeared to be a point by point
refutation. While existentialism was primarily concerned with
the immediate experience of the individual subject in-the-world,
with the question of individual choice and responsibility and
the importance of concrete, historical situations, structuralism
focused on the (unconscious) structures that precede individual
agency and resist historical contingency, and remained
resolutely closed to questions of a moral or ethical nature.
Inevitably, a polemic developed between the two movements,
crystallising around the figures of Sartre and Lévi-Strauss. In
Tristes tropiques, Lévi-Strauss attacked the subjectivist bias of
existentialism, asserting that a philosophy based on personal
experience can never tell us anything essential about society or
humanity and is simply a dramatisation of the individual
(1955: 61; 1984: 58). A few years later, in *The Savage Mind*, he
questioned the obsession of philosophers like Sartre with
history, arguing that their conception of the historical process
was purely relative. The societies studied by ethnologists also
possessed a history, but chose to represent it differently,
constructing their social identity around the repetition of
archetypal situations rather than in relation to a linear
sequence of events (1962b: 329–32; 1966: 249–51). In his turn,
Sartre criticised the abstraction of structural analysis, which
ignored the dialectical realities of concrete relations and of the
historical process. In his view the priority structuralism gave to
autonomous and unconscious structures dehumanised the
subject and excluded the possibility of individual agency. More

generally, he saw structuralism as the intellectual expression of a modern technocratic civilisation which had little use for the kind of critical reflection traditionally offered by philosophy (Sartre 1966: 94–5; see also Dosse 1991: 397–8).

Though some of Sartre's criticisms of Lévi-Strauss and structuralism were not without foundation, it was evident that the general tide had turned in favour of structuralism. Moreover, it could be argued that the rise of Lévi-Strauss as an intellectual celebrity during this period corresponds to a shift in perception as to what the intellectual is or should be. While Sartre belonged to the post-Enlightenment tradition of the intellectual as a moral consciousness and a moral agent (the *intellectuel engagé*, the socially and politically committed intellectual), Lévi-Strauss was seen to represent a new generation, a new breed of intellectual, the *savant* (expert, specialist, scientist), who felt no compulsion to pronounce on moral questions beyond their specialism, even less to take to the streets in defence of their ideals. Whereas Sartre represented the last of a generation of intellectuals operating in an extra- or para-academic environment, Lévi-Strauss's power base was firmly entrenched in the university and, within the university, in the most prestigious of its research institutions.

However, in spite of this 'professionalisation', so to speak, of the intellectual, in the case of Lévi-Strauss it cannot be said that the intellectual's moral mission has been entirely liquidated, rather it has been displaced. While Lévi-Strauss sees the role of the human scientist as first and foremost one of objective research and detached analysis (this is the principal ambition of structuralism), nevertheless there is an ideological dimension to his thought that is to an extent independent of the structuralist project. This has to be viewed in the context of what was, increasingly, the special status of ethnology in the postwar period. The decline of the European powers and the wave of decolonisation which followed the war had caused many to question the pre-eminence of European culture and consciousness and also to criticise its ethnocentrism. In this context it seemed logical that ethnology, as a privileged mediator of non-Western cultures, should become the special focus of such questioning and criticism. Indeed, in the 1950s and 1960s ethnology came to be regarded as a 'new humanism' (Bastide 1964), with a wider vision of humanity than the traditional philosophical version of humanism, whose conception of the individual subject was culture-specific and thus far from achieving the universality it claimed.

A number of texts published in the 1950s and early 1960s indicate that, in addition to establishing the scientific credentials of his discipline, Lévi-Strauss is equally concerned to articulate what might be its possible moral missions. In *Race and History* (1952), for example, he resituates the problem of racial inequality on the more abstract and philosophical level of the problem of human diversity, and suggests that this diversity is increasingly in danger with the spread of Western civilisation (Lévi-Strauss 1973: 377–422; 1978a: 323–62). This concern for cultural diversity is equally a leitmotif of *Tristes tropiques*, which criticises the homogenising influence of Western 'monoculture' and proposes that the example of traditional societies may precisely help us to remedy some of the ills of modern existence (1955: 501–15; 1984: 458–71). Later texts such as *Le Totémisme aujourd'hui* and *La Penseé sauvage* (1962 a and b) demonstrate that the systems of classification used in nonliterate societies possess a rigour at least equivalent to that of Western science, but they also argue that traditional systems of representation provide a measure of social and ecological balance that has been lost in Western culture (1962a: 136–53; 1964: 92–104; 1962b: 324–57; 1966: 245–69).

All of these texts show in Lévi-Strauss a conscience and a sensibility which is not necessarily in contradiction with the more 'scientific' side of his project. While he strongly resists the idea of an applied anthropology – anthropology is a human and not a social science[7] – it is clear that he views his discipline as a repository of alternative values, values different from those of the consumerist and materialistic societies of the West. We can now appreciate more fully the challenge that Lévi-Strauss's version of anthropology represented for philosophy. On the one hand, this anthropology presented itself as a science with philosophical pretensions (structuralism); on the other hand, this science was also a humanism with a more comprehensive vision of humanity and a critical mission that had traditionally been the preserve of philosophy alone. It was Lévi-Strauss's skilful combination of these two registers that explains both the pre-eminence of anthropology in the postwar intellectual scene and the alternately enthusiastic and hostile reactions structuralism received from the philosophical community in France.[8] Whatever the responses to his work, by this point Lévi-Strauss's status as an intellectual celebrity was now beyond question, his reputation rivalling that of Sartre. It remains now to see how that celebrity was extended to an even wider public.

Autobiography and iconography

One can think of a number of French intellectuals who, through the originality of their thought and the quality of their writing, have achieved a measure of celebrity outside of their respective academic specialisations. In the latter part of the twentieth century, intellectual figures such as Derrida, Kristeva, Foucault and Bourdieu all enjoyed international reputations. However, the celebrity of these figures has remained for the most part restricted to the academic and para-academic world, and they rarely impinge on the consciousness of a wider public. In principle, the same should be true of Lévi-Strauss: the two instances or levels of legitimation treated above ensure him a high profile within the French intelligentsia, but they do not in themselves guarantee a more general and enduring celebrity. For this to be possible, there needs to be a wider mediation of his thought and also, inseparably, the *incarnation* of Lévi-Strauss the individual in an identifiable persona. I say inseparably, because the normal condition of a wider public interest in a thinker, beyond the detail of his or her thought, is that this thought should be a source of values, and values need the guarantee of human and affective embodiment. We have already seen how Lévi-Strauss's scientific claims for anthropology were accompanied by a moral message which had particular resonance in the troubled international climate of the 1950s and early 1960s. However, it is arguable that this message would never have acquired such a resonance had it not been for the autobiographical mediation of *Tristes tropiques*.

By all accounts, the publication of *Tristes tropiques* is a defining moment in Lévi-Strauss's career, and a significant moment in the intellectual history of postwar France. The book was not originally Lévi-Strauss's idea. The initial impulse came from Jean Malaurie, the veteran explorer and ethnologist who had recently launched a series named *Terre humaine*, in which the first publication had been his own *Les Derniers Rois de Thulé*. Malaurie had already read Lévi-Strauss's 1948 doctoral thesis on the Nambikwara Indians which, he confessed, he had found very boring, but the photographs accompanying the thesis, he felt, revealed a complex and sensitive character. He therefore asked Lévi-Strauss to rewrite his thesis as a kind of 'philosophical travelogue' on the Indians of the Amazonian forests. The result was a text which, according to Malaurie, set the tone for the entire series (Douin and Portevin 1995: 13).

The book was not entirely without precedent in France. In the 1930s the ethnologist and writer Michel Leiris had published an autobiographical account of his participation in the famous Dakar-Djibouti expedition (1931–1933) (Leiris 1981[1934]). Whatever the merits of Leiris's text, it must be said that *Tristes tropiques* is in a different class altogether, not simply as a piece of literature, but in terms of its performance, what it proposes and what it accomplishes. The book is not an autobiography in the conventional sense of the term: there is no account, for example, of childhood experience or of psychologically formative events. In this respect, *Tristes tropiques* is not a confession; the reader does not immediately get the sense of the disclosure of a personality, of the 'man behind the work'.[9] Rather, the book describes an intellectual itinerary, part ethnological treatise (the chapters on the Nambikwara are often simply transpositions, sometimes verbatim, from the 1948 thesis), part philosophical quest, all of this delivered in a brilliant style reminiscent of Chateaubriand and Proust.[10] If the 'character' of Lévi-Strauss as such is not foregrounded, nevertheless, through the narrative of his professional life there emerges the sense of a persona which is strangely consonant with the discipline he has chosen to practise.

Part of the power of the narrative of *Tristes tropiques* derives from the fact that its structure is that of the classic rite of passage, the spiritual journey, the quest. Typically, this journey could be seen to consist of three parts or stages: the moment of revelation, the young Lévi-Strauss's realisation of his ethnographic vocation; the moment of initiation, the difficult and demanding experience of fieldwork; finally, the moment of social reintegration, the return from the 'exotic' to the 'civilised' and the different tensions and ambiguities this generates. Each of these moments or stages has its own, memorable features or scenes: the protagonist's description of his 'neolithic' affinity with the cultures he has elected to study; the episode of the 'Writing Lesson', a chief's attempted exploitation of the European's 'magic' during his stay with the Nambikwara Indians; the crisis of faith the protagonist experiences as he approaches the end of his initiation, which leads him to write a play (*The Apotheosis of Augustus*) on the reverse side of his fieldnotes. In the final part of the book, appropriately entitled 'The Return', Lévi-Strauss works through the existential dilemmas that precipitated his own crisis of faith, and which are endemic to the ethnographic vocation. He gives an impassioned defence and illustration of his discipline, in terms of both its intellectual integrity and the moral contribution it can make to contemporary civilisation. Particularly important here is his reference to Jean-Jacques Rousseau, who is presented as an important predecessor of the modern science of anthropology, but who also lends an affective resonance to the final pages of the book and crystallises what is its essential nostalgia. For Lévi-Strauss, Rousseau is a kindred spirit, a man not in his place and not of his time, never quite at home in his society or his century. The persona Lévi-Strauss presents in *Tristes tropiques* is likewise a restless soul, a nomadic consciousness, obsessed with the transience of the world and always searching for the past behind the present (1955: 41–3; 1984: 48–51).[11]

On one level, *Tristes tropiques* could be read as the journey in Lévi-Strauss's mind from the complications and the uncertainties of fieldwork to the relative stability of anthropological knowledge. In the fifteen or so years which have passed between the radical doubt of the fatigued ethnographer, dramatised in the play he writes, and the present moment of narration, the ethnographer has become the anthropologist, his social reintegration is in principle complete, the rite of passage has been successfully accomplished. However, the picture is not quite as simple as this: still, at the time of writing, there appears to persist a residual sense of crisis, a residual sense of the disenchantment expressed in the play, and it is this which gives the book its tension and thus its interest. As Lévi-Strauss later confessed, he wrote *Tristes tropiques* at a time when he had largely abandoned his ambition of being elected to the *Collège de France*, having already failed twice in his attempt to give to French anthropology the institutional and intellectual pre-eminence he felt it deserved. As a result of this failure, he considered his university career to be practically finished (Lévi-Strauss and Eribon 1988: 86; 1991: 58). On the professional plane, therefore, his wager, the risk he has taken in his unconventional choice of discipline, ethnology, has not yielded a reward proportionate to that risk and the sacrifice of self it has implied. Viewed from this perspective, *Tristes tropiques* can be seen as a final departure from convention, this time the conventions of his own discipline. Lévi-Strauss was aware when writing the book that it would provoke displeasure amongst his professional colleagues, and tells how the venerable Rivet, director of the *Musée de l'Homme*, abruptly severed relations after the book's publication (Lévi-Strauss and Eribon 1988: 87; 1991: 58).

Of course, in retrospect, it was precisely the unorthodox nature of *Tristes tropiques* which guaranteed the future success of Lévi-Strauss. It is tempting to speculate that, far from damaging his career prospects, it was a positive factor in his subsequent election to the *Collège de France*, and the widely acclaimed literary merits of the text were obviously instrumental in his later admission to the *Académie Française*. More generally, the book inspired a whole new generation of anthropologists and revealed the mysteries of ethnology to a wider public.[12] It described the discipline in a very immediate way, not as a dry, academic subject, but as a lived experience, depicting the adventure and exhilaration, the trials and tribulations of fieldwork, and the existential dilemmas facing the ethnologist. The book showed how these dilemmas were in a sense shared by us all, and how anthropology might help us confront the ambiguities of what was rapidly becoming a postcolonial world.

Tristes tropiques can therefore be viewed as Lévi-Strauss's first exercise in self-mediation, the first significant incarnation of his thought in an identifiable persona. Nevertheless, the construction of this persona is, in the final analysis, a one-way process: it is Lévi-Strauss who is in control of the image he projects. What happened in the wake of *Tristes tropiques*, and the fame that it brought, was that he was increasingly solicited to appear, to speak and to respond, in the qualitatively different format of the interview. In the interviews he has given, from the late 1950s onwards, there has been both an attempt to get the master to explain some of the more difficult aspects of his thought (structuralism is in the ascendant) and a demand for more of the personality behind the persona.[13]

Of course, a certain degree of vulgarisation and self-disclosure is an inevitable consequence of the genre of the interview, even in its more esoteric and academic forms. As distinct from the solitary and singular act of writing, the interview is a dialogue, an interpersonal exchange requiring the immediate presence and the performance of the subject. The public of the interview is no longer a virtual one: it is present in the form of the interviewer, who speaks on behalf of that public; who acts as the delegate and intermediary of their interest and of their curiosity. While it would be difficult to maintain that there is any perceptible distortion of Lévi-Strauss's thought when expressed through this medium, it remains that the structure of the interview of necessity dictates a different framing and a different emphasis. Thus, in some of the more substantial interviews, Lévi-Strauss is encouraged to expand and extend some of the more philosophical and ideological implications of his thought. This is the case, for example, in the series of radio interviews with Georges Charbonnier in 1959, where, questioned on the difference between so-called 'primitive' and 'modern' cultures, he develops the famous distinction between 'hot' and 'cold' societies, the first working in a manner analogous to a steam engine, producing its energy through a basic disequilibrium or difference of potential, the second functioning like a clock, periodically returning to a central point of equilibrium (Charbonnier 1961: 35–48). In the same interview, he is allowed to comment and speculate, at some length, on the different functions of art in traditional and modern societies, and on the future of painting as an art form (Charbonnier 1961: 105–75). Beyond the actual content of these comments and speculations, what is of interest here is how the medium of the interview permits Lévi-Strauss to elaborate on ideas and interests already present in his academic work, but in a setting unconstrained by the normal conventions of academic discourse. His pronouncements on subjects unrelated to his own immediate area of expertise – art, music, painting – show an individual of great sensitivity and culture, and they satisfy what is perhaps one of the essential requirements of the French intellectual: that he or she should never be simply a specialist, that intellectual power should be associated with something more than mere expertise. This can perhaps be linked back to the compulsion to personalise, to individualise, to incarnate, mentioned above. It is as if, by listening to Lévi-Strauss's musings on aesthetic and artistic issues, we gain access to another level of consciousness, and learn something more about the 'real' Lévi-Strauss.

Whatever its inherent limitations and ambiguities, the interview can be seen as another significant instance of the public incarnation of Lévi-Strauss as an intellectual figure. But there is a final form of incarnation which merits our attention, if only briefly, for its power of communication and connotation, and this is the photograph. The photograph could be considered to be the most iconic form of incarnation, to the extent that it can capture and fix the essence of a persona in a way that even the moving (televisual or cinematic) image cannot. The photographs of Lévi-Strauss available in the public domain normally accompany the texts of interviews or appear in special issues of magazines or journals devoted to his work. I will focus here on two of my favourites.[14]

The first photograph is a frequently reproduced one. It was taken by Cartier-Bresson in 1968 and appeared in a feature in *Vogue* in the same year, a clear indication of the international profile of this French academic (Cartier-Bresson 1968: 100–1). As with most photographs of the older Lévi-Strauss, it is taken at his place of work, here the *Collège de France*. The out-of-focus background appears to be a teaching room, reminding us of his role in the institution. His dress is typical of that of a Parisian university professor: semicasual but smart and elegant. The portrait takes the classic three-quarter pose, with the hand resting on the knee denoting a state of rest and contemplation. But the centre of the photograph, without doubt, is in the expression and above all, the look of its subject. The expression, unfaltering, betrays no emotion, but seems firm, even severe. The look, turned away from the observer, like all three-quarter poses, suggests that the subject is not quite here, that he is absorbed in some other thought or design. However, this absence is clearly not that of the idealist, it is not the ascendant look of a future-oriented voluntarism. The straight, horizontal gaze appears instead to be looking elsewhere, anywhere out of this world, whether it be to the exotic societies to which he has devoted his life or to a past which is irremediably lost. If an emotion can be attributed to this look, it is precisely that of nostalgia and melancholy, the '*triste*' of *Tristes tropiques*.

The second photograph again has as its setting the *Collège de France*, but this time the photograph is not a portrait, and the setting, it could be said, is as important as the subject. The subject himself is presented in a long shot, at the centre of the photograph, face and body half in shadow, his right hand raised and left foot forward as if on the point of advancing. The look is direct, but due to the distance and the shadow, inscrutable. However, the centre of this photograph is not the subject, or rather, it is the relationship between the subject and his surroundings. On either side of him, behind, and indeed extending outside the frame of the photograph, above his head and to his right, are identical rows of filing drawers: this is Lévi-Strauss in the archives of the *Collège de France* in 1964. If the first photograph concentrates on the person of the intellectual celebrity, draws us in and invites us to decipher a mood or an attitude, this second photograph conveys the distanced objectivity of the *savant*. While the intellectual or writer is often photographed in his or her study, surrounded by books (there are a number of photographs of Lévi-Strauss in this genre), here the seemingly infinite repetition of the archive, the sheer mass of information it contains, reminds us of what kind of intellectual Lévi-Strauss is, that the thought and theory for which he is responsible are the result of a long and laborious work of erudition, the incessant sifting and processing of data. It is also a graphic reminder of what in Lévi-Strauss's case might be termed the consubstantiality of the intellectual and his work. It shows him in the vaults of an academic institution, the most privileged in France, and it shows his person, his persona as being in a sense co-extensive with the institution and the discipline he represents.

Between them, these two photographs could be seen to represent the two sides or faces of a specific iconography of the intellectual, as incarnated in Lévi-Strauss, and they repeat, in microcosm, the main divisions of this study. On the one hand, there is Lévi-Strauss the anthropologist, human scientist, father of structuralism, member of the *Collège de France* and the *Académie Française*. On the other hand, there is Lévi-Strauss the romantic outsider, the restless and nomadic protagonist of *Tristes tropiques* who feels at home nowhere and who is not of his time. It is this tone of nostalgia, of resistance and contestation, the ambivalent counterpoint of the confident modernity of structuralism, which perhaps provides the key to his enduring celebrity as an intellectual, in that it responds to what seems to be a residual feature of modern secular consciousness: the desire for transcendence.

Notes

1. See, for example, the poll of students, intellectuals and politicians published in the journal *Lire* in 1981 (cited in Pace 1986: 1); more recently, a survey of contemporary French intellectuals in *Le Nouvel Observateur* placed Lévi-Strauss at the head of the different thinkers reviewed, before Gilles Deleuze and Jacques Derrida (Guillebaud 1993: 4).
2. A significant early response was Simone de Beauvoir's enthusiastic review (1949). Before this, Beauvoir had already consulted the proofs of the *Elementary Structures* when writing *The Second Sex* (Lévi-Strauss and Eribon 1988: 77–8; 1991: 51–2).
3. The disputed point of interpretation centres around the Melanesian notion of *hau*, the magical force which ensures that a gift is both received and reciprocated. For a more general discussion of this point in the context of the *Introduction to Mauss*, see Johnson 2003a: 73–4.
4. Typically, Lévi Strauss opens 'The Structural Study of Myth' with the evocation of a kind of tabula rasa, claiming that nothing of note has been accomplished in the anthropology of religion in the past twenty

years, and that for even longer the situation in the subfield of mythology has been 'chaotic' (1958: 227–8; 1977: 206–7).

5. In a special number of the journal L'Arc devoted to Lévi-Strauss's work, the ethnologist Jean Guiart recognises the immense influence Lévi-Strauss has exercised on the shaping of French anthropology, but is at the same time concerned that without the presence and support of this great figure, the discipline would lose its sense of purpose and cohesion (1968: 66–9).

6. In a special number of the journal Esprit, devoted to the recently published The Savage Mind, the philosopher Paul Ricœur famously remarked that Lévi-Strauss's structuralism was a form of 'Kantianism without a universal subject' (1963: 618).

7. 'I do not care for applied anthropology, and I question its scientific value' (Lévi-Strauss 1958: 417, note 1; 1977: 380, note 16).

8. On the ambivalent relationship between philosophy and the human sciences in France, see Dosse 1995: 406–7.

9. Lévi-Strauss has on a number of occasions confessed to his lack of a normal sense of individual identity or personality. This self-effacement is not, as it might appear, simply a manœuvre to protect and preserve a certain everyday privacy; rather, it seems in Lévi-Strauss's case to be a genuine aspect of personal temperament (see Lévi-Strauss and Eribon 1988: 233; 1991: 168).

10. In his interviews with Eribon, Lévi-Strauss reveals that the book was considered as a candidate for the prestigious Prix Goncourt, but that unfortunately as a piece of nonfiction it did not qualify for nomination (Lévi-Strauss and Eribon 1988: 87; 1991: 58).

11. Again in his interviews with Eribon, Lévi-Strauss intimates that the key to his personality lies in the figure of Don Quixote (Lévi-Strauss and Eribon1988: 134; 1991: 93–4).

12. To date, the book has sold over 500,000 copies (Douin and Portevin 1995: 14). It was also for many years on the teaching syllabus for the French baccalauréat.

13. My own, rough estimate is that for the period from 1956 to the present there are more than fifty recorded interviews. These range from the mainly academic register of interviews published in literary and philosophical journals (e.g. Esprit, La Nouvelle Critique, Le Magazine Littéraire) to the more personal angle taken in the more popular media (e.g. L'Express, Mademoiselle, a televised interview with Bernard Pivot in 1984). For a more extensive analysis of Lévi-Strauss's use of the interview, and more generally of the role of the interview in postwar French thought, see Johnson 2003b.

14. Both of these photographs appear in the 1985 special issue of Magazine Littéraire (Grisoni 1985: 43, 47).

CHAPTER 8

'STARLETTE DE LA LITTÉRATURE': FRANÇOISE SAGAN

Heather Lloyd

Françoise Sagan became a major celebrity in 1954 at the age of eighteen, when she won a literary prize, the *Prix des Critiques*, with her best-selling first novel *Bonjour tristesse*. No discussion of celebrity in postwar France would be complete without reference to her, for a number of reasons. Firstly, coming to fame when she did, Sagan was a very early arrival in the postwar firmament of stars, predating Bardot and Hallyday, for example. Secondly, she was truly an icon, in that she was extensively photographed and her image was widely diffused in what, practically speaking, was a pretelevisual age.[1] Thirdly, she quickly came to be seen in France as bearing witness to the values and lifestyle of a new generation: the critic Emile Henriot, discerning in her third novel, *Dans un mois, dans un an* (Sagan 1957), an outlook on life which he believed to be shared by many young French people, commented: 'Her success comes as no surprise; she is representative [of her generation], she bears witness'. ('Il n'y a pas lieu de s'étonner de son succès; elle représente, elle est un témoin' [Henriot 1957: 8]).[2] Fourthly, as an international celebrity, she was viewed abroad as being an emblem of postwar France: in his biography of Sagan, Jean-Claude Lamy reports that when she visited the United States in 1956 the literary magazine *Saturday Review* ranged her alongside Chanel Number 5, Edith Piaf and Camembert as one of the great French exports (Lamy 1988: 197). When translations of her first two novels, *Bonjour tristesse* and *Un certain sourire*, were published in a British book club edition in 1958, the dust-jacket blurb included the comment that 'at twenty-two [she] can claim to be the most celebrated living French person' (Sagan 1958a). Finally, in that she was a writer, she was a distinctively French kind of celebrity, since France, it can be argued, has an unusual tradition of literary celebrity at the heart of its national culture. Priscilla Parkhurst Clark has analysed the status accorded to literature and writers in France in *Literary France: The Making of a Culture* (Clark 1987). Her central concern is with those who achieve the status of 'public writers', writers who are viewed in some sense as spokespersons for the nation on matters of high import, a group in which Sagan is not included. Nevertheless, the strength of the public acclaim which Clark describes as having been accorded to certain writers – Voltaire, Hugo and Sartre being the most salient examples – is convincing evidence of a quintessentially French tradition of the writer as popular celebrity.

But although Sagan emerged as a writer in a country where literary fame was always possible, and although she was to a significant degree shaped by French literary tradition and was even, in a sense, a product of the literary establishment, she was never just a famous writer. In a quite remarkable way, and virtually from the beginning of her career, she moved beyond the limits of literary celebrity to become a star, in the sense in which stardom had come to be understood by the middle of the twentieth century. She was famous as a 'personality', intersecting in her orbit with many other stars and celebrities: Brigitte Bardot, Juliette Gréco, Mélina Mercouri, Christian Dior, Roger Vadim, Jean-Louis Trintignant, Claude Chabrol, Yves Montand, to mention only a few of the most enduring names. The trappings and traditions of 1950s' stardom were all hers: her name became synonymous with '*la dolce vita*' which, both in perception and reality, encompassed driving fast cars, whisky-drinking, night-clubbing in Saint-Germain-des-Prés, partying in St.Tropez, spending freely the large sums of money that she early on accrued from her books, and, once she was old enough to do so legally, frequenting casinos – she adored gaming. She was the subject of innumerable articles and interviews, a trend which was set by the eleven kilograms of press cuttings that *Bonjour tristesse* (Sagan 1954), a novel of under two hundred pages, is reputed to have generated. She was avidly pursued by the popular press – for example, there

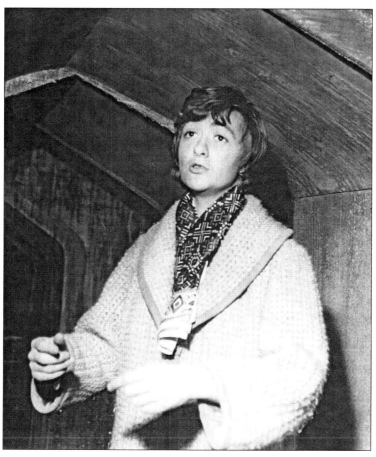

Françoise Sagan: *Sagan in 1975*.
© Collection Petit / DR / Opale.

were reportedly around two hundred photographers at her wedding in 1958 to Guy Schoeller, a publishing executive twenty years her senior. The break-up of the marriage in 1959 made the front page of *France-Soir*. When she gave birth in 1962 to a son, the product of her second marriage, to Robert Westhoff, the happy parents and newborn baby were featured on the front cover of *Paris Match* in that modern-day nativity pose that has entered the iconography of stardom. The subject of all this razzmatazz had, by 1962, it is true, published five novels, acclaimed in varying degrees from a literary point of view, and had ventured into the world of theatre. But her literary output in itself was hardly enough to explain her status as a major national celebrity, and in any case she had become a star on the strength of one novel, her first. Various factors in addition to literary merit are implicated in the rise of the Sagan phenomenon, among them her own background and propensities, the influence of the literary establishment, modernising trends in the book trade, and the emergence in the postwar period of a mass culture that was youth-and leisure-oriented, in a nation which was standing on the brink of redefinition. This essay examines how such factors contributed to the process of the creation and mediation of the star, and considers some of her incarnations as a star, up to the point at which, in the wake of 1968, the nation moved on again and Sagan herself outlived the myth.

'Une jeune fille scandaleuse et un écrivain bourgeois'

A striking and arguably very modern feature of Sagan's celebrity was that, with the publication of *Bonjour tristesse* in March 1954 and the much-publicised award of the *Prix des Critiques* in May of the same year, she shot to virtually instant stardom. Before this, her trajectory is short and easy to chart. She was born Françoise Quoirez in her mother's family home in Cajarc in the Lot (southwest France) in 1935. Her father was a well-off industrialist. The Quoirez's permanent home was in the bourgeois seventeenth *arrondissement* of Paris, though they spent the war years in the Lyons area. By every account she had a happy childhood in a serene and relaxed family setting, though her formal education was somewhat chequered. She was expelled from two of the schools she attended in Paris: from the first, for pranks, and from the second, a convent, for what nowadays would be called an attitude problem but which was referred to then as her 'failure to be deeply spiritual' ('manque de haute spiritualité' [Sagan 1974: 36]). She gained her *baccalauréat* only at the second attempt, at the 'cours Hattemer'. She entered the Sorbonne in the autumn of 1952, cementing a friendship there with the daughter of André Malraux, Florence, who had also been at Hattemer. She failed the first-year *propédeutique* examination and spent the summer of 1953 reworking a novel she had written.

There are just about the makings here of a 'youthful rebel' strand for a copywriter to weave into the subsequent myth. Like

Bardot, she came from a privileged and conservative social background – the journalist and Catholic polemicist Georges Hourdin called her 'unarguably a product of the Catholic upper-middle class' ('un incontestable produit de la bourgeoisie catholique' [Hourdin 1958: 15]) – and her background served to throw into relief not only the racy lifestyle that she so readily assumed on becoming famous, but also the themes of her early novels. Even though discreetly handled, these were judged to be extremely daring. In *Bonjour tristesse* the seventeen-year-old heroine, Cécile, calls the shots in a relaxed, summertime affair she has with a young man, Cyril, on the French Riviera near St.Tropez, while using him in her plot to thwart the marriage plans of her widowed playboy father, Raymond, and Anne, the woman who would be her stepmother. *Un certain sourire* (1956a) recounts Dominique's affair with Luc, an older, married man, the uncle of her student boyfriend. In *Dans un mois, dans un an* (1957) we follow the criss-crossings of nine characters fruitlessly in pursuit of love (usually adulterous) in the *chic* but jaded Parisian social circle of writers, publishers and theatre people. In *Aimez-vous Brahms ...* (1959) a woman of thirty-nine leaves a long-standing relationship to have an affair with a younger man. In *Les Merveilleux Nuages* (1961) the heroine, unfaithful to her neurotic, young, American husband, wrestles with the dilemma of whether or not to leave him.

Models of stardom suggest that it is common for there to be an interplay between the images projected by a star's work and the star's own life. The question of whether the events in Sagan's early novels reflected her own experiences aroused great interest, all the more because the pace at which she pursued the social round and her expressed hedonism and *insouciance* seemed to be much of a piece with the lifestyle of her characters. She moved in social circles which seemed not too far removed from those described in *Dans un mois, dans un an*. Like Dominique in *Un certain sourire* she was attracted to a man much older than herself; having married and divorced the older man, she then, like Josée in *Les Merveilleux Nuages*, married a young American from whom she subsequently separated. And what of her first heroine, Cécile?[3] Reviewing *Bonjour tristesse* in *Le Monde*, Emile Henriot, who was not only a distinguished literary critic but a member of the *Académie Française*, gave academic respectability to the question which was no doubt in other minds: 'Is she already as terrifyingly experienced as her heroine?' ('A-t-elle déjà l'expérience effrayante de son héroïne?' [Henriot 1954: 9]). More brutally,

Bernard de Fallois, reviewing *Un certain sourire* in *La Nouvelle Revue Française*, comments that readers will pick up her latest novel each year and ask themselves 'Let's see, who has Françoise slept with this year?' ('Tiens, avec qui Françoise a-t-elle couché cette année?' [de Fallois 1956: 893]).

In subsequently discussing her image and her rise to fame, Sagan herself commented in her characteristically pithy way on the opposition perceived between the respectability of her background and the subject matter of *Bonjour tristesse*:

> In 1954, I had to choose between two roles that I was being offered: on the one hand that of the author of shocking books, on the other hand that of a middle-class young lady, whereas in fact I was neither of these things ... It would have been truer to say that I was a shocking young lady and the author of middle-class books.[4]

What the phrase 'the author of middle-class books' indicates is that at the source of the Sagan myth is a ferociously well-read young woman who, as an adolescent, had had a series of love affairs with works of literature. She later singled out as having been of special influence Gide's *Les Nourritures terrestres*, which she read at thirteen, Camus's *L'Homme révolté*, which she read at fourteen, Rimbaud's *Illuminations*, read at sixteen, and her great master, Proust – 'Proust, moreover, taught me everything' ('J'appris tout d'ailleurs, par Proust' [Sagan 1984: 150]). When her father asked her to adopt a pseudonym for the publication of *Bonjour tristesse*, it was in the work of Proust that she found the name Sagan. The title of the novel was itself a literary allusion, coming from a poem by Paul Eluard. Sagan, in the words of Brigid Brophy, was 'literate to her fingertips, which hold a pen saturated in French literature' (Brophy 1964: 61). Such was the young woman who provided the raw material for stardom.

The critical acclaim that greeted *Bonjour tristesse* and, subsequently, *Un certain sourire*, is striking for the wealth of literary comparisons that reviewers brought into play. Her writing was deemed to be in the classic mould, with its lucidity of style and perceptive analysis, and among writers to whom she was compared were Colette, Constant, Laclos, La Rochefoucault, Madame de la Fayette and Radiguet. Nor were such comparisons confined to the serious press: *Paris Match* ran its first article on Sagan in its issue of 27 March 1954, complete with a photograph of the author and typewriter, under the heading 'Behind *Bonjour tristesse* is an eighteen-year-old Colette' ('*Bonjour tristesse* révèle une Colette de 18 ans'). A popular, hagiographic work entitled *Bonjour Françoise* took the pursuit of literary affiliation to risible lengths when the authors pointed out not only that Colette died in the year that *Bonjour tristesse* was published, but that George Sand died in the year that Colette was born, and that, in the year that Sagan was born, Henri Troyat had just been hailed as the new Radiguet (Gohier and Marvier 1957: 9, 108). But for all that such linkages may seem contrived, they did serve to confirm Sagan as an important literary phenomenon and part of a coherent literary tradition.

Sagan's moment of anointing in the public gaze was undoubtedly just after she had won the *Prix des Critiques* in May 1954, when François Mauriac, holder of the Nobel Prize for Literature (as he reminded readers) and *doyen* of the French literary establishment, devoted an article to her, 'Le Dernier Prix' ('The Latest Prize'), which appeared on the front page of *Le Figaro* on the first of June of that year. Mauriac, like other critics, praises her novel in the most glowing terms from a literary point of view – 'Its literary merit leaps out at you from the first page, and is beyond question' ('Le mérite littéraire y éclate dès la première page et n'est pas discutable') – and makes the inevitable literary comparison, in this instance with Laclos, author of the great eighteenth-century novel *Les Liaisons dangereuses*. This comparison was a supreme compliment in one sense, but it was double-edged, carrying with it a strong condemnation of the jury's failure to select a spiritually more uplifting work. Mauriac's disapproval is tempered somewhat by his avuncular reference to Françoise Sagan herself as 'a charming eighteen-year-old monster' ('un charmant monstre de dix-huit ans'). The reactions of the 'charmant petit monstre', as she came to be known, were sought by the press and were gratifyingly forthright. Stating that Mauriac enjoys being indignant – 'It's his age' – she continues: 'This is very good for sales. You can count on it that the half a million people who have read what Mauriac has to say will rush out to buy such a shocking book'. ('C'est de son âge' … 'C'est une excellente affaire: vous pensez bien que les 500, 000 lecteurs de Mauriac s'empresseront de lire un livre aussi scandaleux' [Gohier and Marvier 1957: 180]).

A best-seller for a new era

Sagan's comment that Mauriac's indignation would be good for sales shifts the spotlight from the literary to the commercial foundations of her stardom. The birth of the star can only be properly accounted for if we examine first the birth of the best-seller. Through a chance meeting in the summer of 1953, Françoise had got to know Colette Audry who was involved with Sartre's journal *Les Temps modernes*, published by Julliard. It was Audry who advised Françoise about submitting her novel for publication.[5] Within a couple of weeks of her submitting it to Julliard, in January 1954, a contract had been signed and a publication date set for March. Plon, to whom she had also submitted the manuscript, also came up with an offer, but lost out to Julliard's rapid reaction.

The role of her first publisher in the trajectory of Françoise Sagan is extremely important. René Julliard was an energetic and astute player in the postwar French publishing scene, a relative latecomer when compared with his rivals, the well-established firms of Gallimard and Grasset, but in the vanguard as far as marketing techniques were concerned.[6] In that Julliard represented the modern face of French publishing, Sagan's success can be seen as due in part to modernising trends in that field. Christopher Todd describes the general ethos of the book trade at the point at which *Livres de poche*, the first paperbacks to be widely available in France, were launched by Hachette and Gallimard in 1953:

> In France books remained expensive, and it was, for instance, still thought to be a sign of good taste to distribute them with their pages uncut, so that the slitting open of the pages could form part of some sacred ritual for the initiated. A book was seen as an object of reverence to be approached with care, and not for general consumption (Todd 1994: 106).[7]

Although not involved in the launching of *Livres de poche*, Julliard was sufficiently in tune with the times, in the years after the war, to see the advantages of promoting young writers, particularly young women writers. Women were *à la page*. Female suffrage had been introduced in elections just after the war. Simone de Beauvoir had published *Le Deuxième Sexe* in 1949. Five important literary prizes had fallen to women since 1945.[8] Julliard had already published novels by Françoise d'Eaubonne, who was twenty-six on the appearance of her first novel *Le Cœur de Watteau* (1946), and Françoise Mallet (later Mallet-Joris) who was twenty-two on the publication of *Le Rempart des Béguines* (1951), a novel, like *Bonjour tristesse,* with a 'shocking' theme, where a teenage girl falls in love with her father's mistress. Sagan was therefore the third of *'les trois Françoise'*, a youthful female trio for Julliard to set against Grasset's heavyweights *'les quatre M'*: Mauriac, Maurois, Morand and Montherlant (Lamy 1992: 9).

In an interview that she gave in 1977, Sagan said, 'I am an accident that keeps on happening'. ('Je suis un accident qui se prolonge' [Ezine 1977: 5]). Certainly she was, and would continue to be, a very lasting phenomenon, but it is difficult in marketing terms to maintain that her fame was accidental. As a talented young woman writer, she was just what Julliard was looking for in the early 1950s to add to his stable. It was as a young writer, rather than a woman writer, that he chose to promote her. The French literary canon is not short of young writers. Rimbaud's *Illuminations* had been published while the writer was still in his teens; Hugo's poetic gifts had been recognised at an early age. Sagan's contemporary Françoise Mallet was, as noted, scarcely into her twenties on the publication of *Le Rempart des Béguines*. But one young writer in particular provided Julliard with a useful precedent to Sagan. Cocteau's protégé Raymond Radiguet was twenty when his novel *Le Diable au corps,* the story of a schoolboy's affair with a young woman whose soldier fiancé was at the front, became a *succès de scandale* in 1923. The publisher, Bernard Grasset, had heralded the novel's appearance with a strenuous publicity campaign which had included using the cinema – a Gaumont newsclip showed Radiguet supposedly in the act of signing the contract (Boillat 1973: 42–3). Julliard uses that memorable publishing event as a launch-pad for his own new protégée by having printed a wrapper to *Bonjour tristesse* bearing, along with a photograph of Sagan, the phrase 'Devil in the Heart' ('Le Diable au cœur'). This commercial ploy – the forging of a connection between Sagan and Radiguet – not only inscribes her in a literary tradition but gives a strong hint of scandal and points up her precociousness. The use of the photograph on the wrapper also draws attention to her youthfulness while, unwittingly no doubt, setting an agenda in which Sagan's image was to become at least as wellknown as her work.[9]

Having appeared in March, *Bonjour tristesse* had, by the beginning of May, sold a more than respectable 8,000 copies. But by October the sales figure was quoted as 100,000, a figure which, before the paper shortages of World War II, would have meant that a book could be considered a major success (Todd 1994: 3). By September 1955 the wrapper on the novel was announcing that 350,000 copies had been sold. Commenting subsequently on its success, Sagan pointed to its having sold beyond the traditional book-buying constituency: 'What if I had only caught on with the *bourgeoisie*? ... But that wasn't the case.' ('Si je n'avais «pris» que dans la bourgeoisie encore ... ce n'était pas le cas' [Sagan 1974: 47–8]). Sophie Delassein, Sagan's most recent biographer, notes that girls were said to be reading *Bonjour tristesse* surreptitiously, for fear their mothers would find out (Delassein 2002: 41).

It was the award of the *Prix des Critiques* and, as a consequence, the Mauriac review, that led a respectably-selling first novel to become a best-seller of historic proportions. In an interview reproduced in *Réponses*, an important compilation of interviews with Sagan published in 1974, she confirmed that the award of the prize was the catalyst for her fame: 'It was the Critics' Prize that triggered it all off' ('C'est le Prix des Critiques qui a tout déclenché' [Sagan 1974: 46]). In the immediate postwar period, Julliard seems to have been particularly alive to the value of literary prizes as a marketing tool, and particularly adept at using that tool. No fewer than eleven works published by him had carried off prizes since the end of the war.[10] Although *Bonjour tristesse* was not the favourite in 1954 to win the *Prix des Critiques* (a prize which had first been awarded in 1947 for Camus's *La Peste*), it squeaked through by two votes with a jury consisting of some of the most distinguished names in literary criticism.[11] But how was this accolade from the literary establishment to be interpreted? The day after the jury's pronouncement, Henriot featured *Bonjour tristesse* in his literary column in *Le Monde,* where he stated, astonishingly, that the award should not be seen as endorsing the suitability of 'this immoral book' ('ce livre immoral') as reading matter for the general public (Henriot 1954: 9). His comment betrays a fundamental misunderstanding of the function of literary prizes in an increasingly commercialised world, as does that of another distinguished member of the jury, Gabriel Marcel, writing in *Le Figaro littéraire* of 29 May: 'What worries me is the likelihood that this book will do irreparable damage to the image of young Frenchwomen in the eyes of foreigners' ('Ce qui me gêne ... c'est que ce livre risque de porter un coup fatal au prestige de la jeune fille française à l'étranger'). Such attitudes on the part of members of the very jury whose decision propelled her to fame indicate the locus that Sagan would occupy at a unique intersection between, on the one hand, literary tradition and the conservative establishment and, on the other hand, the new, populist, youth- and consumer-oriented value system emerging in the postwar period. There was not quite a clash between the two cultures; rather, in a curious way, they were set to mesh, since it was the literary establishment itself that provided the springboard for the success that Sagan was about to enjoy in the wider, developing social context, in which the cult of youth and the pursuit of leisure and pleasure were to be dominant features. As yet, in 1954, the old guard of the literary establishment did not recognise the cultural transformation that was taking place. Mauriac, while praising Sagan's literary gifts in the highest possible terms, objects to the *Prix des Critiques* having gone to her novel because in his view it fails to bear witness to 'the spiritual life of France which still burns brightly, indeed more brightly than ever, as those of us who remain in contact with the young people of this country well know' ('la vie spirituelle française, brûlante encore, et plus que jamais, nous le savons bien, nous qui demeurons en contact avec la jeunesse de ce pays' [Mauriac 1954: 1]).

In retrospect it is all too clear that 'the young people of this country' with whom Mauriac here claims to be familiar are not the same young people as those whose 'sun, sand and sex' values Sagan delineates, even though she may not ultimately endorse them, in *Bonjour tristesse*. Mauriac's journal of the period, published under the title *Bloc-Notes 1952–57*, gives an indication of the young people he had in mind, since the entry for 10 May 1954 records that on a Whitsun pilgrimage to Chartres Cathedral he had been moved by the presence there of twelve thousand students who had made the journey on foot, and at a most inauspicious moment in the national life:

> What a deafening silence greets those twelve thousand young men and girls of France, assembled beneath the most illustrious vaults of Christendom, in Péguy's cathedral, the day after Dien Bien Phu! … What a deafening silence reverberates throughout France as she stands bereft in 1954![12]

The Battle of Dien Bien Phu, which culminated in a traumatic defeat of the French and effectively ended French rule in Indochina, took place between March and early May 1954, the very period, coincidentally, during which *Bonjour tristesse* was selling so well back home. Mauriac alludes to this curious conjunction in his article in Le Figaro:

> France is living through days of anguish; her fate is being decided at this moment; it will be determined, perhaps, for generations to come. What relevance can there be in a novel written by a little girl who is too clever by far?[13]

Mauriac demonstrates a profound awareness of France being poised at a decisive moment in its history. But out of colonial decline and the traumas of its experiences in World War II, a new, modern France is emerging and finding expression, and in his Figaro article Mauriac fails to recognise Bonjour tristesse as an early manifestation of this modernity.

Mauriac, who was nearly seventy, may be forgiven for not sensing the direction in which the cultural wind was blowing. Bardot had not yet emerged as a star; pop culture had not yet really taken hold; it was not evident that Sagan was the harbinger of massive new trends. But only four years on, in 1958, when Flammarion published Bloc-Notes 1952–57, her quizzical little face featured in the checkerboard design of the cover, one of sixteen famous faces, including those of Sartre, Camus, Malraux and de Gaulle (and the only female one), deemed to be emblematic of the period. In 1958 too, Michel Guggenheim, reviewing contemporary critical attitudes to Sagan, pointed out that, after the publication of her second and third novels, when it became clear that Bonjour tristesse was not just a literary flash in the pan, critics were increasingly seeing Sagan as bearing witness in her works to the new generation and its values (Guggenheim 1958/59: 9–10). Hourdin, writing in Le Monde on the publication of Dans un mois, dans un an in 1957, is no longer arguing the case, as Mauriac had, for the spirituality of French youth: 'You just have to set foot on any beach in the South of France to realise that the characters described by our young novelist are anything but figments of her imagination.' ('Il suffit de mettre le pied sur une plage du Midi pour être convaincu que les personnages décrits par notre jeune romancière sont bien réels' [Hourdin 1957: 8]). The modern world, he grudgingly admits, has seen its own image in the novels of Sagan, and, he continues, the technology that allows lived events to become instantaneously captured by camera and microphone has turned her into a star. By the mid- to late 1950s the new era had arrived, and was seen to have arrived.

Incarnations of the Sagan myth

In interviews and in her own writings Sagan has spoken extensively of the experience of stardom from the inside. If we are to believe her account of what she felt during the presentation of the *Prix des Critiques*, she became immediately aware of the role of the media, and of the artifice involved, in the creation of celebrity:

> The Prize played a big part, it well and truly launched the book. There was a cocktail reception, there were journalists and photographers, my age struck them as being a source of good copy for articles and a good subject for photographs ... When I was presented with the *Prix des Critiques*, I had a split second of lucidity (amidst all the people clinging round me, the photographers, the crazy aspect of the situation) and I suddenly said to myself 'Gosh! This is what they call fame'. What they call the 'spotlight of fame' lasted for a split second, then afterwards it was all just a question of things being given a particular slant, but for a split second I said to myself 'Gosh! This is fame'. And strangely enough I didn't take a lot of pleasure from it. I realised immediately that fame was all about being asked and answering questions, and the truth being given a certain twist.[14]

In view of such clear-sighted detachment – 'I realised immediately that fame was all about ... the truth being given a certain twist' – it was paradoxical that the popular press should seize initially on the idea of her juvenile simplicity. A fortnight after the Mauriac review, *Elle* (14 June 1954) ran an article under the headline 'The baby of the best-seller writers holidays with her family' ('La junior des best-sellers passe des vacances familiales'). At the end of July *Paris Match* (31 July 1954) carried a feature proclaiming 'Françoise Sagan is a simple little girl who earns millions but is afraid of the dark' ('Françoise Sagan petite fille toute simple gagne des millions mais a peur la nuit'). An early photograph taken for *Paris Match* depicts her with her apron on in a dazzlingly modern 1950s kitchen, cooking (or at least putting into the oven something she had prepared earlier) – a truly normal girl. Annabel Buffet, one of her set, points up the provincial element in her social origins as being part of her attraction: '[She is] one of the upper-middle classes of the 17th *arrondissement* of Paris while at the same time being a thoroughgoing little peasant-girl from the Lot' ('[Elle est] à la fois bourgeoise du XVIIe arrondissement de Paris et petite paysanne drue du Lot' [Lamy 1988: 125]).

Between 'bourgeoise' and 'paysanne', however, it was the former image that was to hold sway. There was fascination in the fact that the 'charmant petit monstre' had sprung from the ultrarespectable Parisian bourgeoisie. Her identity as *'une jeune fille rangée'* (a well brought-up young lady) is clearly signalled in the early photographs, which show her dressed in the best possible taste, demurely, even rather staidly. In an interview reproduced in *Réponses*, the interviewer remarks that in the early years her excessive lifestyle had been accompanied by a very discreet style of dressing, typified by the little black dress and the string of pearls (Sagan 1974: 12–13). This somewhat surreal combination of ultrarespectability in dress and credentials, and the subversive values of her novels and lifestyle seems to have mesmerised the public. Judith Graves Miller describes one of the favoured poses in the early photographs as representing Sagan 'dressed in a tailored gray skirt and dark cashmere turtleneck, "at home" in a well-appointed bourgeois interior, [reaching] towards a half-empty bottle of Scotch, cigarette in hand' (Miller 1988: 6).

A much projected aspect of the Sagan myth was the love that this fragile-looking young woman had for fast cars. Nothing in this aspect of the myth seems to have been manufactured (except for the story that she drove barefoot – only at the seaside, she insisted). She had inherited an interest in cars from her father, and cars – two Jaguars and a Gordini, according to an early biography (Gohier and Marvier 1957: 46–7) were the first big purchases that she made with her earnings as a writer. In *Bonjour tristesse* the dénouement occurs when one of the main characters is killed (or kills herself – we do not know) when her car leaves the road. In 1957 life vied with art and took a near-catastrophic turn when Sagan met with an accident driving her Aston Martin. Her injuries were such that she was given the last rites. She was hospitalised for several months and subsequently had to wean herself off the pain-killing drugs to which she had become addicted. The detoxification cure she underwent is agonisingly described in *Toxique* (Sagan 1964).

Although it was undoubtedly a traumatic experience for her, Sagan's accident appears to have consolidated her image as a thoroughly modern, independent young woman devoted to life in the fast lane, and even enhanced her status as a star – Guggenheim records that members of a Sagan fan club in Milan hired a coach to bring them to Paris to express their concern (Guggenheim 1958/59: 10). Commentators were quick to draw a comparison between Sagan and James Dean, killed in a car accident in 1955. *Paris Match* referred to them as 'brother and sister' ('frère et sœur'). Hourdin, writing in *Le Monde* (27 April 1957), notes the narrow artistic base on which their celebrity was founded, James Dean having starred in only three films when he died and Sagan having published only two slim novels, and he comments further: 'Each of them has expressed in their art and attitude to life what is commonly referred to as youth's malaise' ('Ils ont traduit, l'un et l'autre, dans leur art, dans leur attitude devant la vie, ce qu'il est convenu d'appeler le mal de la jeunesse'). Brophy, writing in the early 1960s, by which time Sagan's dress style had become more relaxed than it had been in the mid-1950s, gives her own particular twist to the Dean/Sagan comparison:

> To the *jeunes gens* of this generation Sagan is instantly assimilable ... wearing their kind of clothes, she is, perhaps, a sort of French, female James Dean (himself the last of the stars to possess the real glamour and the first to cast it aside for jeans) ... a James Dean who survived the crash (Brophy 1964: 60).[15]

Regardless of how the Dean/Sagan parallel may be glossed, it undeniably enhances Sagan's star status by strengthening the France-US axis which was already part of the configuration of her legend. Sagan went to the United States as early as spring 1955 for a highly photographed and fêted launch of *Bonjour tristesse* by the US publisher Dutton, and returned for a second visit shortly afterwards. In 1956, she contributed a commentary to a book of photographs of New York. Her second husband, Bob Westhoff, was American, and American characters, and the United States as a setting, figure in early novels. She has recounted meetings with Tennessee Williams, Carson McCullers, Billie Holiday, Ava Gardner and Orson Welles (Sagan 1984; 1993). Of course the literary and artistic connections count less in the making of the myth than the air of jet-setting, up-to-the-minute modernity that the American connection brings to the star construct in this case, to be savoured or deplored depending on your point of view. There were those in the old guard who deplored it. On the publication of *Dans un mois, dans un an,* which sold two hundred thousand copies in a week, Henriot wrote a piece in *Le Monde* in which he compares her work to Coca-Cola, a product which, he argues, has been imposed on France by the modern publicity machine and which is now such a feature of French life that people are no longer receptive to a straightforward critique of its qualities, if any (Henriot 1957: 8).

Sagan expressed her own awareness of her work, and herself, as commodities when she commented: 'I became a commodity, an object: the Sagan phenomenon, the Sagan myth' ('Je suis devenue une denrée, une chose: le phénomène Sagan, le mythe Sagan' [1974: 50]), referring to herself also as having been a commercial phenomenon (1974: 59). She was a gift to the burgeoning mass-circulation press which included *Paris Match* (relaunched in 1949), *Elle* (launched in 1945) and *L'Express* (launched in 1953). There were two aspects to her 'commodification', both providing strong support for the view that stardom is created and sustained by the iterative incarnation of the persona across a range of media. On the one hand, there was the endless stream of interviews and photographs: *Réponses*, the collection of interviews with her compiled in 1974, found material in over eighty different francophone titles. In Bertrand Poirot-Delpech's superb picture-biography *Bonjour Sagan* (Poirot-Delpech 1985), a sizeable proportion of the credits go to *Paris Match* – it seems hard to underestimate the role of *Paris Match* in the star-making business of the 1950s. But on the other hand, apart from the interviews and photo-opportunities, Sagan's own name was a valuable by-line. An attempt was made to invent her as a travel writer, a journalistic role with glamour attached. As early as the autumn of 1954 she was sent by *Elle* with a photographer to the Middle East, the aim being that she would produce a series of travel articles on Jerusalem, Damascus, Beirut and Baghdad. The project does not appear to have come to fruition, though that year three articles by her on Italian towns, Naples, Capri and Venice, did appear in autumn numbers of *Elle*.[16] In 1956, as noted, she provided text for a book of photographs of New York (Sagan 1956b). But the travel-writing role does not seem to have paid off. As she observed in 1960: 'Those weeklies, counting on a fresh young eye, who sent me off at their expense to far-away places, soon thought better of it.' ('Les quelques hebdomadaires qui, comptant sur la fraîcheur d'un jeune œil, m'expédièrent à leurs frais dans des pays lointains s'en repentirent vite' [Sagan 1988 (1960): 189–90]).

Efforts were made to cast her in somewhat meatier journalistic roles. In March 1958 she was invited by Pierre Lazareff, director of *France-Soir*, to be an observer at a murder trial in Versailles and to write up her impressions for the paper.

However, according to her biographer Lamy, of the three articles she wrote, the second was cut and the third not used, on account of her sympathetic attitude to the defendants, one of whom received the death sentence (Sagan 1958b; 1958c). In 1960, she visited Cuba for *L'Express* on the first anniversary of the Revolution. Although she did not get to meet Castro, as had been hoped, the two articles she wrote were well worthwhile for their dry wit and nicely poised judgements (Sagan 1960b, 1960c). At the same time *Paris Match* of 13 August 1960 ran a six-page feature ostensibly on Castro, of which two and one-third pages were taken up with pictures of Sagan in Cuba, including a full-page illustration of her in the swimming pool of her luxury hotel – at least one part of the media was determined not to turn her into a political commentator. At the beginning of the 1960s she was also writing occasional, and, it must be said, somewhat inconsequential pieces for *L'Express* on the cinema.[17]

In the drive for 'intermediality' that is attendant on stardom, it was inevitable that cinema should figure in the Sagan construct. It was early assumed that *Bonjour tristesse* had screen potential. It is reputed that Julliard sold the dramatisation and film rights to Ray Ventura for between three-and-a-half million and five million old francs (reports vary) and that Ventura sold them on to Columbia for sixty million (Gohier and Marvier 1957: 43; Lamy 1988: 173). Big names were used – Deborah Kerr and David Niven in *Bonjour tristesse*, for example, and Yves Montand, Ingrid Bergman and Tony Perkins in *Goodbye Again* (based on *Aimez-vous Brahms..*). However none of the films that were made proved to be particularly enduring. Although she had a small part in *Goodbye Again*, Sagan herself took little interest in the film versions, telling Jean Seberg, the young American actress who played Cécile, that she did not care whether or not Seberg 'betrayed' the character (Gohier and Marvier 1957: 187). She had turned down a suggestion by Otto Preminger, the director of *Bonjour tristesse*, that she play the part herself (Lamy 1988: 174). Audrey Hepburn, who had played Gigi in the film adaptation of Colette's novel, is said to have turned it down on moral grounds. Sagan's biographers relate (Gohier and Marvier 1957: 187; Lamy 1988: 174–5) that a competition was arranged by Hélène Gordon-Lazareff, the editor of *Elle*, to find a young hopeful to play Cécile, and that, out of fifteen hundred applicants, fifteen were chosen for an audition in July 1956, among them Mijanou, the sister of Bardot. But no-one was picked on that occasion, and Preminger spotted Seberg later in America.

The story of the *Elle* audition is incomplete without reference to the fact that Sagan herself failed to turn up, an early example of her refusal, reputedly, to be subsumed by her celebrity status. Another famous anecdote relates that she refused to leave a skiing holiday in Mégève to return to Paris for an interview arranged by her publishers with journalists from *Life*. Further evidence that she was impatient with the uses to which celebrities could be put is her disparaging reference in *Toxique* to (unnamed) acquaintances '[who] persist in drivelling on in travel magazines' ('[qui] s'obstinent à bégayer dans les revues du tourisme' [1964: 16]). The celebrity determined to live his or her own life is a familiar enough theme in star discourse, but in Sagan's case it seems clear that she did indeed refuse to be merely a construct or commodity, and her own zest and creativity led her into new areas, thereby paradoxically strengthening her image. Her friendship early on with the young composer Michel Magne led to her writing the lyrics of four songs recorded by Juliette Gréco in 1956. She describes embarking upon her first play, *Château en Suède* (1960d), to entertain friends just after she had finished *Dans un mois, dans un an* (1984: 81), though, when it reached the stage, Anouilh, Cocteau, Mauriac and Sartre were at the gala performance. She got to St.Tropez before it was famous: in *Avec mon meilleur souvenir* (Sagan 1984: 109–24) she describes its tranquil charms in 1954 or 1955 – she is unsure of the dates – when she first arrived there with her brother, before it achieved celebrity status as the place where Vadim shot *Et Dieu créa la femme* with Bardot in 1956. Having become one of the movers and shakers of the St.Tropez set (as featured in *Paris Match*, 13 August 1960) she transferred her affections to the infinitely less glitzy setting of Normandy, buying an impressive property there at Equemauville in 1960 with winnings from a good night at the Deauville casino. There is plenty of evidence to support Brophy's observation that 'Sagan writes her own lines' (Brophy 1964: 60). But her independence simply nourished her star status by multiplying the opportunities for the mediation of her image.

Surviving stardom

In 1975, a collection of photographs of Brigitte Bardot by Ghislain Dussart, destined for coffee tables everywhere, was published with an introduction by Sagan (Sagan and Dussart 1975). No doubt conscious of the parallels between herself and

Bardot – she points out that they are the same age – she praises BB for having remained a human being in spite of all the efforts of the media to turn her into an object. The subtext is that she, Sagan, has likewise been through the mill of stardom and has emerged with a strong self-image and creative role intact. Fundamentally Sagan was a writer, with an urge to communicate through the written word, and primarily to narrate, and as such she survived stardom. In her own words: 'I have left stardom behind me and I have become a person with a skill' ('J'ai passé le cap de la célébrité et je suis devenue quelqu'un qui a un métier' [Sagan 1974: 54]).

In the decades that followed her making of this observation, and virtually until her death in 2004, Sagan remained in the public eye in France both as a writer and as a perennially newsworthy individual.[18] But when did she cease to be a star? In that her stardom was predicated to a large degree on her youth and on her image as an *enfant terrible*, it had a built-in sell-by date. From a literary point of view, a distinction may be drawn between most of the novels she wrote up to and including *Des bleus à l'âme* (1972), with their confessional tone and subtle psychological probing, and subsequent novels, which Miller characterises as relying on 'more melodramatic techniques: exaggerated emotions, an increase in coincidences and surprises, more intricate plots and even subplots' (Miller 1988: 18). There is no doubt also that a retrospective mode is in operation in the explicitly autobiographical aspects of *Des bleus à l'âme* (1972), and with the publication of *Réponses* (1974),[19] and in the Bardot book (1975). By this time not only was the wild-child approaching middle age, but French society had itself crossed the watershed of May 1968.

Referring back to that heady period, Sagan related that when militant students occupying l'Odéon recognised her at a meeting there and castigated her for having turned up in her Ferrari, her response was that it was not a Ferrari, it was a Maserati (Sagan 1998: 103). But although she was in her Maserati and not on the barricades, it may be argued that Sagan had already contributed more than her bit to the trends that culminated in May 1968. Her works were often criticised for their failure to engage with any great political or humanitarian issues, but she did lend her celebrity to a number of liberal causes. In 1960, she was one of the signatories of the 'Manifeste des 121' supporting the right of French soldiers not to serve in the Algerian war, and in the same year she wrote an article in *L'Express* defending the cause of a young Algerian woman,

Djamila Boupacha, alleged to have been tortured under interrogation by French military personnel (Sagan 1960a). This one article, 'La jeune fille et la grandeur', where 'grandeur' was an ironic allusion to the greatness of France, redeems a score of her other trivial excursions into journalism. Her identification with the cause of Algerian independence resulted in her home being the target of OAS plastic-bombers. She also signed the 'Manifeste des 343', an expression of the support of 343 famous Frenchwomen for legal abortion, published in *Le Nouvel Observateur* of 5 May 1971.

But more important than the stand she took on specific issues was the pervasive influence that she exerted in the 1950s and 1960s both through her novels and her lifestyle, which together expressed the hedonistic and youth-oriented values that set the tone for things to come. In particular she foregrounded in her works women's awareness and autonomy in the sexual arena, prior to the rise of the Women's Liberation Movement in France and well before the legalising of contraception under the *Loi Neuwirth* of 1967. Thirty years on from *Bonjour tristesse*, she summed up succinctly what that novel represented in the mid-1950s:

> It was not to be tolerated that a girl of seventeen or eighteen should make love, without being in love, with a boy of her own age and not be punished for it. What was deemed unacceptable was that she did not fall head over heels in love with him and was not pregnant by the end of the summer … And the other unacceptable thing was that this same girl should know all about her father's love affairs and should discuss them with him and consequently should be complicit with him on matters which until then, as far as between parents and children was concerned, had been quite unmentionable.[20]

Achieving celebrity status early in a period of cultural transformation as she did, Sagan appears both to have set trends and to have reflected and responded to an emerging ethos. Susan Weiner, whose astute analysis of the reception of women writers in France in the 1950s gives pride of place to Sagan and *Bonjour tristesse*, comments:

> By writing a novel in which the heroine offhandedly loses her virginity and, more seriously, sabotages her father's relationship with a lover who is too much like a mother, Sagan seemed to question the daughter's position in the family and in society: her female protagonist's as well as her own. Sagan as a daughter-

figure was symptomatic of the slow process of change that young women, and young women writers, were undergoing in postwar France (Weiner 1993: 98).

Alfred Cismaru sees her as having articulated the sense of insecurity and *ennui*, a watered-down form of existential *Angst*, that was the price of liberty from conventional frameworks and value systems, and he observes somewhat lugubriously: 'She would not have found the vast audience she did, or have been so successful, had she not captured the widespread mood of her time which aims to bandage our disquietude with the illusory dressing of amorality' (Cismaru 1965/66: 458).

These evaluations relate to Sagan as a writer in tune with the times, but they do not fully explain the fact of her stardom, which, as we have seen, rested on a striking paradox. While her bourgeois identity and her anointing by the conservative literary establishment gave her a special status in a country where traditional values were highly prized, that initial status was rapidly transmogrified by a modernising network of publishing people, newspaper editors, cinema folk and the like into popular celebrity of the most up-to-date kind. But Sagan the writer and Sagan the star never lost sight of each other. The phrase '*starlette de la littérature*', which encapsulates the meshing of the traditional and the modernising tendencies, comes from one of the best commentators on Sagan – herself (Sagan 1974: 54). She was of course not merely a starlet, but one of the stars of postwar France. Moreover, as a writer, she had the capacity, and happily had the will, to discourse engagingly and perceptively on her own stardom, commenting, for example, on the way in which she consciously lent herself to the legend:

> It took quite a long time for me to understand that what I needed was a mask and that I needed to put that mask on. I assumed the mask of my legend, and my legend ceased to bother me.[21]

Even in her final collection of essays, *Derrière l'épaule* (Sagan 1998), she was continuing to deconstruct unflinchingly, and from her own experience, the notion of celebrity:

> One of the great rewards and advantages of celebrity is that it causes you to tire of yourself. When you are presented with half a dozen or a dozen images of yourself, true or false, you end up by being sickened by them and by turning away from them: the fact is that you no longer seek to see through others' eyes that eternal adolescent you once were.[22]

Notes

1. Television was not widespread in France in the 1950s. Writing in 1958, Georges Hourdin commented: 'A daily newspaper and several illustrated magazines find their way into every home. Every house has a radio. Soon – in a few years' time – there will be a television set in every house too'. ('Il pénètre dans chaque foyer un journal quotidien et plusieurs magazines illustrés. Dans chaque maison on trouve un poste de radio. Il y aura bientôt sous chaque toit – laissons passer quelques années – un poste de télévision' [Hourdin 1958: 48]).
2. Other contemporary commentators who saw Sagan as bearing witness to the spirit of the times are quoted by Michel Guggenheim (1958/59: 9–10).
3. Referring to her first meeting with René Julliard, the publisher to whom she had submitted the manuscript of *Bonjour tristesse*, Sagan relates: 'He said that he liked my book a lot and that he hoped it wasn't autobiographical because generally speaking, where that was the case, it was the only book a person wrote. I assured him that there was no such sinister tale in my private life'. ('Il disait qu'il aimait beaucoup mon livre, qu'il espérait que ce n'était pas autobiographique car alors, généralement, on n'en écrit pas d'autre. Je lui ai assuré que non, qu'il n'y avait pas d'histoire sinistre de ce genre dans ma vie privée' [Sagan 1974: 43]).
4. 'En 1954, j'avais à choisir entre les deux rôles qu'on m'offrait: l'écrivain scandaleux ou la jeune fille bourgeoise, alors que je n'étais ni l'un ni l'autre ... J'aurais été plutôt une jeune fille scandaleuse et un écrivain bourgeois' (Sagan 1974: 13–14).
5. Audry is said also to have advised Françoise to alter the ending of her novel to make it more ambiguous (Delassein 2002: 36).
6. In the 1920s Julliard had pioneered book clubs in France with his *Sequana* series. For an account of his career as a publisher, see Jean-Claude Lamy's biography *René Julliard* (Lamy 1992).
7. Todd contrasts the relative lateness of the appearance of the *Livre de poche* series with the appearance of Penguin paperbacks in Britain in 1935 and of the *Marabout* series in Belgium in 1949.
8. Lucille Frackman Becker (1989) lists the following: Prix Goncourt (1945) – Elsa Triolet, *Le Premier Accroc coûte deux cents francs*; Prix International du Premier Roman (1949) – Geneviève Gennari, *Les Cousines Muller*; Prix Femina-Vacaresco (1951) – Marguerite Yourcenar, *Mémoires d'Hadrien*; Prix Fémina (1953) – Zoë Oldenbourg, *La Pierre angulaire*; Prix Goncourt (1954) – Simone de Beauvoir, *Les Mandarins*.
9. Julliard's quest for youthful authors and his capacity for making waves are confirmed in the strange case of Minou Drouet, a seven-year-old girl reputed to have written a number of poems, among them 'Arbre, mon ami' ('My friend the tree') which Julliard judged to be of sufficient interest to distribute to critics in a limited edition in 1955. *Paris Match*, in an item about Julliard's new discovery (6 August 1955), comments gleefully that a seven-and-a-half-year-old child is making Françoise Sagan look like an old lady. The Minou Drouet affair became a *cause célèbre*, the question being whether Minou's domineering adoptive mother had exercised undue influence in the composition of the poems. Julliard himself was the publisher for an investigatory book treating the affair from a sceptical point of view (Parinaud 1956). One can infer from his robust attitude to the Minou Drouet affair that he must have taken in his stride rumours

shedding doubt on the precise authorship of *Bonjour tristesse*. These rumours were speedily quashed (Lamy 1992: 166, 227).

10. Robert Kanters, himself a member of the jury that awarded the *Prix des Critiques* to *Bonjour tristesse*, refers in his memoirs to Julliard's success at producing prize-winning writers in the postwar years: 'When it came to manoeuvring in the battle for prizes, he definitely benefited from the fact that the old publishing houses had still not repositioned themselves strategically' ('Il profitait sans doute du fait que les vieilles maisons d'édition n'avaient pas encore retrouvé leurs positions stratégiques dans la guerre de manoeuvres des prix' [Kanters 1981: 191]).

11. *Le Monde* (26 May 1954: 9) published a list of the jury members as follows: Emile Henriot, Gabriel Marcel, Mme Dominique Aury, Marcel Arland, Georges Bataille, Maurice Blanchot, Jean Blanzat, Roger Caillois, Henri Clouard, Jean Grenier, Armand Hoog, Robert Kanters, Robert Kemp, Pierre Loewel, Thierry Maulnier, Maurice Nadeau and Jean Paulhan.

12. 'Ces douze mille garçons et filles de France, réunis sous les voûtes les plus illustres de la chrétienté, dans la cathédrale de Péguy, au lendemain de Dien-Bien-Phu, quel silence les accueille! ... Quel silence, partout, dans cette France désemparée de 1954!' (Mauriac 1958: 87).

13. 'La France vit des jours d'angoisse: son destin se noue en ce moment; il va être déterminé pour des générations peut-être. Qu'est-ce que cela a à voir avec le roman d'une petite fille trop douée?' (Mauriac 1954: 1).

14. 'Ce prix a joué un grand rôle, il a lancé le livre pour de bon. Il y a eu un cocktail, des journalistes, des photographes, mon âge les a frappés, ça leur a paru une bonne matière à articles et à photos ... Quand j'ai reçu le prix des Critiques, j'ai eu une seconde de lucidité (parmi tous ces gens accrochés à moi, ces photographes, ce côté dément de la situation), je me suis dit brusquement: "Tiens, c'est ce qu'on appelle la gloire." Ça a duré une seconde, ce qu'on appelle le "soleil de la gloire", après, ça n'a plus été que par des biais, mais une seconde, je me suis dit: "Tiens, c'est la gloire." Et bizarrement, je n'avais pas beaucoup de plaisir; j'ai su tout de suite que la gloire c'était des questions et des réponses et une manière de biaiser avec la vérité' (Sagan 1974: 46, 49–50).

15. Surprisingly enough, the James Dean comparison was still resonating forty years later when, in reacting to news of Sagan's death, Edmonde Charles-Roux, president of the *Prix Goncourt* jury, said of her that 'she lived dangerously, like many artists, like James Dean' (quoted in *Le Monde* 26–27 September 2004: 16).

16. These are cited in Kaiser's bibliography of Sagan writings as having appeared in issues of 27 September, 4 October and 11 October 1954 respectively (Kaiser 1973: 107, 108).

17. Bibliographical details of Sagan's cinema articles from *L'Express* are given in Kaiser (1973). A number of them are reprinted in Sagan et al. (1988).

18. This is borne out in the lively portrait provided by a recent biographer, Sophie Delassein, in *Aimez-vous Sagan ...* (2002), which includes detailed accounts of various well publicised legal proceedings in which she was involved, as well as giving an account of her friendship with, and public support for, François Mitterrand. Obituaries following Sagan's death on 24 September 2004 did not fail to refer to her brushes with justice involving drugs and tax matters, and her role, albeit minor, in the '*affaire Elf*', one of the great scandals affecting French public life in the 1990s.

19. Later works in which Sagan speaks in her own voice are *Avec mon meilleur souvenir* (1984), *Répliques* (1992), … *et toute ma sympathie* (1993) and *Derrière l'épaule* (1998).

20. 'On ne tolérait pas qu'une jeune fille de dix-sept ou dix-huit ans fît l'amour, sans être amoureuse, avec un garçon de son âge et n'en fût pas punie. L'inacceptable étant qu'elle n'en tombât pas éperdument amoureuse et n'en fût pas enceinte à la fin de l'été … L'inacceptable était ensuite que cette jeune fille fût au courant des amours de son père, lui en parlât et acquît de ce chef avec lui une complicité sur des sujets inabordables jusque-là entre parents et enfants' (Sagan 1984: 43).

21. 'J'ai mis assez longtemps à comprendre qu'il me fallait un masque, le mettre sur ma figure. J'ai mis le masque de ma légende et elle a cessé de me déranger' (Sagan 1974: 52).

22. 'C'est l'une des grandes récompenses, l'un des grands avantages de la célébrité: elle vous fatigue de vous. Quand on vous présente cinq ou douze images, vraies ou fausses, de vous-même, vous finissez par vous en dégôuter et vous en détourner : c'est qu'on ne cherche plus dans l'œil des autres cet éternel adolescent que nous avons été' (Sagan 1998: 114).

CHAPTER 9

THE ONLY ACT IN TOWN: CHARLES DE GAULLE

John Gaffney

Introduction: the scenery and the actors

It may seem odd to compare the cultural phenomenon of stardom with politics, and probe the extent to which stardom and a star system might exist here too. In approaching French politics in this way, however, we can shed light on its very singular nature, its preoccupation with the personalisation of leadership, and on how de Gaulle – the biggest star since Napoleon – influenced French politics. In one sense, as regards our study of the 1950s and 1960s, de Gaulle was the biggest star of them all: in 1958, he returned to public life after twelve years in obscurity; was hailed as a saviour (by some as an arch villain); dominated the national and international media; changed the regime, the Fourth Republic (1946–1958); into his own, personalised Fifth Republic with himself as the main player; and in many ways, made France itself a star again. And throughout the 1960s, he was almost the only star in the political firmament. In this case study, we shall take a 'star' to mean a political figure – Charles de Gaulle, in this case – who acts in the political arena by virtue of widespread public recognition of his exceptional talent.[1] Recognition of such talent facilitated the acquisition of power, and performance when in power consolidated personal leadership, and laid the foundations of subsequent claims by others to stardom.[2] By framing an analysis of de Gaulle in this way, two contradictory aspects to the problem are illuminated, the first of which places de Gaulle alongside the stars of the 1950s and 1960s, sharing characteristics of followership (fandom), media fame, and all the paraphernalia of image making; and the second of which demonstrates the limitations of such a 'modern' interpretation, and shows how de Gaulle illustrates that a very old and mythical view of France is deeply embedded in the French imagination. De Gaulle was both a 'modern' in French politics and an expression of a complex, chivalric tradition in French political culture. He was modern in that he used all the modern media to promote his image: newsreels, radio, the press conference and television (plus all the marketing tools of political campaigns at election times) (Chalaby 2002: 151–76). He was acutely sensitive to his public persona – his 'image' – observing protocol (he behaved in a near-monarchical way), yet also fond of ignoring protocol, a good illustration being his love of the *bains de foule* (poorly translated into English as 'walkabouts'), diving into crowds, shaking hands, touching, being touched, surrounded by his adoring fans.

In a sense, both stardom and modern politics are the products of the rise of mass society. And in this, at least, they share an essential, almost defining feature, namely, mediation. This is a commonplace in the study of film stars or pop stars. In politics, it is often omitted from analysis, but is essential here; that is, that the twentieth century politician has in many forums no 'reality', but is what can be called an 'imagined persona' (Gaffney 2001: 120–33). In cabinet meetings or in his office, de Gaulle, negotiating with ministers or a foreign head of state or government, was real enough; but this was not the case for the rostrum, the radio and the television camera. There, an image appears, a persona who has ascribed qualities, and who responds and corresponds to an expected and recognisable behaviour or comportment. In the modern period, the mediation of the politician is an essential feature of his or her political reality. The 'image' is all the more convincing in that there obviously is a real person laying claim to the persona. In the de Gaulle period, the 'media men' were already becoming well established, and would go on into the current period, developing what they saw as the fine art of creating, sustaining or improving the image of the politician. The analogy with the film star is therefore appropriate; what the public saw was not de Gaulle but an 'imagined' de Gaulle.

De Gaulle in 1959.
© La Documentation française. Photo Jean-Marie Marcel.

The fact that this imagined persona, in fact, corresponded very closely to the real person is of interest but is not the essential point. The fact that politics and politicians are mediated through newspapers, press conferences, political occasions and so on, makes the comparison with, say, the film industry a fruitful one, and political authority can well be studied from the perspective of mediation.

Where such an approach can obscure understanding is through the persuasive sense that this is the explanation of modern politics, that the hidden persuaders can market politicians like soap powders, and that that is explanatory of political life; that, in a sense, an Americanisation of politics has taken place. The study of de Gaulle, however, reveals or strengthens the sense of how French-specific such stardom is, both in its appeals to French history and traditions, and in its relation to a long tradition of political leadership. This point will be developed later in this analysis. Here it can be pointed out that not only were the myths and memories de Gaulle appealed to French, but that appealing to them in the way he did had a long pedigree in French politics. Moreover, not only the way in which de Gaulle came to power, but also the Fifth Republic itself (particularly through its concerted use of referenda) established a direct relationship between the leader and the people. This plebiscitary tradition also has a long French pedigree, and de Gaulle's use of the referendum was revived from Bonapartism, and in the modern period was a form of bypassing the modern political parties, in this way setting up an imagined, exclusive and apparently unmediated (i.e. unobstructed) relationship between the leader and the people. The treatment of de Gaulle as a star by the French helped him set up the new Republic, and the Fifth Republican system, in turn, encouraged the idea of the star as playing a central role. Subsequently, the consolidation of the Republic saw the institutionalisation of stardom through the constitutional reform of 1962, which introduced the election of the president by direct suffrage. But de Gaulle also reflected or interpolated an even older tradition in French culture, that of the chivalric knight, and when in power, the chivalric king. These points will be discussed further below. Here I shall simply list – and note their oddity in the life of a modern, 'ordinary' democracy, where knights ride out and dragons are slain only in Walt Disney cartoons – that the 'ingredients' of a chivalric tale are: the long, lonely trials and desert crossings of the hero in his quest to right a wrong; combat with dragons and giants and triumph against the odds; being wounded but constant in the service of a beautiful queen; a period of self doubt, and the acquisition of grace and wisdom; and the return of the hero to the castle and the restoration of the kingdom. There are, of course, variants on this theme. But de Gaulle brings this mythical world into politics; in a word, bringing into the political and institutional a deep cultural strain, normally kept out of the institutional, particularly in modern democracies. De Gaulle brought the ancient cult of the hero into everyday politics. This had existed – unstably – in the modern period, in monarchical politics with kings, and with Napoleon and other strong leaders. Now in this new age of modern democracy where hero-worship was more focussed upon the Beatles (whose first French tour was in 1964) than upon political leaders, de Gaulle's new republic brought adulation to the heart of daily politics.

In this way, the general theatricality of French politics increased significantly as a result of the highly personalised political system of the Fifth Republic (1958–). The use of theatrical metaphors to describe political life is generally so overworked as to be banal. Well worn phrases about the political 'stage', 'actors', 'exits' and so on are all staples of political journalese. To an extent, perhaps as with all clichés, they reflect a certain reality: political life is public, is mediated by images of leaders who correspond to various archetypes in given political cultures. And there is a public language, a ritual and a performative aspect to politics. In the case of the French Fifth Republic, however, perceiving politics as theatrical, as dramatic, has a truly substantive claim for two reasons. One concerns the political context (the set), one the politicians (the actors).

There is another reason why treating de Gaulle in this way, that is to say in terms of context and performance is appropriate. As was discussed both in the introductory chapter of this book and above in relation to de Gaulle, one of the quintessential features of postwar French stardom is its dynamic interplay of old and new. Of all the case studies in this book, de Gaulle is perhaps the clearest example of this. In terms of the time he came from and the time he governed; the discourse he used and the method of its mediation; the values he represented and those over whose emergence he presided; and so on, the old and the new are intertwined in de Gaulle so as to make it analytically counterproductive and, in fact, counterexplanatory to separate them out, as it was the clash of the two in his performance which had such politically strategic impact. Their significance will be analysed here both in terms of context and in terms of performance.

Context

One of the essential features of the French political context is that the political culture has a rich and dramatic history, and therefore offers great potential for 'performance'. This is in part because politics has been so contested; and with each contest (e.g. the Revolution, the Commune), new heroes (and martyrs) arose; with new ideals to strive for, and perhaps die for. In the French case, perhaps much more than in the case of, say, US or UK history, there was only consensus about the greatness, not about the details; and the interpretation of events such as the Revolution made history and analysis themselves part of the political landscape. This, too, has lasted till the present day. Politics, therefore, does not create consensus, only the agreed need for all and each to take a stand. In the case of de Gaulle, for example, it was very difficult, both in 1958 and later, to be other than for him or against him. French politics did not easily confine itself to detached observation. This context means that appeals to political action in the service of history are always seen as needing to be dramatic. Until World War II, however, one of the essential qualities of French democracy and republicanism had been that it was or would have itself impersonal. No one should be indispensable in a democracy. In part, the reason for this emphasis was the virulence and volatility of personal leadership in French history – very often it was 'heroes' who destroyed or threatened to destroy public freedoms: Louis XIV, Robespierre, Napoleon, Charles X, Louis Napoleon, Pétain and others trampled on freedoms, and were themselves often the expression of a chivalric, romantic view of politics in which personal action and power were seen as a means of (re)establishing a desired, antidemocratic order. The innovation of Gaullism was that it created a situation in which personal stardom was put to the service of democracy and republicanism.

In some ways, de Gaulle expresses Barthes and Morin's idea that stars incarnate ancient myth in modern form. De Gaulle saw life as a quest. He believed in heroes, believing himself to be one of them, and he believed in the need to serve the community as if serving were an act of devotion. He believed, therefore, in chivalric notions of trials, struggle, lonely fortitude, and a love of France that goes even beyond the chivalric (Lancelot and Guinevere) to the Freudian (Oedipus and his mother). And his own 'return' in 1958 is akin to the celebration of the hero by the crowd upon his triumphal return. All this was in an age of rock and roll, Saturday night TV variety and quiz shows, sputniks, atomic bomb tests, food mixers and design-icon cars like the Citroen DS. What perfect irony that the car de Gaulle was in in one of several assassination attempts (22 August 1962), a car riddled with bullets, and from which he stepped – the old from the new – divinely unharmed, was, as the images flashed to news agencies around the globe showed, a Citroen DS. It is crucial to an understanding of postwar France to take account of this true anachronism: that the agent of France's momentous and belated leap into the twentieth century, unlike in any comparable country, was a figure who expressed perfectly France's ancient, even mythical, history.

As regards political stardom, de Gaulle's credentials as the person who would solve France's 1958 crisis were strong, and – of great significance for the founding of the regime in 1958 – already 'mythical'. As an almost unknown young general/ junior minister, disgusted with the armistice signed by Marshal Pétain in 1940, de Gaulle flew to London and, on 18 June 1940, broadcast on the BBC, urging the French to continue the war against Germany. This immediate and solitary act gave him the status of the first Resister. He gradually gained in popularity and strength throughout the war years, entering Paris in 1944 as the leader of liberated France. As head of the provisional government, he tried to create a strong executive power, but was thwarted by his parliamentary opponents. Contrasting his own vision and mission with their mediocrity and self-interest, he resigned in January 1946 and entered the political wilderness for twelve years. The decolonisation process, which took place during this period, raised one intractable problem: Algeria (due partly to its constitutional status, partly to the strong European population living there). The intractability of the Algerian question between 1954 and 1958 provoked a crisis of state authority, as government after government fell, unable to impose itself in the face of terrible violence and near army mutiny. De Gaulle's return to power in 1958 was, therefore, of a particular kind: as if destined. Two features or consequences of this are important as regards the subsequent influence of his stardom in political life. First, it was his very own victory, a triumph for him as a person. His road to triumph was mythical in its proportions: the lonely certainty of 1940; the trials, dangers and gradual coalescing of support in the war years; initial triumph and universal acclamation in 1944 (here the legend could have ended); rejection by a fickle people and their intermediaries; a second desert crossing; lonely, aloof integrity; and the second and final triumph and acclamation in 1958. This heady story would therefore characterise the early years of the Fifth Republic, in that the personal adventure of one person was the foundation of the regime's legitimacy. In terms of the politics of stardom, this does indeed seem a good tale, shot through with all the qualities of the ideal story of the star. It also means that with such an illustrious background, de Gaulle's stardom transcended the normal categories of political support. It also turned France itself into an ideal co-star. This is how it was represented, moreover, in de Gaulle's own thought. His memoirs in particular treat the relationship to France in this way (though one might argue that for him France was the star and he the co-star, but the relationship is the same). They begin:

> All of my life, I have had in my mind a very particular idea of France. It is shaped as much by feeling as by rational thought. The emotional part of me imagines France quite simply like a fairy tale princess or the madonna in a painting, and fated to have an unusual and glorious destiny. Instinctively, I feel that providence created France in order that she acheive great triumphs or else undergo great misfortunes (De Gaulle 1954a: 1).[3]

This is the most quoted piece of all de Gaulle's writing. For the purpose of this chapter, not only the wondrous and the chivalric – in fact, story-book – aspect to the quotation and sentiment, but also the very personal ('ma'[my], 'je'[I], 'me'[for me/in me], 'moi'[me], 'j'ai'[I have]) relationship of (a boy?) to a mother figure, the (Oedipal?) dreams of glory, the notion of a teleological destiny and, of course, the notion that the self is crucial to the world and almost creative of it, should be noted. It is startling that such a fairy tale should inform the politics of a modern, democratic state, because the second and equally important feature of de Gaulle's coming to power in 1958 was that it imposed upon the new Republic and upon France itself (and upon French history) his own version of history. This is significant for the politics of stardom. De Gaulle's lack of political party support after the Liberation was due partly to fundamental disagreement about what France was by 1945: the eternal France of suffering, resolve and triumph, i.e. the fairytale France of de Gaulle's imagination, or the modern, practical democracy which had emerged from the chastening experience and mediocrity of imagination of the 1940–1944 period. The re-emergence of de Gaulle as a kind of saviour in 1958 meant that his view (his vision and envisioning) was imposed upon political life in contradiction to the less dramatic politics that were emerging everywhere else.

The Fifth Republic, therefore, heightened the role of symbolic politics by bringing to the heart of the system the 'performance' of individuals or, rather, at this time, one individual, and his reactivation of appeals to French history and a dramatic view of political action. The world of symbolic politics is much wider than the formal political one. It teems with myths and traditions, national and subnational identities, memories, histories and allegiances, which are 'envisioned' by the individual who in this way both articulates and transcends discrete political, social and ideological constituencies and thus can be legitimated (through election but not only in this manner) by the national community.

Let us, therefore, use the framework of stardom to appraise the performance of this unusual example of modern political leadership. Three of the essential characteristics of the film star, particularly, in fact, in the 1950s, were their star quality or qualities, their difference from others, and their relationship to immediate support and to the public at large. De Gaulle's political performance can be analysed in terms of the following: what were de Gaulle's star qualities; how was he seen as being different from rivals; and what was his relationship to his various audiences?

Star qualities and character traits

By the time de Gaulle was on the threshold of power in 1958, the details of his stardom were nationally known. His courage as a soldier on active service in World War I was both legendary and true. His fearlessness, and the semimystical nature of his facing imperturbably great physical danger throughout his life added near-superhuman qualities to his persona; his aforementioned baffling escape from an assassination attempt in 1962 further increased his national popularity. A second element of his public 'character' was his devotion to an ideal, which lay outside his own self-interest, and because according to himself only he could see it, this involved him even more in being the only instrument for achieving the ideal. The political result of this was that despite his persona being exculpated from the charge of egotism, the focus upon him sharpened. This was compounded by the notion of his having acted upon this devotion by being the first to resist. The 'man of 18 June' (1940) in this way envisioned something others could not see. A third trait was his Cassandra quality: having 'understood' the need for changes in military strategy during World War I, being ignored when imploring the High Command in the 1930s to develop tank warfare, warning the country that the Fourth Republic was unworkable, etc. The result of these traits in such emphatic form distinguished him from all other politicians. It should also be noted that de Gaulle's political (and military) performance was 'real' in that he did the things that were ascribed to him, but that many of these acts elevated him to legendary or mythical status.

Differentiation from others

De Gaulle was in many respects 'outside' the political system, and not only of the Fourth Republic. In the 1930s, as a young officer, he distinguished himself by his opposition to military orthodoxy; from 1940 to 1944 he was truly outside the system, condemned to death for treason/desertion. Throughout the war, moreover, he was outside the very inner circle of other Allied leaders; in 1946, he broke with the political elite setting up the Fourth Republic; in the late 1940s, his party, the Rally of the French People (RPF), was considered as being outside the system; and by the 1950s, he was considered a relic of the past. De Gaulle's political effect in 1958 was such, however, that his coming to power on his own terms enhanced even further the role of the personal within the political.

De Gaulle's perceived character traits (courage, devotion, wisdom), and the fact that he and they were so publicly known, meant that he was seen as having a particular way of seeing and doing things. This in turn meant that de Gaulle had a *style*. It was a style organised around the idea that he was the emanation of France itself, and that, of his political generation, only he possessed it. Any attempt by others to appropriate it would have meant instant ridicule. The result of de Gaulle's difference meant that he could not, in fact, succeed in political life unless a crisis occurred, and if it did, as it did, he would then become an exclusive winner. By refusing to compromise on anything in the name of his vision of France, and ever comporting himself publicly as if this were the only question at issue, de Gaulle could only be rejected by 'everyday politics', until such time as that broke down and he became the only recourse. The conditions, therefore, of such a return to power in 1958 meant that he would govern with a personal authority rare even in French political history.

De Gaulle's comportment thus consolidated his character or persona. In public and semipublic forums (e.g. conversations with party leaders or foreign politicians) his style was highly rhetorical, with a historical sweep to his discourse and an incantatory tone. (He was also 1.94m tall.) In a time of crisis such a style enhanced still further the majesty of the person and his purpose. This rhetorical style was perceived as having real depth, moreover, in that his speeches and memoirs, what may be termed his 'discursive persona', were real. Unlike many politicians, he wrote his own speeches.[4] His public voice was the authentic product of his private thought. The end result of these qualities, a particular public comportment and a particular discursive style, informed the early Fifth Republic, so that leadership within it was highly personalised, highly sensitive to protocol, declamatory and forcefully patriotic, and each of these to the point where the scale of the character, once he was president, had created, in turn, a corollary question: was France even imaginable now without this person? Such incarnation is rarely seen in political life.

De Gaulle's larger-than-life character and uncompromising comportment, therefore, posited a perceived integrity. He appeared to always take the hardest, most uncompromising, road to power: in 1940 when he fled France, in 1946 when he resigned as Prime Minister, and in 1958 when he agreed to return only if invited by the legitimate institutions. He was, therefore, always perceived as concerned about power for a reason other than its own sake. The concomitant effect of this was to increase differentiation still further in that, as he projected vision, steadfastness and integrity, so his opponents, in a sense the whole political class, appeared lacking in these qualities – the practical politicians seemed to lack vision, the believers in democratic compromise seemed to lack steadfastness, and the political class generally, almost by its nature rather than its action, seemed to lack integrity.

De Gaulle's extreme differentiation also meant that the notion of the 'authenticity' of the private man was brought to the fore within the political realm. Given that the private man was seen to possess such integrity, the conferring of authority upon him to re-establish the authority of the state was akin to a private conferring by each individual. All of de Gaulle's action was based upon the idea that he was in a relationship with the French people. This point will be developed in the next section of this chapter, but suffice it to say here that if a political relationship is imagined as a personal one in which personal qualities count, then once authority to act has been conferred, the right of the recipient to act has an intensity which significantly increases his scope to act. This is not to say that de Gaulle was universally supported or liked, in 1958 or at any other time. What is interesting, however, is how he enjoyed respect beyond his 'natural' constituency or constituencies; it was clear, for example, that disciplined communists voted for him in 1958, even though the party opposed him and likened him to a fascist. Conversely, once it became clear soon after his coming to office that de Gaulle was going to give Algeria independence, the violent sense of betrayal of a large proportion of the European Algerians, was more akin to acute personal deception than to ordinary political disapproval.

The corollary of this is not only that his own presidency would be conducted in an inordinately personal way, but that by bringing to the heart of the political institutions such a personalised relationship, he ensured that, in spite of his own view that France would degenerate once again without him, this imagined personal relationship between 'the people' and the President, would become a mainstream effect of political relations within the Fifth Republic. This will be discussed in the conclusion. Let us look, now, at his relationship to his various audiences.

De Gaulle's three audiences: the core, the political elites, the people

To an extent, like all stars, de Gaulle was 'promoted' (by a political entourage) and sustained from below by the ascription of qualities by 'the people', and by the co-operation of intermediary actors and institutions. De Gaulle, more than many other political figures, did appear to possess certain personal qualities. Irrespective, however, of whether the qualities ascribed to de Gaulle were indeed possessed by him, he also had a core support group which acted as a machine whose function was to act in all circumstances on his behalf: consulting with him constantly, organising support for him from 1940 onwards, setting up the Gaullist Rally of the French People in 1947; offering active and concerted support during the Algerian crisis of 1958, and so on. All political actors of this type need such a support network, one of whose functions is to construct and then maintain the appearance that in spite of such allegiance, no such machinery exists; that 'the General' stood alone.

The core initially succumbed to, later sustained, and ultimately refashioned and mass-marketed the mythology itself. This group comprised about one hundred people. These were the '*compagnons de la première heure*', those who rallied to de Gaulle in 1940 at his London base through his broadcasts on the BBC (Viansson-Ponté 1963). It began as a military rather than political rally – it was first soldiers (and seamen and airmen) who 'heard the call' (to resist), and simply obeyed this new source of authority. Many who constituted this group were young (men), creating a sense of a chivalric brotherhood. The circumstances and emotions – and subsequent memory – were dramatic, even life changing. And belonging to this group involved a kind of mystical 'recognition' of the leader.

The core, therefore, gave a great deal of practical help and, through the nature of its commitment, performed the original mythmaking role (this would be particularly significant in terms of his image among the two other groups). The core group was supplemented by several waves of subsequent support, much of which would turn out to be more reliable and politically effective (for example, members of the political class that joined him in Algiers in 1943, rather than the soldiers who joined him in London in 1940). This group had a significant effect upon the next group (the wider political elite) by demonstrating through practical example that the leader had a governing team. Throughout World War II and also the Fourth Republic, de Gaulle was able, by and large, to depend upon this core support.

The wider elites came into de Gaulle's orbit as the Algerian crisis developed in 1958, mainly as a result of his being increasingly seen as 'the only person' to solve the crisis. One after another, the political parties formerly hostile to him 'went over' to him, as did the bureaucracy in Algiers, the army, the European Algerians, much of the indigenous population, and then the metropolitan French. Significantly, the party leaders – even among these the normally unimpressionable Socialist leader, Guy Mollet – described these meetings with him in May/June 1958 in terms reminiscent of the cohort of 1940 in London, that is, as a near-mystical experience, of meeting someone of an almost superhuman character. Interestingly, each of the elements of the wider elites which rallied to de Gaulle saw in him different things: for the Socialists, he – rather than the supporters of *Algérie française* – was a republican; for the army, he – rather than the Fourth Republic's elite – was concerned with military glory; for *Algérie française* he was concerned with the empire; for the mainstream Right he was anticommunist; and so on. And for each group, he was this plus something more, corresponding to their notion of a national saviour (of varying degree depending upon the level of devotion of each element). It is also the case that various members of his 'core' moved into contact with each of these discrete supportive elements – the whole making up a stampede of support at the critical moment of May-June 1958. Even parties opposed to him such as the French Communist Party (PCF) were not unaffected. As previously mentioned, even though the PCF opposed him, many PCF supporters supported him, and many party members admired him. After his death, everyone 'has been, is, or will be a Gaullist' (a été, est ou sera gaulliste) (Sabatier and Ragueneau 1994: 496); but in terms of his popularity at the time we can see that the publics were like tributaries, flowing into one another until he was carried to power on a single stream of support.

In 1958, de Gaulle was 'recalled' to power by the political elite, with the tacit then later explicit approval of the country. The conditions of such a return were a combination of deep trends in French history, a political culture which recognised strong leadership, the activity of his core support (a particular type of allegiance to him, a particular type of activity on his behalf), his own image and comportment (maintaining his personal style in all public forums while offering reassurance of his integrity and the integrity of the republican tradition) and of course chance, contingency and circumstance (by 1958 de Gaulle was no longer expected ever to return to power; such reversals of fortune are irresistibly seen as 'destiny').

The period 1958–1962 saw the celebration, then institutionalisation, of the relationship of de Gaulle to the third audience, the public at large. He secured this in a series of moves across the political spectrum, involving the loss of support of some of the units in the second group (essentially because of Algerian independence) and even some of the inner core support. De Gaulle moved, between 1958 and 1962, away from his *Algérie française* support and the more virulent elements of the military, and even away from some of his own core support (in 1962, he moved from supporting the hardline Michel Debré as his first prime minister to championing the more flexible Georges Pompidou), using for these purposes the support of the established political parties until he provoked these, too, into hostility over his proposal to embed presidential legitimacy in direct election. He then dissolved the National Assembly and in the subsequent parliamentary elections of 1962 his new party defeated the established political parties and then pushed through constitutional reform so that from then on (1965) 'the nation', rather than a restricted electoral college, would elect the president. The use of national referendums (four in this first four-year period) gave a popular framework to these shifts.

With regard to the third group, it is worth pointing out that it too, like de Gaulle himself, like French politics itself, was a combination of real and mythical elements. The 1962 reform gave 'the people' a reality in that their choosing future presidents would be a real act performed by real people, but in order to do/be so, they also entered into a mythologising process in which they became de Gaulle's 'nation', enacting as it were de Gaulle's interpretation of France. We can see, therefore, that essential to de Gaulle's leadership style is not simply the people's approval of him, but his depiction of their approval, and their acquiescence in his interpretation of their relationship. One can make a parallel with the film star's fan magazine and the way in which communion is depicted. In de Gaulle's discourse, his 'understanding' of the feelings and knowledge of the confidence of the people are strong features. Extending the parallel, we can also say that de Gaulle's use of referendums – there was always a subject, such as Algeria or constitutional reform, but they were also votes of confidence – were akin to box-office figures or record sales, demonstrating approval in both him and his performance. In terms of the wider question of stardom, it is also interesting here to comment on two details of this relationship: intimacy and disdain.

De Gaulle's 'intimacy' with 'la nation' (the nation), was a relationship that was direct, unobstructed by obstacles (such as political parties). He displayed great confidence in '*la France profonde*', and especially in his own credentials to speak on behalf of it. He also displayed a deep love for France, and for the shared mission with the French people to serve and protect France. In all his discourse there was a conferring of greatness upon the French, a recognition of them by him, and therefore a valorising of them.

This recognition of the French by de Gaulle, however, was of a very particular type. Its intimacy and immediacy allowed no nuance permitting, say, the existence of social class differences or of the possibility of uncertainty as to the nature of the France so proclaimed and loved. Moreover, the 'je' (I) of de Gaulle was never absorbed into the 'vous' (you) of 'the French' (Gaffney 1993: 1–9); de Gaulle's own thrill at the *bains de foule* he often indulged in, especially in his early years as President, never altered the fact of his distinctiveness. In fact, integral to the intimacy was a disregard for individuals, as distinct persons, and even a personal disdain for the crowd. De Gaulle's personal comportment was highly aristocratic: referring often to himself in the third person, allowing others to worry about – and he to disdain them for it – 'the price of artichokes' (i.e. daily life), a true dislike of the political parties (in the name of their being part rather than whole, but ignoring their representative function), and through his dislike of them, in fact, an attitude to democracy itself which was ambivalent to say the least. De Gaulle's attitude to democracy would merit another chapter, but what one can say here is that the two features informing his relationship to the people, namely, intimacy and disdain, mirror very accurately in many cases the attitudes of stars to their audience. There follows just one illustration of what might be called intimacy in action, which offers many insights into the nature of de Gaulle's approach, his style of leadership and attitude to democracy.

As mentioned above, de Gaulle thrived on the protocols surrounding Fifth Republican presidential democracy, imposing, for example, on himself and others, an astonishing, monarchical set of procedures of deference and ritual in the Elysée palace, his official residence (Alexis 1999; Fleurdorge 2001: 206–10). He also, as previously noted, threw such protocols into high relief when he broke the protocolary comportment he had himself brought into the institutions. He often ignored his own constitution, for example. Perhaps the most memorable example was his flouting of international protocol when he proclaimed 'Vive le Québec libre!' ('Long live free Quebec!'), advocating that Quebec develop its own independence movement on a visit to Canada as the guest of the Canadian government (De Gaulle 1999: 1051–2). Another good illustration was his 1961 television (and radio) appeal. It was not in itself an unconstitutional act or a breaking of protocol, but it was indeed a moment when he as it were stepped down from his Olympian heights and almost through the television screen into the homes of the French population to appeal to them for support.

In April 1961 there was a serious army coup attempt in Algiers, essentially because the military and the European Algerians had realised that de Gaulle was going to grant independence to Algeria after all. It was intended that the coup would spread to the mainland (just as it had in 1958 in the wave of military threats, which had helped bring de Gaulle to power). Much of the high command remained loyal to de Gaulle, and it was by no means going to be necessarily a decisive coup, but the danger was real enough. Interestingly, throughout modern history France has used conscription, in principle to ensure that France could defend the country if it were in danger and save the Revolution and its gains if ever these were threatened. Bizarrely, one of the greatest dangers to the Revolution throughout the nineteenth and twentieth centuries was the army itself. In many ways, conscription became a way of countering the politicised, antirevolutionary, professional elements within the military. Ordinary soldiers, straight from school, the farm or the factory, called up for 18 or 24 or 28 months, were far less likely to entertain ideas about toppling a regime than hardened, right-wing, professional soldiers. And in many ways it was the former, and their indirect relationship to de Gaulle, who saved the day. De Gaulle's broadcast of 23 April 1961 was stunning – a real performance (De Gaulle 1999: 736–8). He had gone on television explicitly to talk to the French people, in particular those families, parents, who had recently acquired new TV sets and whose sons were serving as conscripts in the army and in Algeria. The text was short and had urgency, but it was the closing lines which were the most memorable: 'French women, French men, help me!' (Françaises, Français, aidez-moi!) he implored, into the television camera. However bold and authoritarian the TV appeal may have been (with de Gaulle wearing military uniform), the speech ended thus with the sudden breaking of all de Gaulle's usual tone (and he failed to add the usual 'Vive la république, vive la France' [Long live the republic, long live France']) and a reaching out to his audience, almost declaring his weakness, at a moment when his greatest strength was needed, to the French families sitting in their living rooms watching the television, or listening to the radio. As they sat, de Gaulle's own metaphorical falling to his knees, imploring them, suddenly conferred upon *them* the power to rise up against a coup, while implying strongly that without them he was unable to cope. This saturnalian gesture, with the king telling his subjects that without them in France's hour of need, he had no power, was a true expression of de Gaulle's attitude to 'the nation': there was intimacy but in the name of France, an intimacy that underlay the whole relationship but which only displayed itself like this in crisis; an intimacy that conferred upon the ordinary French people a heroic status that carried with it necessary heroic obligations (although in reality these would not be realised); and an intimacy that wilfully demonstrated how fragile was de Gaulle's own authority without them (and in fact how fragile all French regimes were). The result was dramatic: French public opinion remained unequivocally behind de Gaulle, the authority of the pro-de Gaulle generals prevailed; the rebels were characterised not as heroes trying to save the integrity of the state but as villains to be tracked down and arrested. The conscripts, home on leave or returning to service from their families – many listening to their new transistor radios – obeyed de Gaulle and their parents. Never had the media (TV, radio, newspapers and newsreels) and leader-people relations, opinion and political and military decision-making been in such a powerful combination. And, in fact, the result was a leap into contemporary society. No more coups would occur to this generation of baby boomers (although in 1968 they would stage their own near-revolution); their TV sets were essentially for variety shows and their transistors for listening to pop music. France would never again be threatened from within by a military coup. Ironically, the authoritarian, monarchical de Gaulle, who had come to power against the background threat of just such a coup, had saved democracy and pushed France forward into the consumer age. And in this, the nature of de Gaulle's relationship to 'the people' was crucial. His three audiences, moreover, were crucial to the political situation. These audiences – core supporters, political elites and people – interacted with one another in varying degrees and at different times. The essential characteristic of de Gaulle's relationship to his core support was his simple assumption of its existence and purpose. In terms of the elites, in particular the political parties, his essential relationship was one of disdain; and when in 1958 they did go over to him, he himself treated them as if they were either the core or the people, never recognising in their partisan allegiance their democratic function. In terms of the third audience group, perhaps the single most important thing to note was its imaginary character; that in spite of the existence of a real population and electorate, the essential nature of the relationship between this political star and his support was an imaginary one, full of the ascription of qualities, special understandings and intense emotion, none of which necessarily reflected a reality.

Conclusion

This study reveals that political context and political action are strongly interdependent. In the case of de Gaulle and French politics, a rich political culture contained within it sensitivity to strong, personal leadership, where, essentially, democratic forms were seen as antithetical to it. The paradox of modern France was that, even though the notion of 'media personalities' was beginning to take shape in postwar French politics, it was de Gaulle, re-enacting old leadership forms, who imposed himself upon contemporary politics and society, bringing into contemporary democratic politics the myth of the hero and the myth of eternal France. This in turn affected political institutions and subsequent political practice and discourse, so that de Gaulle's register, style, memory, discourse, iconography and so on entered the mainstream of political reference and exchange.

It is also clear from this study that a support network was nevertheless necessary for such a political adventure. De Gaulle did not simply emerge. The role of the support network was, in fact, to ensure the illusion of natural emergence. There was a structure to his support that was vigorous and mutable, for practical and strategic reasons. A final observation that can be drawn from this analysis is that such politics involved a kind of 'invention' of France by de Gaulle which was subscribed to by the people, and that this involved willing or tacit acquiescence by the latter in also imagining, if not France, then themselves in the way de Gaulle imagined them, and a recognition by them of, on the one hand, his heroic qualities: courage, devotion to a cause, and vision; and, on the other, his difference: from the parties, from their leaders, from adversaries and, most importantly, from themselves.

To a certain extent, by introducing the reform of the constitution in 1962, whereby subsequent Presidents would be elected by direct universal suffrage, de Gaulle ensured the continuation of both the political system and its concomitant star system, even though such was de Gaulle's prestige that his was a seemingly impossible act to follow. Interestingly, the workmanlike, down-to-earth style of his successor, Georges Pompidou, can be seen as part of the system; as can the variants of presidential stardom, which followed him. Not all presidential aspirants needed to be stars in the Gaullist manner, but some kind of stardom became an imperative of political imagery and strategy. This might involve notions of: coming in from 'outside'; having a vision of and for French society; enjoying a complex and privileged relationship to the French nation; and having a relationship of power to a political base or movement while either dissimulating it or mythifying it by making it chivalric by treating the movement itself as a microcosm of French society itself. These features were not only tolerated by the political system set up by de Gaulle, but became its motor. Over and above de Gaulle's effect upon the conditions of success of his successors, his type of fame had a further effect, namely a posthumous stardom of mythical proportions, which has informed French politics since.

Notes

1. Gender-specific pronouns will be used in this chapter. Not only the political actors, but also the mythology itself was almost exclusively male. This study itself reveals that it was not simply the case that, as in all democracies, although, constitutionally, the law is nonsexist, there remained obstacles to equality; in France, at least, it was the mythology itself which exerted such inordinate pressure on formal political institutions, and it was this mythology which was almost exclusively male-oriented. In much of its logic and imagery, it was a modern version of the chivalric tradition, or that of the warrior-philosopher. For analysis of how this impacts on women in politics, see Footitt 2002.
2. Although it should be treated with care, Max Weber's notion of charismatic authority, a personal authority ascribed to particular leaders and seen as transcending the authority of office, law, or tradition, is helpful. See Gerth and Wright Mills 1977: 51–5, 246ff., 245–52. See also Kane 2001.
3. (My translation). 'Toute ma vie, je me suis fait une certaine idée de la France. Le sentiment me l'inspire aussi bien que la raison. Ce qu'il y a, en moi, d'affectif imagine naturellement la France, telle la princesse des contes ou la madone aux fresques des murs, comme vouée à une destinée éminente et exceptionnelle. J'ai d'instinct, l'impression que la Providence l'a créée pour des succès achevés ou des malheurs exemplaires'.
4. All of Charles de Gaulle's memoirs, speeches and other works were published in Paris by Plon from the 1950s onwards (De Gaulle 1954–). Also, the bibliography on Charles de Gaulle (periodically updated) is published by the Charles de Gaulle Institute in Paris, and lists all of the books and articles on him (over 1,500 books and 10,000 articles) (Institut Charles de Gaulle 1981).

CONCLUSION

John Gaffney and Diana Holmes

For France, the quarter-century between the end of World War II and the early 1970s was a period of extremely rapid social change – economic, political and demographic – which informed the lived experience of millions of individuals. These years were characterised particularly by the strong pull of a new modernity, in difficult and often acute tension with the past. The new emerged, but strongly informed by the old, as well as by the progressive and oppressive possibilities of a new, fast-moving, consumerised culture that expanded in the context of a remarkable and sustained economic boom. In this fertile period of French history, the interaction between dramatic newness and powerful tradition created a dynamic yet fragile society, uncertain of its direction, and both heavily influenced by and resistant to a globalising, American culture.

This was the period of the development of mass culture, with its curious interpenetration of the real and the imaginary, its capacity to formulate new mythologies that not only express but also shape and direct the dreams, fears, aspirations and anxieties of the majority. It is not by chance that in that decade three of France's major intellectuals – Lévi-Strauss, Barthes and Morin – devoted influential works to the theorisation of mythology, with the two last specifically addressing the way that new forms of popular culture produce new and potent forms of myth. Stars, whom Morin likens to the gods of antiquity, play a vital role in mass culture, acting out emotions, conflicts, ways of negotiating a changing world in a realm that the public knows to be, in part, fictional, but that can also be recognised as real. '[Stars] concentrate in themselves the mythological and the practical powers of mass culture', wrote Morin in 1962, (...) the super-individuality of the Olympians is what makes modern individuality possible'.[1]

We have seen that the era's new media were crucial to the production of stardom. The sudden development of technologies of mass-communication, the growing ubiquity of visual images (the photographic easily becoming the iconographic) in magazines and advertising, and the media's appetite for interviews, radio and TV appearances all made possible a new sense of familiarity with celebrities. In this market-oriented economy, everything, including 'high culture', was more likely to be packaged and made attractive through emphasis on the individual and on 'lifestyle', lending the process of star formation an irresistible dynamism. Though each star studied here had exceptional talents, qualities or abilities, to move from celebrity within a specific field to immediate, mass recognition, and to the occupation of a significant role within the national imagination, required the construction of a public persona through radio, the printed press, cinema or television – or all of these. Fame began with success in a specialised domain – discussed here are cinema, music, sport, literature, the university and politics – but then spread outward through the next circle of a wider but still specialised public and on, through the media, to a mass audience for whom the celebrity became not just a performer in a specific field, but a part-fantasised figure who invited curiosity, identification and fascination.

Stardom and stars, and their consumption, were inextricable elements of the new modernity. The notion of the individual's right to pleasure and freedom of choice was part of the discourse of the new consumerism, but it also helped to shape the nascent generational consciousness of the young, and would feed into the spirit of social contestation that exploded in May 1968. The 'scripted' individualism of the stars themselves provided a model for the young's new sense of entitlement: a young woman of any social class, in Paris or the provinces, might dream of a life touched by the glamour and agency evoked by Bardot; her male counterpart might hope, if not to join a rock 'n' roll band, at least to go and watch one, and to absorb some of the glamour, energy and vibrant youthfulness it represented.

But we have also seen that stars, rather than simply fostering dreams and aspirations by representing an ideal,

matter to their public because they embody and give satisfying
form to the contradictions of personal and national identity
produced by a particular historical moment. The French – like
other Europeans – both welcomed a more global, US-inspired
culture with its promise of freedom, excitement and confident
control of the material and social world, and feared for the loss
of cherished values, identified as 'national', even though
precisely what those values were varied according to class and
political allegiance. As France emerged from the ravages of
World War II into the bright lights of the late 1950s and
swinging 1960s, we need to bear in mind the politically
dramatic nature of that emergence: the politically paralysing
effects of the decolonisation process and the postwar regime,
only twelve years old in 1958, broken on the rack of the
unsolvable Algerian problem. The ability to embody at once
confidence and anxiety, modernity and tradition, assertion
and vulnerability was a characteristic that linked many of the
stars of the period. De Gaulle, the heroic leader, constantly
emphasised his devotion to a beautiful fragile France; beneath
Bardot's assertive, vibrant sexuality ran the public knowledge
of her repeated suicide attempts, and their echo in the deaths
of many of the heroines she played; Sagan's sophisticated
lifestyle, like that of many of her characters, included a
marked element of self-destruction. Poulidor was loved
because he was both heroic and the eternal loser; Hallyday
incarnated at once the good, patriotic French boy and the
alienated rebel. The stylish modernity of the New Wave
brought to the screen a series of brittle, doomed heroes, and in
Godard's films moved towards a searing critique of the
deadening power of the new consumerism.

The age of celebrity would take different directions after
May 1968: no statesperson has since matched the iconic status
of de Gaulle; later intellectuals have not shaped and marked
their era to the same extent as Sartre, Beauvoir, Barthes or
Lévi-Strauss; Hallyday remains the best-known figure in
French pop music; the international fame of Bardot has not
been equalled by any French star since; and very few authors
have come close to achieving Sagan's position as a household
name in France and an internationally recognised face, name
and image. Poulidor's significance for a national audience
remains an exception, and Godard remains the film director
who has most firmly imprinted his name and his vision on
twentieth-century France. Each of our stars belongs to the
constellation of postwar celebrity, and each in their way

encapsulates, embodies and interpellates the contradictory dynamism of those years.

Note

1. '(Les stars) concentrent en eux les pouvoirs mythologiques et les pouvoirs pratiques de la culture de masse. Dans ce sens, la surindividualité des olympiens est le ferment de l'individualité moderne' (Morin 1976 (1962): 147–8).

BIBLIOGRAPHY

(Where relevant, the original date of publication is given in brackets after the date of the edition referred to.)

Achard, M. 1998. *Souvenirs souvenirs*. Paris: Flammarion.
Age tendre et tête de bois. 1963a. 'Deux cowboys de la chanson: Charles et Johnny', no.3, March, 8–11.
——— 1963b. 'Spécial western', no.6, June, 22–9.
Agulhon, M. 2000. *De Gaulle: histoire, symbole, mythe.* Paris: Plon.
Alexis, J.-P. 1999. *Au protocole du général de Gaulle.* Paris: Perrin.
Alion, Y. 1989. *Brigitte Bardot.* Paris: J'ai lu.
Anderson, B. 1991. *Imagined Communities: Reflections on the Origin and Spread of Nationalism.* Revised Edition. London and New York: Verso.
Anon 1961. 'Movies Abroad: Larcenous Talent', *Time* 77, 12, 17 March: 55–6.
Anon 1965a. 'Une rencontre nommé Godard', *Cinéma 65*, 92, January: 16–18.
Anon 1965b. 'Courrier', *Cinéma 65*, 94, March: 87–8.
Audé, F. 1981. *Ciné-modèles, cinéma d'elles.* Lausanne: Editions l'Age d'Homme.
Augendre, J. 1991. *Le Tour 1991: Panorama d'un siècle.* Issy-les-Moulineaux, Société du Tour de France. (Unpaginated.)
Austin, G. 2003. *Stars in Modern French Film.* London: Arnold.
Badinter, E. 1986. *L'Un est l'autre.* Paris: Odile Jacob.
Bardot, B. 1996. *Initiales B.B. – Mémoires.* Paris: Grasset & Fasquelle, Livre de poche.
——— 2003. *Un cri dans le silence.* Paris: Editions du Rocher.
Barnes, J. 2002. 'Tour de France 2000', in *Something to Declare.* London: Picador, 79–97.
Barthes, R. 1953a. *Le Degré zéro de l'écriture.* Paris: Seuil.

—— 1953b. 'Visages et figures', in *Esprit* 204, July.

—— 1957a. *Mythologies*. Paris: Seuil.

—— 1957b. 'Le Tour de France comme épopée', in *Mythologies*. Paris: Seuil, 110–21.

—— 1960a. *Sur Racine*. Paris: Seuil.

—— 1960b. *Eléments de sémiologie*. Paris: Seuil.

—— 1964a. *On Racine,* trans. R. Howard. New York: Hill and Wang.

—— 1964b. *Essais critiques*. Paris: Seuil.

—— 1966. *Critique et vérité*. Paris: Seuil.

—— 1967a. *Writing Degree Zero,* trans. A. Lavers and C. Smith. New York: Hill and Wang.

—— 1967b. *Elements of Semiology,* trans. A. Lavers and C. Smith. New York: Hill and Wang.

—— 1967c. *Système de la mode*. Paris: Seuil.

—— 1972. *Mythologies,* trans. A. Lavers and C. Smith. New York: Hill and Wang.

—— 1973. *Le Plaisir du texte*. Paris: Seuil.

—— 1975. *The Pleasure of the Text,* trans. R. Millar. New York: Hill and Wang.

—— 1993. *Oeuvres complètes, I, 1942–1965*. Paris: Seuil.

—— 2002a. *Comment vivre ensemble, 1976–1977*. Paris: Seuil/IMEC.

—— 2002b. *Le Neutre, 1977–1978*. Paris: Seuil/IMEC.

Bastide, R. 1964. 'L'ethnologie et le nouvel humanisme', *Revue philosophique de la France et de l'étranger*, 4, October-December: 435–51.

Bastide, S. 2003. 'Drame sur le Tour', special report on the Tour de France 'Cent ans d'histoires', *Dernières Nouvelles d'Alsace*, 24 July.

Beaurenaut, J.-P. 1996. *Poulidor, coeur d'or* (Television documentary, TF1, 55 minutes).

Beauvoir, S. de. 1949. 'Les Structures elémentaires de la parenté', *Les Temps modernes*, 49: 943–9.

—— 1954. *Les Mandarins*. Paris: Gallimard.

—— 1972 (1959). *Brigitte Bardot and the Lolita Syndrome*, New York: Arno Press & the New York Times.

—— 1972 (1953). *The Second Sex,* trans. H.M. Parshley. Harmondsworth: Penguin Books.

—— 1976 (1949). *Le Deuxième Sexe*. Paris: Gallimard, Livre de poche, vol. 1.

Becker, L.F. 1989. *Twentieth-Century French Women Novelists*. Boston: Twayne.

Bergala, A. 1990. 'Godard a-t-il été petit?', *Cahiers du cinéma*, hors série, November: 28–9.

Bernert, P. 1991. 'Et Dieu créa Bardot', in *Le Roman vrai de la IIIe et de la IVe République 1870–1958, 2ème partie 1919–1958*, ed. G.Guilleminault. Paris: Laffont, 1080–112.

Berstein, S. 1989. *La France de l'Expansion: 1958–1969*. Paris: Seuil.

Berstein, S. and Milza, P. 1991. *Histoire de la France au XXe Siècle: 1945–1958*. Paris: Complexe.

Blondin, A. 2001. *Tours de France: Chroniques de "L'Equipe", 1954–1982*. Paris: La Table Ronde.

Boillat, G. 1973. *Un maître de 17 ans*. Neuchâtel: Editions de la Baconnière.

Brierre, J.-D. 2003. *Johnny Hallyday: Histoire d'une vie*. Paris: Fixot.

Brophy, B. 1964. 'Françoise Sagan and the Art of the Beau Geste', *Texas Quarterly*, 7, winter: 59–69 (also in *The London Magazine*, February 1963: 47–59).

Cartier-Bresson, H. 1968. 'Claude Lévi-Strauss: a Portrait', *Vogue*, 152, 1 August: 100–1.

Chalaby, J. 2002. *The de Gaulle Presidency and the Media*. Basingstoke: Palgrave.

Charbonnier, G. 1961. *Entretiens avec Claude Lévi-Strauss*. Paris: Plon.

Chorus. 2003. *Les Cahiers de la chanson, Johnny Hallyday*, no. 43. Spring 2003. Brezolles: Les Éditions du verbe.

Cinéma 65. 1965. 'Godard par Godard', *Cinéma 65*, 94, March: 46–75.

Cismaru, A. 1965–66. 'Françoise Sagan's Theory of Complicity', *Dalhousie Review*, vol. 45, winter: 457–69.

Clark, P.P. 1987. *Literary France: The Making of a Culture*. Berkeley: University of California Press.

Clément, C. 1993. 'Leçons de structuralisme appliqué', *«Claude Lévi-Strauss: Esthétique et structuralisme»*, *Magazine Littéraire*, 311, June: 22–6.

Clément, C. and Casanova, A. 1973. 'Un ethnologue et la culture', *La Nouvelle Critique*, 61, 242, February: 27–36.

Colette. 1928. *La Naissance du jour*. Paris: Flammarion.

Dauncey, H. 2003. 'French Cycling Heroes of the Tour: Winners and Losers', in *The Tour de France, 1903–2003: A Century of Sporting Structures, Meanings and Values*, ed. H. Dauncey and G. Hare. London: Frank Cass, 103–27.

——— ed. 2003. *French Popular Culture: an Introduction*. London: Arnold.

Dauncey, H. and Cannon, S., eds. 2003. *Popular Music in France: From Chanson to Techno*. Aldershot: Ashgate.

De Fallois, B. 1956. 'Un ouvrage fort bien fait', *Nouvelle Revue Française*, 7: 892–8.

De Gaulle, C. 1944 (1932). *Le Fil de l'épée*. Paris: Berger-Levrault.

——— 1954a. *Mémoires de guerre I*, Paris: Plon.

——— 1954b. *Discours et messages*. Paris: Plon.

——— 1999. *Allocutions et Messages*. Paris: Plon.

Delassein, S. 2002. *Aimez-vous Sagan …* Paris: Fayard.

Delerm, P. 1997. 'Le Tour de France', in *La Première Gorgée de bière et autres plaisirs minuscules*. Paris: Gallimard, 39–40.

Delmas, J. 1965. 'Godard et ses fans', *Jeune cinéma*, 7, May: 7–9.

Desbarats, C. and Gorce, J.-P. 1989. *L'Effet Godard*. Paris: Milan.

Dosse, F. 1991. *Histoire du structuralisme, I. Le champ du signe, 1945–1966*. Paris: La Découverte.
——— 1995. *L'Empire du sens. L'Humanisation des sciences humaines*. Paris: La Découverte.
Douin, J.-L. and Portevin, C. 1995. 'Jean Malaurie: l'aventurier des mondes perdus', *Télérama*, 2394, 2–8, December: 10–16.
Dries, J.-M. and Dries, R. 1996. *Anquetil, champion de légende* (Television documentary, TF1, 75 minutes).
Dupuy and Berberian. 2003. 'A chacun son Tour: Dupuy & Berberian', in *L'Equipe Magazine*: 70–71.
Duval Smith, A. 1996. 'Brigitte Bardot denies race hatred charge', *The Guardian*, 20 December: 10.
Dyer, R. 1979. *Stars*. London: BFI.
——— 1987. *Heavenly Bodies: Film Stars and Society*. New York: St Martin's Press.
Ellis, J. 1982. 'Star/Industry/Image', in *Star Signs. Papers from a Weekend Workshop*. London: BFI, 1–12.
L'Equipe Magazine. 2003. Special issue on 'La France du Tour', no. 1102, 5 July.
Estève, M., ed. 1967. *Jean-Luc Godard: au-delà du récit*. Paris: Lettres Modernes, collection 'Etudes Cinématographiques'.
Ezine, J.-L. 1977. 'Françoise Sagan, un accident qui dure', *Nouvelles littéraires*, 7, April: 5.
Fleurdorge, D. 2001. *Les Rituels du président de la République*. Paris: PUF.
Fondation Charles de Gaulle. 1998. *De Gaulle et le RPF*. Paris: Colin.
Footit, H. 2002. *Women, Europe and the New Languages of Politics*. London: Continuum.
Fotheringham, A. 2004. 'McEwen knees up as Tour salutes legend Poulidor', *Irish Independent*, 14 July: 57.
France-Dimanche. 1956. 'Et pourtant si! Ils divorcent!', 21–27 December.
——— 1960. 'La Défaite des mauvaises femmes'. 14–20 January.
French Cultural Studies. 1997. Special issue on Edgar Morin, Vol. 8: 24.
Gabriel, F. 2002. 'L'or en Barthes', *Les Inrockuptibles* 367, 4–10 December: 36–40.
Gaffney, J., ed. 1988. *France and Modernisation*. Aldershot: Avebury.
——— 1993. 'Political Language', in *French Today*, ed. C. Sanders. Cambridge: Cambridge University Press.
——— 2001. 'Imagined Relationships; Political Leadership in Contemporary Democracies', *Parliamentary Affairs*, 54, 1: 120–133.
Gaitti, B. 1998. *De Gaulle Prophète de la Cinquième République*. Paris: Presses de Sciences Po.
'Génération 68'. 2003. *L'Histoire*, no.274, March, 62–7.
Gerth, H.H. and Wright Mills, C. 1977. *From Max Weber*. London: RKP.

Gildea, R. 1996. *France Since 1945*. Oxford: Oxford University Press.

Givray, C. de. 1957. 'Nouveau traité du Bardot … suivi du petit A.B.B.Cédaire', *Cahiers du Cinéma* 12, 71, May, 42–6.

Gledhill, C., ed. 1991. *Stardom: Industry of Desire*. London: Routledge.

Gohier, G. and Marvier, J. 1957. *Bonjour Françoise!* Paris: Editions du Grand Damier.

Goodbody, J. 2003. 'Elite Calling for Armstrong', in 'The Game: Tour de France', supplement to *The Times*, 30 June: 10.

Grall, X. 1962. *La Génération du djebel*. Paris: Desclée de Brouwer.

Grignon, C. and Passeron, J.-C. 1989. *Le Savant et le populaire. Misérabilisme et populisme en sociologie et en littérature*. Paris: Gallimard.

Grisoni, D.-A., ed. 1985. *'Claude Lévi-Strauss'. Magazine Littéraire*, 223, October.

Grosdemouge, J.-M. 1999. *Génération copains, musique et presse 'yéyés': la jeunesse française dans les années soixante*. Unpublished manuscript supplied by the author, adapted from a Maîtrise dissertation, *Un mouvement musical et social: les yéyés. La jeunesse française à travers Salut les copains et Nous les garçons et les filles, 1962–9*. Paris: Université Paris X-Nanterre.

Guggenheim, M. 1958–59. 'Françoise Sagan devant la critique', *The French Review*, 32: 3–13.

Guiart, J. 1968. 'Survivre à Lévi-Strauss', *«Claude Lévi-Strauss», L'Arc*, 26: 66–9.

Guillebaud, J.-C. 1993. 'Dossier: la pensée en 1993. Quand les intellectuels ne veulent plus être "des politiques"', *Le Nouvel Observateur*, 1508, 30 September-6 October: 4–14.

Guitar Collector. 2003. *Hors série, Johnny Hallyday, Tous les Scopitones 1960–1967*. Studio Press, St Ouen (93), May (includes DVD of Hallyday's Scopitones).

Haizfeld, J. 1996. 'Le seul: Jean-Luc Godard, 66 ans, sort "For Ever Mozart" et dit deux ou trois choses qu'il sait de lui', *Libération*, 3 December: 52.

Harris, T. 1991 (1957). 'The Building of Popular Images, Grace Kelly and Marilyn Monroe' in *Stardom: Industry of Desire*, ed. C. Gledhill. London: Routledge, 40–44.

Hawkins, P. 2000. *Chanson: The French Singer-songwriter from Aristide Bruant to the Present Day*. Aldershot: Ashgate.

Hennegrave, O. 2001. *Les Grands Duels du Sport: Anquetil–Poulidor* (Television documentary, Arte, 52 minutes).

Henriot, E. 1954. 'La vie littéraire', *Le Monde*, 26 May: 9.

—— 1957. 'Dans un mois, dans un an', *Le Monde*, 11 September: 8–9.

Holmes, D. 1994. 'Angry Young Women: Sex and Conflict in Best-selling First Novels of the 1950s', in *Violence and Conflict in French Culture*, ed. R. Gunther and J. Windebank. Sheffield: Sheffield Academic Press, 199–214.

Hourdin, G. 1957. 'Françoise Sagan et son temps', *Le Monde*, 21 September: 8.

—— 1958. *Le cas Françoise Sagan*. Paris: Editions du Cerf.

Houston, P. 1961. 'Uncommitted artist?', *Sight and Sound*, 30: 64–5.

—— 1980. 'Orson Welles' in *Cinema: A Critical Dictionary. Vol II: The Major Film-makers*, ed. R. Roud. London: Secker & Warburg, 1055–68.

Institut Charles de Gaulle. 1981. *Bibliographie internationale sur Charles de Gaulle*. Paris: Plon.

Johnson, C. 2003a. *Claude Lévi-Strauss: The Formative Years*. Cambridge: Cambridge University Press.

—— 2003b. 'Introduction' and 'Lévi-Strauss in his interviews' in *Thinking in Dialogue: The Role of the Interview in Post-war French Thought*, (special issue) *Nottingham French Studies*, 42, 1, Spring: 1–4, 33–47.

Jouffa, F. and Barsamian, J. 2003. *Johnny, 60 ans* (includes CD containing interviews). Paris: L'Archipel.

Kaiser, J.R. 1973. 'Françoise Sagan: A Bibliography of Her Works (1954–1972)'. *Bulletin of Bibliography and Magazine Notes*, 30, 3: 106–9.

Kane, J. 2001. *The Politics of Moral Capital*. Cambridge: Cambridge University Press.

Kanters, R. 1981. *A Perte de vue*. Paris: Editions du Seuil.

Kelly, M. 2000. 'Demystification: A Dialogue Between Barthes and Lefebvre' in *The French Fifties* (*Yale French Studies*, 98), ed. Susan Weiner, 79–97.

Kofman, M. 1996. *Edgar Morin: From Big Brother to Fraternity*. London and Chicago: Pluto Press.

Laborde, C. 1998. *Duel sur le volcan*. Paris: Albin Michel.

Lacouture, J. 1984–86. *De Gaulle*. 3 vols. Paris: Seuil.

Lamy, J.-C. 1988. *Sagan*. Paris: Mercure de France.

—— 1992. *René Julliard*. Paris: Julliard.

Larkin, M. 1997. *France Since the Popular Front: 1936–1996*. Oxford: Clarendon Press.

Lavau, G., ed. 1983. *L'Univers politique des classes moyennes*. Paris: FNSP.

Leiris, M. 1981 (1934). *L'Afrique fantôme*. Paris: Gallimard-Tel.

Lesage, J. 1979. *Jean-Luc Godard: A Guide to References and Resources*. Boston: G.K. Hall & Co.

Lévi-Strauss, C. 1949. *Les Structures élémentaires de la parenté*. Paris: La Haye/Mouton.

—— 1950. 'Introduction à l'œuvre de Marcel Mauss', in Mauss, M., *Sociologie et anthropologie*. Paris: PUF, ix–lii.

—— 1955. *Tristes tropiques*. Paris: Plon.

—— 1958. *Anthropologie structurale*. Paris: Plon.

—— 1962a. *Le Totémisme aujourd'hui*. Paris: Plon.

—— 1962b. *La Pensée sauvage*. Paris: PUF.

—— 1964. *Totemism*, trans. R. Needham. London: Merlin Press.

—— 1966. *The Savage Mind*. London: Weidenfeld & Nicolson.

—— 1969. *The Elementary Structures of Kinship*, trans. J. Harle Bell, J.R. von Sturmer and R. Needham. Boston: Beacon Press.

—— 1973. *Anthropologie structurale 2*. Paris: Plon.

—— 1977. *Structural Anthropology 1*, trans. C. Jacobson and B. Grundfest Schoepf. Harmondsworth: Penguin.

—— 1978a. *Structural Anthropology 2*, trans. M. Layton. Harmondsworth: Penguin.

—— 1978b. *Introduction to the Work of Marcel Mauss*, trans. F. Baker. London: Routledge.

—— 1984. *Tristes Tropiques*, trans. J. Weightman and D. Weightman. Harmondsworth: Penguin.

—— and Eribon, D. 1988. *De Près et de loin*. Paris: Odile Jacob.

—— and Eribon, D. 1991. *Conversations with Claude Lévi-Strauss*, trans. P. Wissing. Chicago: University of Chicago Press.

Londres, A. 1996. *Les Forçats de la route*. Paris: Arléa.

Looseley, D. 2003. *Popular Music in Contemporary France*. Oxford: Berg.

Malraux, A. 1971. *Les Chênes qu'on abat*. Paris: Gallimard.

Martin, A. 1996. *Waiting for Bardot*. London and Boston: Faber & Faber.

Martin, A. 2003. *Johnny Hallyday de A à Z*. Paris: Prélude et fugue.

Mauriac, F. 1954. 'Le Dernier Prix'. *Le Figaro*, 1 June: 1.

—— 1958. *Bloc-Notes 1952–57*. Paris: Flammarion.

Mendras, H. and Cole, A. 1988. *Social Change in Modern France*. Cambridge: Cambridge University Press.

Miller, J.G. 1988. *Françoise Sagan*. Boston: Twayne.

Morice, J. 2003. ' "La dernière aventure télévisuelle": Entretien avec le cinéaste Hervé Le Roux', *La Folie du Tour, 1903–2003*, special issue of *Télérama* (hors série): 38–41.

Morin, E. 1956. *Le Cinéma ou l'homme imaginaire: essai d'anthropologie*. Paris: Editions de Minuit.

—— 1957. *Les Stars*. Paris: Seuil.

—— 1960. *The Stars*, trans. R. Howard. New York: Grove Press.

—— 1963. 'Salut les copains II: Le "yé-yé"', *Le Monde*, 7–8 July, 12.

—— 1967. *La Commune en France. La Métamorphose de Plodémet*. Paris: Fayard.

—— 1969. Morin, E., Paillard, B., et al. *La Rumeur d'Orléans*. Paris: Seuil.

—— 1970. *The Red and the White: Report from a French Village*, trans. A.M. Sheridan-Smith. New York: Pantheon.

—— 1971. *Rumor in Orleans*, trans. Peter Green. New York: Pantheon.

—— 1972 (1957). *Les Stars* (third edition). Paris: Le Seuil, collection *Points*.

—— 1976. *L'Esprit du temps I and II*. Paris: Grasset.

—— 1984. *Sociologie*. Paris: Fayard.

—— 1989. *Vidal et les siens*. Paris: Seuil.

—— 1992a [1959]. *Autocritique*. Paris: Seuil.

—— 1992b. *The Nature of Nature*, trans. J.-L. Roland Bélanger. New York: P. Lang.

Mulvey, L. 1989 (1975). 'Visual Pleasure and Narrative Cinema', in *Visual and Other Pleasures*. Bloomington: Indiana University Press, 14–26.

Nick, C. 1998. *Résurrection*. Paris: Fayard.

Nourrissier, F. 1960. *B.B. 60*. Paris: Grasset.

Ollivier, J.-P. 1994. *Raymond Poulidor: La Véridique Histoire*. Grenoble: Glénat.

—— 2000. *Le Tour de France: Lieux et étapes de légende*. Paris: Arthaud.

Pace, D. 1986. *Claude Lévi-Strauss: The Bearer of Ashes*. London: Routledge and Kegan Paul.

Pagnoud, G. 1977. *Le Livre d'or de Poulidor*. Paris: Solar.

Parinaud, A. 1956. *L'Affaire Minou Drouet, petite contribution à une histoire de la presse*. Paris: Julliard.

Piaget, J. 1971. *Structuralism*, trans. and ed. C. Maschler. London: Routledge and Kegan Paul.

Piel, R., with Terbeen, F. 1976. *Merci Poulidor!* Paris: Calmann-Lévy.

Pires, M. 2003. 'The Popular Music press', in Dauncey and Cannon 2003: 77–96.

Poirot-Delpech, B. 1985. *Bonjour Sagan*. Paris: Herscher.

Poulidor, R., with Dirand, G. and Joly, P. 1977 (1968). *La Gloire sans maillot jaune*. Paris: Calmann-Lévy.

Prédal, R. 1965. 'Godard et la critique', *Jeune cinéma*, 8, June-July: 30–32.

Prévost, A.F. 1733. *Manon Lescaut*. Amsterdam: la Compagnie.

Rearick, C. 1997. *The French in Love and War: Popular Culture in the Era of the World Wars*. New Haven and London: Yale University Press.

Reed, E. 2003. 'The Economics of the Tour, 1930–2003', in *The Tour de France, 1903–2003: A Century of Sporting Structures, Meanings and Values*, ed. H. Dauncey and G. Hare. London: Frank Cass, 103–27.

Ricœur, P. 1963. 'Structure et herméneutique', *Esprit*, 322, November: 596–627.

Rigby, B. 1991. *Popular Culture in Modern France*. New York and London: Routledge.

—— 1997. 'The "Anthropological" in Morin's Cultural Analysis', *French Cultural Studies*, 8, 333–40.

Rigoulet, L. 2003. 'Raymond Poulidor: La défaite lui va si bien', in *Télérama*: 51–5.

Rihoit, C. 1986. *Brigitte Bardot. Un mythe français*. Paris: Olivier Orban.

Rochefort, C. 1961. *Les Petits Enfants du siècle*. Paris: Grasset.

Rorty, R. 1967. *The Linguistic Turn: Essays in Philosophical Method*. Chicago: University of Chicago Press.

Ross, K. 1995. *Fast Cars Clean Bodies: Decolonization and the Reordering of French Culture*. Cambridge: MIT Press.

Sabatier, G. and Ragueneau, P. 1994. *Le Dictionnaire du gaullisme*. Paris: Albin Michel.

Sagan, F. 1954. *Bonjour tristesse*. Paris: Julliard.
––––– 1956a. *Un certain sourire*. Paris: Julliard.
––––– 1956b. *New York. Textes de Françoise Sagan*. Paris: Tel.
––––– 1957. *Dans un mois, dans un an*. Paris: Julliard.
––––– 1958a. *Bonjour tristesse* and *A Certain Smile*, trans. Irene Ash. London: World Books.
––––– 1958b. 'Les assassins du parc de Saint-Cloud aux assises de Versailles. Impressions d'audience de Françoise Sagan sur la première journée du procès', *France-Soir*, 22 March: 7.
––––– 1958c. 'Jean-Claude Vivier et Jacques Sermeux seront fixés sur leur sort tard dans la journée. Impressions d'audience de Françoise Sagan sur la 2e journée du procès', *France-Soir*, 23–24 March: 6.
––––– 1959. *Aimez-vous Brahms ...* Paris: Julliard.
––––– 1960a. 'La jeune fille et la grandeur', *L'Express*, 16 June: 5.
––––– 1960b. 'Cuba. Une promenade au soleil', *L'Express,* 4 August: 20–21.
––––– 1960c. 'Cuba. Ce n'est pas si simple', *L'Express,* 11 August: 23–24.
––––– 1960d. *Château en Suède*. Paris: Julliard.
––––– 1961. *Les Merveilleux Nuages*. Paris: Julliard.
––––– 1964. *Toxique*. Paris: Julliard.
––––– 1972. *Des bleus à l'âme*. Paris: Flammarion.
––––– 1974. *Réponses*. Paris: Jean-Jacques Pauvert.
––––– 1984. *Avec mon meilleur souvenir*. Paris: Gallimard.
––––– 1988 (1960). 'Lettre de Suisse', in Sagan, F., Dupré, G. and Nourissier, F. *Au marbre: chroniques retrouvées 1952–1962*, ed. J.-M. Parisis. Paris: Quai Voltaire : 189–92.
––––– 1992. *Répliques*. Paris: Quai Voltaire.
––––– 1993. *... et toute ma sympathie*. Paris: Julliard.
––––– 1998. *Derrière l'épaule*. Paris: Plon.
Sagan, F. and Dussart, G. 1975. *Brigitte Bardot*. Paris: Flammarion.
Sagan, F., Dupré, G., Nourissier, F. 1988. *Au marbre: chroniques retrouvées 1952–1962*. J.-M. Parisis, ed. Paris: Quai Voltaire.
Sartre, J.-P. 1966. 'Jean-Paul Sartre répond'. *'Sartre aujourd'hui', L'Arc,* 30: 87–96.
Sennett, R. 2002 (1977). *The Fall of Public Man*. Harmondsworth: Penguin.
South Bank Show: Johnny Hallyday (television documentary), LWT/ITV, May 2004.
Stacey, J. 1991. 'Feminine Fascinations: Forms of Identification in Star-Audience Relations' in *Stardom: Industry of Desire*, ed. C. Gledhill. London: Routledge, 141–163.
––––– 1994. *Star Gazing: Hollywood Cinema and Female Spectatorship*. London: Routledge.
Stafford, A. 1997. '"Dégel", Hegel and the Launch of *Arguments*', *French Cultural Studies*, 8, 283–9.
Taylor, J.R. 1981. *Hitch*. London: Abacus.

Télérama (hors série) 2003. Special issue on 'Johnny Happy Birthday Rock 'n' Roll!' Paris: Télérama SA.

Télérama (hors série) 2003. Special number on 'La Folie du Tour, 1903–2003'. Paris: Télérama SA.

Tenzer, N. 1998. *La Face cachée du gaullisme.* Paris: Hachette.

Tinker, C. 2005. *Georges Brassens and Jacques Brel: Personal and Social Narratives in Post-war Chanson.* Liverpool: Liverpool University Press.

Todd, C. 1994. *A Century of French Best-sellers.* Lampeter: Edwin Mellen Press.

Touchard, J. 1978. *Le Gaullisme.* Paris: Seuil.

Truffaut, F. 1954. 'Une certaine tendance du cinéma', *Cahiers du Cinéma,* 31, January, 15–29.

—— 1968. 'Truffaut on Truffaut', interview by Yvette Romi, *Nouvel Observateur,* 200, 9 September: 52–4.

Vadim, R. 1986. *D'une étoile l'autre.* Paris: Editions de la Seine.

Various. 1974. 'Table ronde d'Evreux', *Image et Son* 174, June: 78–88.

Vautier, R. 1972. *Avoir vingt ans dans les Aurès.* France (film).

Viansson-Ponté, P. 1963. *Les Gaullistes.* Paris: Seuil.

—— 1971, 1972. *Histoire de la république gaullienne,* 2 vols. Paris: Fayard.

Vigarello, G. 1992. 'Le Tour de France', in *Les Lieux de mémoire, III, Les France: 2. Traditions,* ed. P. Nora. Paris: Gallimard, 884–925.

Vincendeau, G. 1987. 'The Mise en Scène of Suffering: French Chanteuses Réalistes', *New Formations,* 3, Winter: 107–28.

—— 1992. 'The Old and the New: Brigitte Bardot and 1950s France', *Paragraph,* 15, 1, March: 73–96.

—— 2000. *Stars and Stardom in French Cinema.* London: Continuum.

Weiner, S. 1993. '*Le Repos de la critique*: Women Writers of the Fifties', *French Literature Series,* 20: 93–102.

—— 2001. *Enfants Terribles: Youth and Femininity in the Mass Media in France, 1945–1968.* Baltimore: Johns Hopkins University Press.

Winock, M. 1986. 'Trop fort pour être aimé: pourquoi la France préférait Poulidor à Anquetil', *Le Monde,* 17–18 August. (Reproduced in 'Les Archives du Monde', supplement to *Le Monde,* 27–28 June 2004: 69–71.)

—— 1987. 'Le Complexe de Poulidor', in *Chronique des années soixante.* Paris: Seuil, 138–42.

Websites

Discohallyday: http://www.chez.com/discohallyday/menu.htm (accounts of concert performances).

Johnny Hallyday Le Web: http://www.hallyday.com.fr/ (a comprehensive source of information).

RFI Musique: http://www.rfimusique.com/siteEn/accueil/index.asp (detailed biographies of French popular music artists including Hallyday).

Le Site du Scopitone: http://scopitone.free.fr/ (discussion of Scopitones).

NOTES ON CONTRIBUTORS

Philip Dine is Senior Lecturer in French at the National University of Ireland, Galway. He is the author of *Images of the Algerian War: French Fiction and Film, 1954–1992* (Clarendon Press/OUP, 1994) and *French Rugby Football: A Cultural History* (Berg, 2001). He has published widely on representations of the French colonial empire, including particularly decolonisation, as well as sport, leisure and popular culture in France.

John Gaffney is Professor of French Government at Aston University. He has authored and edited ten books, most recently on the French presidential and legislative elections of 2002 (Ashgate, 2004). He has authored forty chapters and articles, most recently in the journals *Political Studies, Parliamentary Affairs,* and *European Security.*

Diana Holmes is Professor of French at Leeds University. She writes and teaches on nineteenth- and twentieth-century literature, particularly writing by women, and on film. Publications include *French Women's Writing 1848–1994* (Athlone, 1996), *François Truffaut* (Manchester University Press, 1998), *100 Years of European Cinema: Entertaining Ideologies*, co-edited with Alison Smith (Manchester University Press, 2000); *Rachilde: Decadence, Gender and the Woman Writer* (Berg, 2001) and *Romance and Readership in Twentieth-Century France: Love Stories* (Oxford University Press, 2006). She is co-editor of the Manchester University Press series *French Film Directors.*

Christopher Johnson is Professor of French at Nottingham University and specializes in postwar French thought. He is author of *System and Writing in the Philosophy of Jacques Derrida* (Cambridge University Press, 1993), and *Claude Lévi-Strauss: the Formative Years* (Cambridge University Press, 2003). He is a member of the editorial board of *Paragraph – a Journal of Modern Critical Theory.*

Heather Lloyd is Senior Lecturer in French at Glasgow University. With interests in French narrative literature of both the eighteenth and twentieth centuries, she has published an edition of Diderot's *La Religieuse* (Bristol Classical Press, 2000), as well as a study of *Bonjour tristesse* (University of Glasgow French and German Publications, 1995).

Alison Smith is Lecturer in European Film Studies at the University of Liverpool, with special interest in the French cinema. She has published various articles on French film of the late 1960s and the 1970s in *French Cultural Studies, Modern and Contemporary France* and *Studies in French Cinema.* She is the author of a book on the films of Agnès Varda (Manchester University Press, 1998), and of *French Cinema in the 1970s: The Echoes of May* (Manchester University Press, 2005).

Chris Tinker is Senior Lecturer in French at Heriot-Watt University, Edinburgh. He has teaching and research interests in modern and contemporary French Studies, particularly popular music, film and media. He has published various articles on the French singer-songwriter tradition and is author of *Georges Brassens and Jacques Brel: Personal and Social Narratives in Post-war Chanson* (Liverpool University Press, 2005).

Susan Weiner is the author of *Enfants Terribles: Youth and Femininity in the Mass Media in France, 1945–1968* (Johns Hopkins University Press, 2001). Her articles have appeared *in Esprit créateur, French Cultural Studies* and *Contemporary French Civilization.* She was Assistant and later Associate Professor at Yale University. She is currently at work on a novel.

INDEX

Lightning Source UK Ltd.
Milton Keynes UK
02 February 2011

166784UK00001B/70/P

9 780857 451606